John Pentland Mahaffy

Alexander's Empire

John Pentland Mahaffy

Alexander's Empire

ISBN/EAN: 9783743308251

Manufactured in Europe, USA, Canada, Australia, Japa

Cover: Foto ©ninafisch / pixelio.de

Manufactured and distributed by brebook publishing software (www.brebook.com)

John Pentland Mahaffy

Alexander's Empire

The Story of the Nations.

ALEXANDER'S EMPIRE.

THE STORY OF THE NATIONS.

Large Crown 8vo., Cloth, Illustrated, 5s.

1. ROME. ARTHUR GILMAN, M.A.
2. THE JEWS. Prof. J. K. HOSMER.
3. GERMANY. Rev. S. BARING-GOULD.
4. CARTHAGE. Prof. A. J. CHURCH.
5. ALEXANDER'S EMPIRE. Prof. J. P. MAHAFFY.
6. THE MOORS IN SPAIN. STANLEY LANE-POOLE.
7. ANCIENT EGYPT. Prof. GEORGE RAWLINSON.
8. HUNGARY. Prof. A. VAMBÉRY.
9. THE SARACENS. A. GILMAN, M.A.
10. IRELAND. Hon. EMILY LAWLESS.
11. CHALDEA. Z. A. RAGOZIN.
12. THE GOTHS. HENRY BRADLEY.
13. ASSYRIA. Z. A. RAGOZIN.
14. TURKEY. STANLEY LANE-POOLE.
15. HOLLAND. Prof. J. E. T. ROGERS.
16. MEDIÆVAL FRANCE. GUSTAVE MASSON.
17. PERSIA. S. G. W. BENJAMIN.
18. PHŒNICIA. Prof. GEO. RAWLINSON.
19. MEDIA. Z. A. RAGOZIN.
20. THE HANSA TOWNS. HELEN ZIMMERN.
21. EARLY BRITAIN. Prof. ALFRED J. CHURCH.
22. THE BARBARY CORSAIRS. STANLEY LANE-POOLE.
23. RUSSIA. W. R. MORFILL.

London:
T. FISHER UNWIN, Paternoster Square, E.C.

Digitized by the Internet Archive
in 2010 with funding from
University of Toronto

http://www.archive.org/details/alexandersempire00maha

BUST OF ALEXANDER THE GREAT.
(British Museum.)

ALEXANDER'S EMPIRE

BY

JOHN PENTLAND MAHAFFY, D.D.,

Prof. of Anc. Hist. in the University of Dublin,

AUTHOR OF "SOCIAL LIFE IN GREECE FROM HOMER TO MENANDER,"
"RAMBLES AND STUDIES IN GREECE," "A HISTORY OF GREEK
CLASSICAL LITERATURE," ETC.

WITH THE COLLABORATION OF

ARTHUR GILMAN, M.A.,

AUTHOR OF "THE STORY OF ROME," ETC.

FIFTH EDITION

London

T. FISHER UNWIN

PATERNOSTER SQUARE

NEW YORK: G. P. PUTNAM'S SONS

MDCCCXC

Entered at Stationers' Hall
By T. FISHER UNWIN.
COPYRIGHT BY G. P. PUTNAM'S SONS, 1887
(For the United States of America).

ALEXANDRO LEEPER LL.D.
Coll. SS. Trin. apud Melb. Præposito
D D D
TOTO ORBE SEJUNCTUS
TOTO CORDE CONJUNCTUS
AUCTOR

PREFACE.

THE story of the conquests of Alexander has been told many times, and his name is familiar in our mouths as household words; but the history of the different portions of the great Empire that he founded, how they rapidly gained and lost their independence, and finally were absorbed into the dominions of Rome, is by no means equally well known.

It was not to be expected that such a conqueror as the great Macedonian should leave behind him any single successor equal to the task of holding his vast Empire together, and it is therefore no matter of surprise that it was speedily broken up; but there is, nevertheless, a deep interest in tracing the progress of disintegration, in the course of which one ruler after another was obliged to resign his power, and the inner life of the world was completely transformed.

The succession of violent deaths that mark the story, indicate clearly the condition of society at the period; but, as we thread our way through the labyrinth of bloody wars and assassinations, we find our attention happily distracted by studying the influence, which is perceptible in them all, of the ideas that Alexander impressed upon the peoples that he conquered. It is one of the purposes of this volume to present this complex truth distinctly to the reader, and to show also how considerably Rome was influenced by the ideas of conquered Greece, as well as to indicate the manner in which Hellenistic influences modified the characteristics of the dominant people.

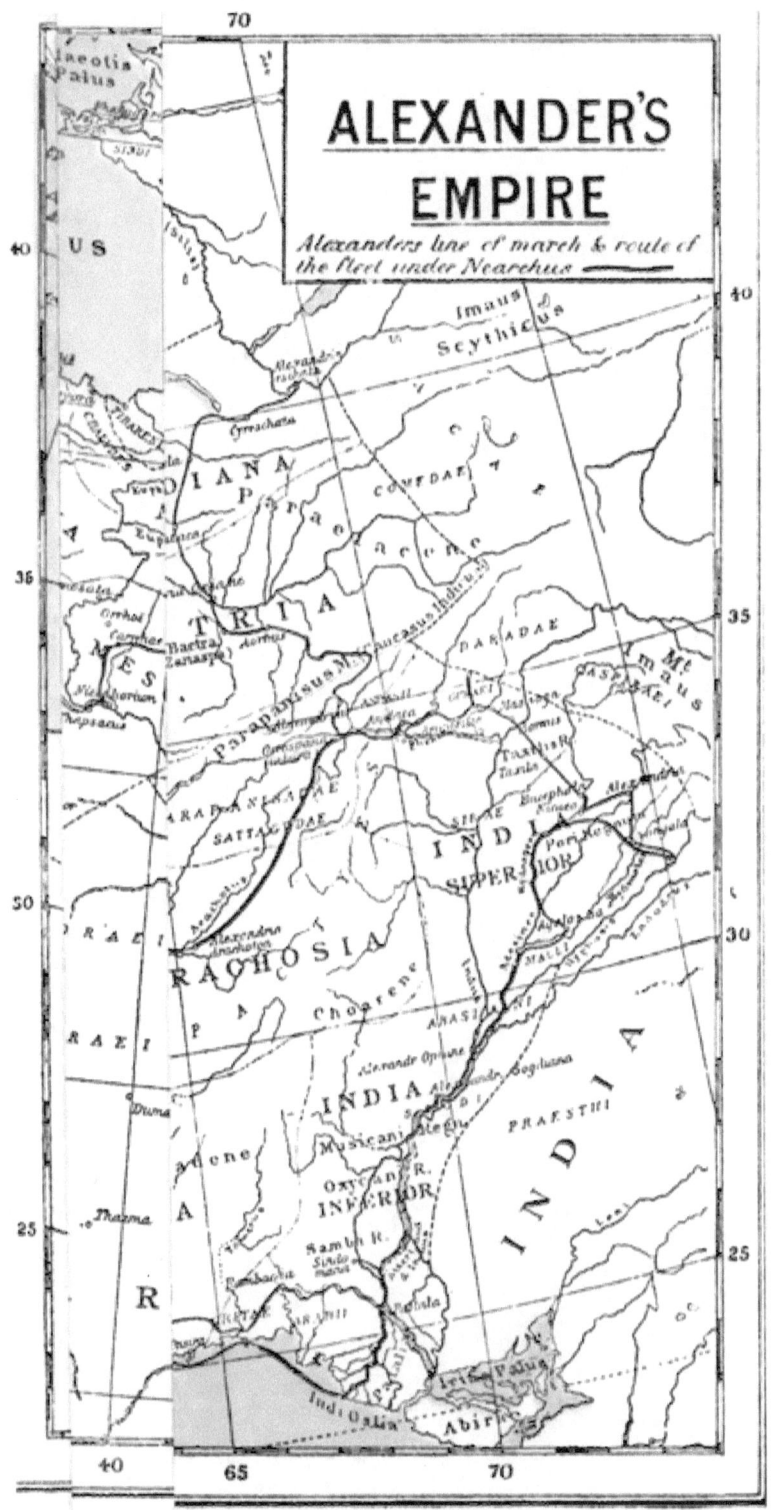

CONTENTS.

PAGE

I.

ALEXANDER'S PLACE IN HISTORY 1–3
The influence of a single genius, 1—The rise of Alexander a turning-point in Greek history, 2—The scope of this book, 3.

II.

YOUTH AND ACCESSION OF ALEXANDER . . . 4–11
Philip of Macedon, 4—The character of Olympias, Alexander's mother, 7—Philip assassinated, 7—Alexander's companions, 8, 9—His early training, 9—Experiences gained while serving in the heavy cavalry, 9—His conquest of Greece, 10, 11.

III.

THE STRUGGLE FOR THE SUPREMACY OF THE WORLD
(B.C. 334–330) 12–30
Alexander's army, 12—The start for the East, 13—The battle of Granicus, 15—Plan of the campaign, 16-19—The victory of Issus, 20-23—The battle of Arbela, 24—Alexander in Persia, 24-27—Darius Codomannus, 28.

IV.

THE MACEDONIAN EMPIRE AND ITS LIMITS UP TO
ALEXANDER'S DEATH (B.C. 323) . . . 31–42
The Persian Empire, 31, 32—The conquest of its three divi

sions, 32, 33—Alexander's march, 34—Wild schemes of mastering the whole world, 35—Passage of the Hindukush, 36—The whole of the Punjab in Alexander's hands, 36—His troops refuse to go further, 36—His return, 37—Hellenistic influences on India, 37—At Babylon Alexander reorganizes his army, and also his vast dominions, 38, 39—Punishment of offending governors, 39—The king in his camp, 40, 41—His death, 41—The confusion that followed, 42.

V.

THE PROBLEM OF THE SUCCESSION (B.C. 323-313) . 43-54

The claimants to the throne, 43—Philip Arridæus made titular king, 44—Division of the empire, 45—The successors in the provinces, 45, 46—The wars of the Succession, 47—The attack on Egypt, 47, 48—The Lamian War, 48—The fate of Demosthenes, 49—The Diadochi, 49—The careers of Eumenes, Seleucus, and Casander, 50-52—The fate of Alexander's child, 53—Cleopatra, 54.

VI.

THE LATER WARS OF THE DIADOCHI DOWN TO THE BATTLE OF IPSUS (B.C. 313-301).—THE CAREER OF DEMETRIUS 55-68

The general epoch of Hellenism, 55—Monarchy becomes the form of government, 55, 56—The reasons why, 56—The principle of Federation developing, 57—The five masters of the spoil, 58—Demetrius's attack on Rhodes, 59-61—The Rhodian Republic and Federation, 62—Antigonus' attempts for universal mastery, 65—The fortunes of Seleucus, Lysimachus, and Ptolemy, 65-67—The fate of Demetrius, 67, 68.

VII.

FROM THE BATTLE OF IPSUS TO THE INVASION OF THE CELTS (B.C. 301-278) 69-75

A new epoch for the Diadochi, 69—Their family relations, 70—Ptolemy's children, 71—The family quarrel, 72—The death of Seleucus, 73—Keraunos' career, 73—The state of Alexander's Empire in 280 B.C., 74, 75.

VIII.

THE INVASION OF THE CELTS (GALATIANS) AND ITS CONSEQUENCES 76-84

Another epoch, 76—The Galatæ, 79—The effects of their invasion, 80—The monument of Ancyra, 83—The welding together of the feelings and interests of the Hellenistic world, 84.

IX.

KING PYRRHUS OF EPIRUS 85-88

Pyrrhus, the Epirot king, 85—His marriages, 85, 86—His early career, 86—His ineffectual efforts to check the advance of Rome, 86—Pyrrhus' struggles in Greece and Macedonia, 87—His death, 87—The question of supremacy between the East and the West, 88.

X.

THE GOLDEN AGE OF HELLENISM 89-95

The three great kingdoms: (1) Macedonia, 89—(2) Egypt, 89—(3) Syria, 90—The lesser powers, 90-92—Homonymous towns, 92, 93—Who were the people who inhabited these towns? 93, 94—Hellenistic city life, 95.

XI.

THE NEW LINES ADOPTED BY PHILOSOPHY UNDER THE DIADOCHI 96-110

A succession of philosophers, 96—Plato, 96—Aristotle, 97—The philosophers out of tune with the politics of the day, 98—The monarchy of Alexander, 99—The effects of the Forty-five Years' War, 99, 100—Three new systems of philosophy, 102—Epicurus, 103—His teaching, 104—The Stoics, 105—The differences of the two schools, 105, 106—Quietists, 106—The old schools at Athens, 107—The opening of the golden age, 108—The New Comedy, 109, 110.

XII.

THE STAGES OF HELLENISM IN THE THIRD CENTURY B.C. 111–114

A curious coincidence, 111—A chronological table, 112—The Syrian wars, 113.

XIII.

THE THREE YOUNG KINGS.—A SKETCH OF ANTIGONUS GONATAS, HIS ACTS AND CHARACTER 115–141

Antigonus Gonatas, 115—His first great victory, 116—Pyrrhus, 116—Career of Antigonus, 117—His difficulties with Greece, 118—His last years, 119—Ptolemy Philadelphus, 102—Alexandria, 120, 121—Its chief features, 121—The great mart of Europe and Asia, 121—Athenæus' account of the feast that inaugurated Philadelphus' reign, 122—The policy of Ptolemy Phil., 133—His amours and his griefs, 134—His death, 135—Antiochus Soter, 135—Antioch, 136—The Septuagint, 137—Theos succeeds to the throne, 137—The events of his reign, 138—Bactrian Hellenism, 139—Açoka adopts the Buddhist creed, 140—Buddhist missionaries in the Hellenistic world, 140—Diffusion of Greek, 141.

XIV.

SCIENCE AND LETTERS AT ALEXANDRIA IN THE DAYS OF PHILADELPHUS 142–155

Little in Science and Literature left to us, 142—The University, 142—The Museum and the Library, 143—The Librarians, 144—Erudition at Alexandria, 145—Three original developments in literature, 146—The pastoral idyll, 146—Specimens of Theocritus' work, 147-150—The other poets, 151—Love in Alexandrian literature, 151—The tragic and comic poets, 152—The Septuagint, 153—Influence of a common language, 154—Euclid, 155.

XV.

THE THIRD GENERATION OF HELLENISM.—THE THREE GREAT KINGDOMS . . . 156–162

Chronological table of the third generation of Hellenism, 156

—Ptolemy Euergetes, 157—His campaigns, 157, 158—His character and achievements, 159, 160—The strides of science, 161—Demetrius' struggles, 161, 162.

XVI.

The Rise of the Achæan League under Aratus.—His Policy 163-169

Plutarch's "Lives," 163—Early history and youth of Aratus, 164—His training, 164—His great ambition, 167—A successful adventure at Sicyon, 167, 168—Aratus and the Achæan League, 168—Aratus' policies and career, 168, 170.

XVII.

King Agis of Sparta.—The Political Theorists of the Day 170-175

The opinions respecting monarchy, 170, 171—Monarchy in Sparta, 171—Sparta in Plutarch's day, 171—Socialism, 172—Agis's proposals, 172—The young king's fate, 173—The relations of Aratus and Antigonus to Agis, 173-175.

XVIII.

The Rise and Spread of Federations in the Hellenistic World.—The Achæan and other Leagues.—Union becomes Popular 176-183

The "city-states" of Greece, 176—Autonomy deep set in the Greek mind, 176—Federation, 177—Guarding against pirates, 178—Constitution of the Achæan League, 179—The preponderance of the wealthy, 180—Aratus's policy, 180, 181—The Ætolian League, 181—Its worst point, 182—Mr. Freeman on the Constitution of the Leagues, 182, 183—Other Leagues, 183.

XIX.

THE EVENTS OF KING DEMETRIUS II.'S REIGN.—
THE FIRST INTERFERENCE OF THE ROMANS
IN THE EMPIRE OF ALEXANDER . . . 184-186

Demetrius II., 184—His career, 184, 185—Roman interference, 185—The cloud in the west, 186.

XX.

COMMERCE AND CULTURE AT PERGAMUM AND
RHODES 187-198

The movements of Ptolemy Euergetes and Antiochus Hierax, 187—Attalus I., 188—The Dying Gladiator, 188—The Pergamene dynasty, 189—Rhodes, 190—The character of its people, 193—The culture of the Rhodians, 193—The Rhodian navy, 194—Presents to Rhodes after an earthquake in 227 B.C., 194-198—The Rhodian system, 198.

XXI.

THE RISE OF ANTIGONUS DOSON AND CLEOMENES
(B.C. 229-223) 199-206

The rise of two leaders, 199—Antigonus Doson, 200—His movements, 200, 201—Cleomenes, 202—His rival Aratus, 203—The fears of the League, 204—Cleomenes' *coup d'état*, 204, 205—His policy, 205—Cleomenes as king, 206.

XXII.

THE CLEOMENIC WAR (B.C. 224-221) TO THE BATTLE
OF SELLASIA.—THE POLICY OF ARATUS . 207-217

The position of Aratus, 207—He proposes an embassy to Antigonus, 208—Cleomenes wants hegemony, 208—His quarrel with the League, 209—The war that ensued, 209—The conduct of Aratus, 210—Antigonus master of the situation, 211—His subsequent policy, 212—Early wars of Antiochus III., 213—Cleomenes forsaken by Ptolemy, 214—The battle of Sellasia, 215—Cleomenes' last days in Egypt, 215, 216—The end of Antigonus Doson, 216, 217.

XXIII.

THE CONDITION OF THE HELLENISTIC WORLD IN 221 B.C. 218-224

Roman invasion postponed a generation, 218—Hellenism in the Far East, 219, 220—Bonds of the civilized world, 220, 221—Hellenistic literature, 221, 223—Developments of positive science, 224.

XXIV.

THE LAST INDEPENDENT SOVEREIGNS OF THE EMPIRE.—THE FATE OF ANTIOCHUS III. AND PTOLEMY IV. (PHILOPATOR) . . . 225-233

Chronological table, 225, 226—Antiochus "the Great," 226—The insurgent Molon, 227—Achæus' revolt, 227—Various operations, 228—The battle of Raphia, 229—The treacherous surrender of Achæus at Sardis, 229, 230—His fate, 230—Antiochus' Eastern campaign, 230, 231—Returns to Antioch, and entitled "the Great," 231—The career of Ptolemy at Alexandria, 232—His death, 233.

XXV.

THE CONDITION OF PERGAMUM AND RHODES . 234-236

Condition of Byzantium, 234, 235—The Galatians in Thrace, 235—Great outcry in the trading world, 235—The Rhodians instigate a war, 236—The point gained, 236—Attalus, 236.

XXVI.

THE REIGN OF PHILIP V. OF MACEDON, UP TO HIS INTERFERENCE IN EASTERN AFFAIRS.—HIS WARS IN GREECE 237-243

Philip V. peacefully succeeds to the throne, 237—Troubles from the Ætolians, 237—The struggle, 238—The coming storm, 238—Demetrius of Pharos, 239—Philip's treaty with Hannibal, 240—Philip's cruelty and injustice, 240—Romans incite war with Philip, 241—With Philopœmen he successfully resists a coalition, 241—Romans displeased at the making of peace, and their attitude towards Philip, 242—A turning-point in the history of Alexander's Empire, 242, 243.

XXVII.

STATE OF THE HELLENISTIC WORLD FROM 204 TO 197 B.C.—THE FIRST ASSERTION OF ROME'S SUPREMACY 244-258

Philip's policy of annoyance and insult, 244—His treaty with Antiochus III., 247—His aggressions and cruelties, 247, 248—The accession of Ptolemy Epiphanes, 248—The Regents Tlepolemus and Sosibius, 251—The attack on Egypt, 252—Rome's assistance is accepted, 252—Antiochus' proposal, 252—The people of Abydos, 253—Rome's second war with Philip, 254—The battle of Cynoscephalæ, 255, 256—The attitude of the Roman general towards Philip, 256, 257—The first blow struck from the West at the Empire of Alexandria, 257—Macedonian humiliation, 257, 258.

XXVIII.

THE HELLENISTIC WORLD FROM B.C. 197-190—THE SECOND ASSERTION OF ROME'S SUPREMACY.—MAGNESIA 259-266

Flamininus in Greece, 259, 260—Philip and Antiochus become enemies, 261—Roman struggle with Antiochus in Europe, 262—The supremacy of the sea secured by the Romans, 263—Their success at Magnesia, 264—The death of Antiochus, 265—The Galatians subjugated, 265—The Romans become plunderers, 265, 266.

XXIX.

THE HELLENISTIC WORLD FROM THE BATTLE OF MAGNESIA TO THE ACCESSION OF PERSEUS (B.C. 190-179) 267-284

Return to Egyptian affairs, 267—The fate of Tlepolemus, 267—Epiphanes' coronation, 268—The Rosetta Stone, 268-271—The decree of Memphis, 272—Pergamum and Rhodes, 275—The powers depend on the beck of Rome, 276—All the world at Rome, 277—Affairs for ten years after Magnesia, 278—Last years of Philip, 279—Roman policy shifting, 280—Rome and the Leagues, 281-283—Death of Philopœmen, 283.

XXX.

THE STRUGGLE OF PERSEUS WITH THE ROMANS.—THE THIRD ASSERTION OF ROME'S SUPREMACY.—PYDNA (B.C. 168) 285–295

Perseus succeeds to the throne, 285—His waiting policy, 285—The feeling between Greece and Rome, 286—Analogies to modern problems, 287—Perseus' first demonstration against Rome, 288—His want of decision, 289—Degeneration of Roman character, 289—L. Æ. Paullus brings the war to a close, 290—The Romans' treatment of Macedonia, 291—of the Epirotes and of Eumenes, 292—of Rhodes, 293—of their allies, 294—The history of Polybius, 295.

XXXI.

THE LAST SYRIAN WAR, AND FOURTH ASSERTION OF ROMAN SUPREMACY.—THE CIRCLE OF POPILIUS LÆNAS (B.C. 168) 296–299

Antiochus IV., king of Syria, 296—His attack upon Egypt, 297—Popilius Lænas' famous circle in the sand, 298—Roman interference, 298—The Empire of Alexander, completely broken, sinks into dependence upon Rome, 299.

XXXII.

THE INFLUENCE OF HELLENISM ON ROME . . 300–310

Early Roman intercourse with Greece, 300—Influence of the Greeks upon Roman literature, 301—The desire to attain Hellenistic culture, 302—The influence of the Greek play upon Roman morality, 303—The baseness of Roman diplomacy, 304—Roman Hellenism, 305—Some curious details from Polybius, 306—Greek art at Rome, 307—The reaction upon the East, 307, 308—A great gain to the civilized world being secured, 309—Roman architecture, 309, 310.

LIST OF NAMES EASILY CONFOUNDED 311

INDEX 315

LIST OF ILLUSTRATIONS.

	PAGE
COIN OF ALEXANDER THE GREAT	3
THE MONUMENT OF LYSIKRATES	5
MAP OF THE BATTLE OF THE GRANICUS	13
PLAN OF THE BATTLE OF ISSUS	17
MOSAIC OF THE BATTLE OF ISSUS. (FROM POMPEII)	21
MAP OF BATTLE OF ISSUS	25
PLAN OF BATTLE OF ARBELA	29
COIN OF PHILIP II. OF MACEDON	42
COIN OF DEMETRIUS I.	54
COIN OF DEMETRIUS I.	59
THE NIKE OF SAMOTHRACE, A MONUMENT SET UP BY DEMETRIUS I.	63
COIN OF PTOLEMY II.	74
THE DYING GALATIAN (GLADIATOR)	77
FROM THE FRIEZE ON THE GREAT ALTAR AT PERGAMUM	81
COIN OF ANTIOCHUS IV.	83
COIN OF ACHÆUS, SYRIAN PRETENDER	88
EPICURUS	101
COINS OF ANTIOCHUS III. AND PTOLEMY V.	111
AN IONIC CAPITAL	124

LIST OF ILLUSTRATIONS.

	PAGE
CORINTHIAN CAPITALS	124, 125
CORINTHIAN PILASTER	125
PYLON (PORTAL) OF A TEMPLE, EDFU	128
A TEMPLE AT PHILÆ	128
PILLAR FROM PHILÆ	129
STATUE OF OSIRIS	129
PERSONIFICATION OF THE CITY OF ANTIOCH, WITH THE RIVER ORONTES	133
COIN OF SELEUCUS III. OF SYRIA	141
PLAN OF THE RUINS OF EPHESUS, WITH THE SITE OF THE TEMPLE OF DIANA	165
COINS OF RHODES AND PERGAMUM	187
COIN OF PHILETÆRUS	188
THE LAOCOON	191
THE TORO FARNESE	195
COIN OF RHODES	197
COIN OF ANTIOCHUS III.	220
COIN OF PTOLEMY V.	233
COIN OF PHILIP V. OF MACEDON	243
THE VENUS FROM MILO	245
FIGURINE FROM TANAGRA	249
PLAN OF TEMPLE OF DIANA AT EPHESUS	269
PLAN OF EGYPTIAN TEMPLE	273
COIN OF PERSEUS, KING OF MACEDON	284
COIN OF ANTIOCHUS IV.	296
COIN OF LEPIDUS TUTOR REGIS	298

THE STORY OF ALEXANDER'S EMPIRE.

I.

ALEXANDER'S PLACE IN HISTORY.

MOST of the great changes in the world's history come about gradually, and wise men can see them coming, for it is very hard to run counter to the nature of average men, and all great advances and degradations of society are the result of persistent causes; but a few times, since our records have been kept, there has arisen a single genius, who has done what no number of lesser men could accomplish, who has upset theories as well as dominions, preached a new faith, discovered some new application of Force, which has given a fresh start to the world in its weary and perplexed struggle for a higher life. These few great men have so changed the current of affairs, that we may safely say they have modified the future of the whole human race. At any rate they have taught us what might and dignity is attainable by man, and have so given us ideals by which the commonest of us can estimate his worth and exalt his aspirations.

So, too, there have been gigantic criminals and imperial fools who have wrecked the peace of the world, and caused the "ape and tiger" elements, which were repressed by long and anxious struggles, to break out afresh in their savagery.

We desire in this book to tell the story of one of the greatest men that ever lived—to tell very briefly of his personal achievements, and to show how long his work, and how far his influence, extended. Most Greek histories stop with the fall of republican liberty under the conquests of Philip of Macedon, the father of our hero; nor is this a bad place to stop in the history of Greece, for with Alexander the stage of Greek influence spreads across the world, and Greece is only a small item in the heritage of the Greeks. All the world, too, made up their minds that the rise of Alexander was a great turning point, when an older volume of history was finished, and a new one begun. Nobody ever thought of going back beyond Alexander and his conquests to make a historic claim, or to demand the restoration of ancient sovranties. His conquests were regarded as perfectly lawful, the world as his natural heritage, his will as a lawful testament. So, then, we may begin with him without much retrospect, and see what he founded, and what he did for the advance of the world.

The fragments of his Empire were great Empires in themselves, and were the main channels of culture and civilization until the Roman Empire swallowed them up; and so far we will follow them, though even after their absorption they did not cease to affect history, and the capitals of the Alexandrian

Empire were long the foremost cities in the Roman world. But this would take a far longer book, and more knowledge than any one man possesses, and must be set down in other books by other men. Even within the limits which are here laid down, thousands of details must be omitted, for the history of Eastern Europe and its wars in the century after Alexander is more complicated than can well be imagined and described. We must try to sever the wheat of important events from the chaff of raids and campaigns, and leave some distinct memories in the reader's mind.

COIN OF ALEXANDER THE GREAT.

II.

YOUTH AND ACCESSION OF ALEXANDER.

NOTHING is so obscure as the law—if there be a law—by which genius is produced. Most of the men who have moved the world in science and letters have sprung from obscure parents, have had obscure brothers and sisters, and have produced obscure children. It was not so with Alexander. His children were not indeed allowed to come to maturity, but we have no evidence to show that they resembled or approached him in genius. His parents, on the other hand, were people of great mark.

His father, Philip of Macedon, was the ablest monarch of his day, and had by war and policy raised a small and distracted kingdom into the leading power in Eastern Europe, in fact, into the imperial chiefdom of the Greeks, though his people were only on the boundaries of Hellenedom. His long diplomatic and military struggles against the Greeks are fully recounted in all the histories of the life and time of Demosthenes, and we need not repeat them here. His successful efforts to educate his nobility have been compared to those of Peter the Great to civilize the Russian grandees of his day. There is no man in our century to compare with him but Victor

This monument (of Lysikrates) is one of the earliest in the Corinthian order, and was erected in Athens at the very time of Alexander's invasion of Asia (335 B.C.). It marks the taste of the epoch.

Emanuel, who started as King of Sardinia, and ended as King of United Italy, utilizing politicians like Cavour, incendiaries like Mazzini, and enthusiasts like Garibaldi, for his steady and long-determined policy. In his private life, too, Philip was not unlike the galant and gallant king.

He had married in early life a handsome Epirot princess, whose family then represented a kingdom not inferior to his own. This princess, Olympias, is not known to us during Philip's young and happy days, when she was watching the growth of her only child, a boy of splendid beauty and from the first of extraordinary promise. But as he grew up, educated in all that a king should know, not only of sport and pastime, of war, but also of science and letters under no less a teacher than Aristotle, her jealousy for his rights was intensified by jealousy for her own. The king's advancing years and enlarged responsibilities had not stayed his vagaries; the house of Macedon had always been by custom polygamous; successions to the throne were generally introduced by domestic tragedies, fratricides, exiles; and Philip's reign, from its beginning to its close, made no exception. Hence, at the birth of a new son, by another princess, and the declared claims of the infant's relations on the ground of old quarrels and suspicions concerning Olympias, the estrangement between Philip and his eldest son became almost complete; Olympias and Alexander even retired from court to the queen's ancestral dominions; the young prince had a narrow escape of his life, and so bitter was the feeling that, when Philip was suddenly assassinated (B.C. 336), owing to a private revenge in some far obscurer affair, Olympias and Alexander were openly charged with having suborned the murderer.

All that we know of Alexander, especially in his youth, belies such a suspicion. His famous utterance when they proposed to him a night attack on Darius at Arbela—οὐ κλέπτω τὴν νίκην, *I steal no victory*—was the motto of his life. Olympias, a woman of furious temper, unbridled ambition, and absolute devotion to her son, is perhaps more justly suspected, but as her crime would be far less heinous, so her innocence or guilt is of little moment in history; but that the greatest career in the world should have started with a parricide, would be indeed a horrible fact.

The other claimants however did not stand against him for an instant; he abolished them without ceremony or mercy, and assumed the purple at the age of twenty, to control a kingdom made up of loyal and warlike Macedonians, disloyal and treacherous Greeks, rebellious and turbulent Illyrians and Pæonians—in fact, of nothing but disorder and fermentation, if we except the companions of his youth and the soldiery who knew and loved him. He had, moreover, a very well-trained army under experienced generals, three of whom, Antipater, Parmenio, and Antigonus must have been steady and able counsellors. It was the old habit of the kings to have the sons of nobles brought up as peers with the royal princes—a habit which Philip had largely extended, and these were first pages at court, then companions of the boy, then household officers about him. At the retired and quiet Mieza (the situation of which cannot now be determined), where the royal prince was trained by Aristotle, he became the intimate of Ptolemy, Seleucus, Lysimachus, and the other famous generals who afterwards formed his brilliant staff. Some of these had even incurred his father's displeasure in the late quarrel, and had left the court with him in disgrace.

They had not only been the companions of his studies, but of his field sports, for which the glens and forests of Macedon were famous, and never, down to the times of Perseus, who was conquered by the Romans two hundred years later, did the royal house neglect its preserves of game, where the young nobles learned the qualities of war by the hardy sports of old days, when the spear and the knife required far braver men than our modern rifles, to meet the bear and the wolf. So convinced was Alexander of the value of these sports, that he always despised formal athletic training and competitions at public festivals, and held that the pursuit of dangerous games by astuteness and endurance produced a quite different race from the practising of special muscles for a competition in the arena. It is the contrast between the *Turnen* of the German, and the field sports of the English youth, in its ancient form.

Alexander and his companions had, however, not been without the experience of these things in actual war; in Philip's campaign of ten months in Bœotia and Phocis, which had been doubtful enough till the final day at Chæronea, the prince had served in the heavy cavalry, and at that battle he had successfully led the charge which helped to decide the day. There he had learned what his father seems never to have realized, that in the heavy cavalry of Macedon they had a military arm which might turn the fortunes of the world. The Greeks had so few horses, and the country was so unfavourable for working them, that in the older Greek battles they were of little importance. If the irregular horse of Thessaly, or the Persian squadrons, occasionally encountered Greek infantry, it could easily avoid them by keeping in rocky or mountainous positions, and in neither case was there hostile infantry which could take advantage of this manœuvre. Now in addition to Philip's phalanx, which could crush any ordinary open array, and the field artillery which was Alexander's first development out of the siege trains of his father, there was a disciplined force well drilled and in hand, with which, as we shall find, he won almost all his battles.

All these things would have made no mark in history but for the man that wielded them, and when we read the wonderful accounts in Plutarch, and other late biographers, of his boyish achievements, we should readily accept them, but for the fact that his contemporaries seem to have had no notion of the wonder with which they had to deal. Demosthenes and his friends thought him only an ordinary boy; the Thebans were of the same mind, for after he had received their submission, and gone away to fight the northern barbarians, they revolted; but in a few days' fighting, in which he first showed his talent for tactics, Alexander penetrated across the Danube, and across the great mountains which separated Macedonia from

Illyria ; he forced passes, and crossed rivers ; he fought with artillery which threw stones and darts three hundred yards, and he suddenly reappeared in Greece, when they thought he was either killed or defeated among the barbarians. With swift and terrible vengeance he fell on Thebes and destroyed it ; to Athens and the rest of Greece, now terrified into abject embassies, he granted generous terms ; to the Spartans, who stood aloof in sullen refusal, he gave no thought but contempt, for he had no time to subdue them. He was not a year on the throne when he stood forth a greater and more powerful sovereign than his father, with his empire united in the bonds of fear and admiration, and ready to carry out the long premeditated attack of the Greeks on the dominions of the Great king.

III.

THE STRUGGLE FOR THE SUPREMACY OF THE WORLD (B.C. 334–330).

NO modern general could possibly have started on a campaign with the means at Alexander's disposal. He had indeed a splendid army of all branches, heavy infantry, light infantry, slingers and archers, artillery such as the ancients could produce without gunpowder, and cavalry, both Thessalian and Macedonian, fit for both skirmishing and the shock of battle. If its numbers were not above 40,000, this moderate force was surely as much as any commander could handle in a rapid campaign with long marches through a hostile country. Ancient authors, who were mostly pedants knowing nothing of war, speak as if two or three hundred thousand men could be marched across a continent without trouble. Xerxes was even supposed to have led some millions into Greece. But all this is absurd, and we know very well that as the commissariat and appointments of more than 40,000 men, marching great distances through strange country, would tax the ablest modern Quartermaster-General, with railroads to help him, so any larger army would have been simply useless to Alexander. He had already secured his passage into Asia by means of the

I.

BATTLE OF THE GRANICUS.

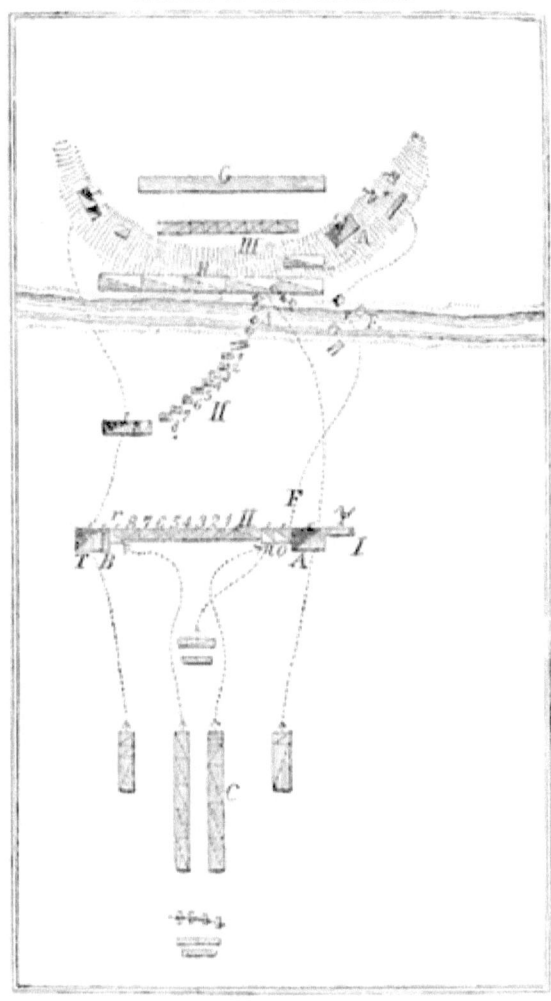

C, The approach of the Macedonian army changing into battle order I, viz.: T, Thessalian cavalry; B, Allied (Greek) cavalry; r, Thracian cavalry; 1-8, Divisions of the phalanx or heavy infantry; n, o, Light infantry; H, The Hypaspists or foot guards; F, The division of cavalry and light infantry sent forward to attack the Persian left flank; ψ, The Agriani and other archers and light troops; A, Alexander's heavy cavalry, which decided the battle. II, Represents the actual attack on R, The Persian cavalry. III, The subsequent attack on the Greek mercenary infantry G, which had been kept in the background by the Persians.

The plans are borrowed from Rüstow and Köchly's book on Greek tactics.

troops which Philip had sent to the Hellespont and the Troad just before his death; but he had no large fleet, and the warships of Phœnicia would have effectually stopped him, had he delayed. This was another reason for collecting no huge army, and it was very well known that a small number of disciplined troops, such as the Greek troops of Xenophon or Agesilaus, were as well able to meet myriads of barbarians, as the victors of Plassy or Assaye to win their victories under very like circumstances.

After a Homeric landing on the coast near Ilium, and sacrifices to the Ilian goddess at her ancient shrine, with feasts and games, the king started East to meet the Persian satraps, who had collected their cavalry and Greek mercenary infantry on the plain of Zeleia, behind the river Granicus (B.C. 334). Here he fought his first great battle, and showed the nature of his tactics. He used his heavy infantry, divided into two columns or phalanxes as his left wing, flanked by Thessalian cavalry, to threaten the right of the enemy, and keep him engaged while he delivered his main attack. Developing this movement by a rapid advance in echelonned squadrons thrown forward to the right, threatening to outflank the enemy, he induced them to spread their forces towards their left wing, and so weaken their left centre. No sooner had he succeeded in this than he threw his heavy cavalry on this weak point, and after a very severe struggle in crossing the river, and climbing its rugged banks, he completely broke the enemy's line. The Persian nobles did all they could to retrieve their mistake; they threw themselves into the gap, and fought heroically with Alexander and his companions; it seemed a mere accident that they did not succeed in killing him, and so altering the world's history. Here was indeed a distinct fault in his tactics; he constantly and recklessly exposed his own life, and so risked the whole campaign on the chance of his own escape. For though he was an excellent soldier, active, strong, and highly trained, delighting in the excitement of a hand-to-hand struggle, and so affording a fine example to his officers, it is agreed that the guiding spirit should not involve itself more than is necessary in the heat and turmoil, as well as the great risk, of personal combat.

We cannot undertake to give the details of Alexander's campaigns, which would in themselves fill this volume, and for ordinary readers they are not worth remembering. We shall merely follow out the leading points.

He did not strike straight into Asia, for this would have left it possible for Mentor and Memnon, the able Rhodians who commanded on the coast for Darius, either to have raised all Asia Minor against him, or to have transferred the war back to Macedon. Indeed, this was the policy which they urged on the Persian nobles, but it was put aside as the plan of shabby Greeks, and not of chivalrous Aryan barons; for the Persians were far more like the mediæval knights and barons than any Greeks, even the noblest, and looked upon them merely as so many useful mercenaries, to fight infantry battles, while the aristocratic service was the cavalry. In this respect the Persians were far nearer the Macedonians in sentiment, and we may

II.

PLAN OF BATTLE OF ISSUS (preliminary movements).   Cf. p. 24.

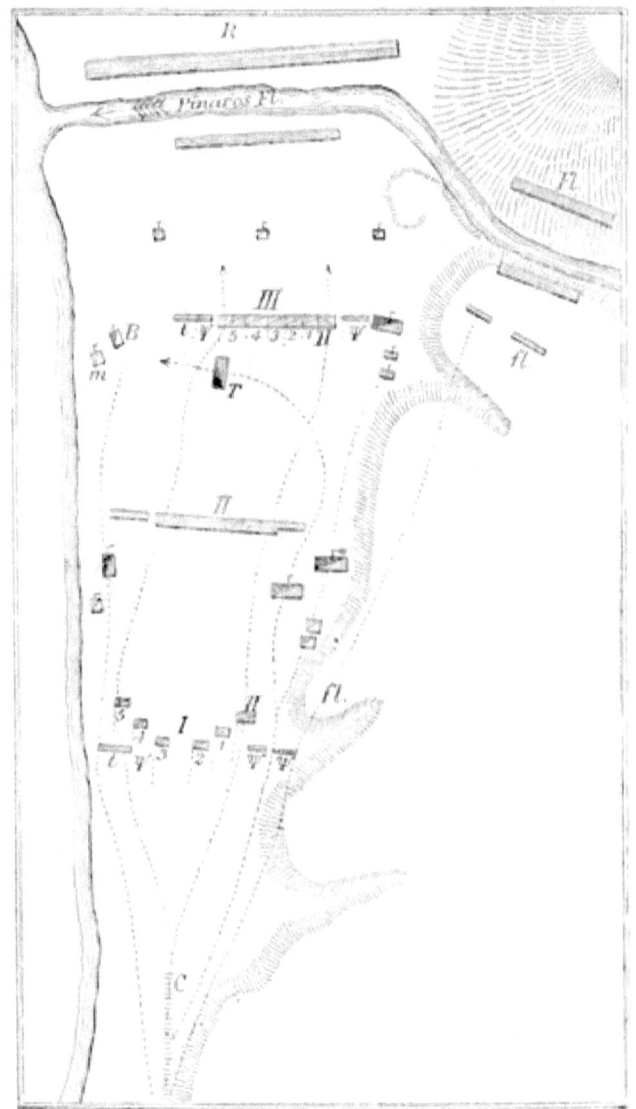

Cf. the letters of the last map. *A*, is the flanking force, protecting Alexander's right; *K*, is the Persian force, with a detachment thrown forward across the river: *T*, a detachment brought across to strengthen Alexander's left, when his right seemed secure.

be sure they so far enlisted Alexander's sympathy. However the policy of Memnon was cautious and wise, and we see that the king knew it, for he left pursuing the beaten force, and turned south to subdue the coasts of the Persian empire. This would prevent their superior fleet not only from landing on his rear, but from acting on Greece and Macedon, for ancient fleets required not only land supplies, but harbours to stay in ; they could not lie out at sea like our men of war, and for this purpose even the islands of the Levant were insufficient. So then he seized Sardis, the key of all the highroads eastwards ; he laid siege to Halicarnassus, which made a very long and stubborn resistance, and did not advance till he had his rear safe from attack.

Even with all these precautions, the Persian fleet, under Memnon, was producing serious difficulties, and had not that able general died at the critical moment (B.C. 333), the Spartan revolt, which was put down the following year in Greece, would have assumed serious proportions. Alexander now saw that he could press on, and strike at the headquarters of the enemies' power—Phœnicia and the Great king himself. He crossed the difficult range of the Taurus, the southern bulwark of the Persian Empire, and occupied Cilicia. Even the sea was supposed to have retreated to allow his army to pass along a narrow strand under precipitous cliffs. The Great king was awaiting him with a vast army—grossly exaggerated, moreover, in our Greek accounts—in the plain of Syria, near Damascus. Foolish advisers persuaded him, owing to some delay in Alexander's advance, to leave his favourable position, where the advantage of his hosts of cavalry was clear. He therefore actually crossed Alexander, who had passed on the sea side of Mount Amanus, southward, and occupied Issus on his rear. The Macedonian army was thus cut off from home and a victory necessary to its very existence. The great battle of Issus was fought on such narrow ground, between the sea and the mountains, that neither side had room for outflanking its opponent, except by occupying the high ground on the inland side of the plain (B.C. 333). This was done by the Persians, and the banks of a little river (the Pinarus) crossing their front were fortified as at the Granicus Alexander was obliged to advance with a large reserve to protect his right flank. As usual he attacked with his right centre, and as soon as he had shaken the troops opposed to him, wheeled to the left, and made straight for the king himself, who occupied the centre in his chariot. Had Darius withstood him bravely and for some time, the defeat of the Macedonians' left wing would probably have been complete, for the Persian cavalry on the coast, attacking the Thessalians on Alexander's left wing, were decidedly superior, and the Greek infantry was at this time a match for the phalanx. But the flight of Darius, and the panic which ensued about him, left Alexander leisure to turn to the assistance of his hard-pressed left wing, and recover the victory.

It may be mentioned here, as it brings the facts together for the reader, that the very same thing took place at Arbela, the next and last great battle for the supremacy of the world at that crisis. There, too,

MOSAIC OF THE BATTLE OF ISSUS (FROM POMPEII).

while Alexander's feint at outflanking the enemy's left, and his furious charge upon the king in the centre, was successful, his left wing was broken, and in danger of complete destruction. It was only his timely charge on the rear of the attacking force which saved Parmenio's phalanx. So true is it that Alexander *never won a battle with his phalanx*. He saw at once that Persian discipline was not such as could bear the defeat or death of the king. Therefore a charge in close squadrons of heavy cavalry, if brought to bear at the proper moment, and after the enemy's line has been weakened or disturbed by manœuvring, was certain to give him the victory.

At Issus, too, the Persian grandees showed a loyalty equal to any instance in the days of mediæval chivalry, and sacrificed their lives freely in defence of their pusillanimous king. In this battle, too, Alexander committed the fault of risking his person—he was actually wounded—by way of contrast to his opponent.

The greatness of this victory completely paralyzed all the revolt prepared in his rear by the Persian fleet. Alexander was now strong enough to go on without any base of operation, and he boldly (in the manifesto he addressed to Darius after the battle) proclaimed himself King of Persia by right of conquest, who would brook no equal. Nevertheless, he delayed many months (which the siege of Tyre cost him, B.C. 332), and then, passing through Jerusalem, and showing consideration for the Jews, he again paused at the siege of Gaza, merely, we may suppose, to prove that he was invincible, and to settle once for all the question of the world's mastery. He delayed again for a short while in Egypt, when he regulated the country as a province under his sway, with kindness towards the inhabitants, and respect for their religion, and founded Alexandria; nay, he even here made his first essay in claiming divinity; and then, at last, set out to conquer the Eastern provinces of Darius' empire.

The great decisive battle in the plains of Mesopotamia (B.C. 331)—it is called either Arbela or Gaugamela [1]—was spoken of as a trial of strength, and the enormous number of the Persian cavalry, acting on open ground, gave timid people room to fear; but Alexander had long since found out, what the British have found in their many Eastern wars, that even a valiant cavalry is helpless, if undisciplined, against an army of regulars under a competent commander. The Persians, moreover, committed the fatal mistake of letting Alexander choose the time and point of his attack, when the effect produced by disciplined troops is almost irresistible. The rapid evolutions of serried columns or squadrons have always had this effect upon irregulars. The Macedonian had again, however, failed to capture his opponent, for which he blamed Parmenio, whose partial defeat and urgent messages for help had compelled the king to turn at the first moment of pursuit and save his hard-pressed left wing. So then, though the issue of the war was

[1] It was on almost the same spot that another of those battles which have decided the fate of empire was fought in the year 750 A.D., when the black flag of Abbas waved victoriously over the Saracenic partizans who founded a new dynasty on the ruins of the Amiades. See "The Story of the Saracens," chap. xxxv.

III.

BATTLE OF ISSUS (decisive movements).

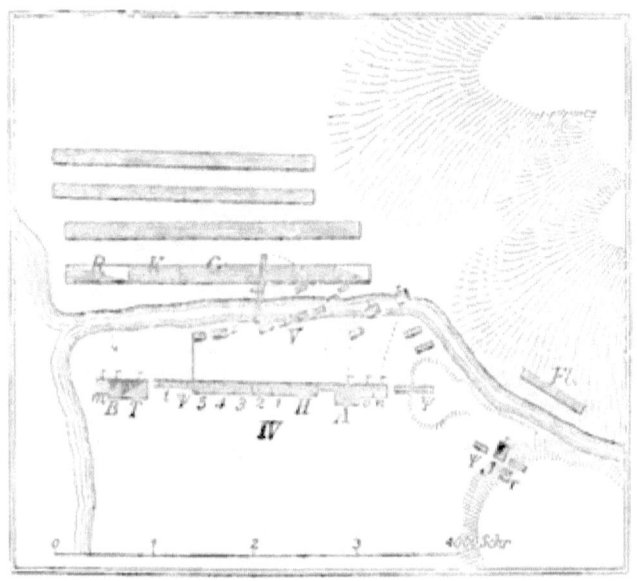

Explanation of MAPS II. *and* III.—The same letters hold good for the various divisions of Alexander's army as in the previous maps.

Five successive positions in Alexander's advance are given here and in the previous map, as he came in narrow columns through the passes of Mount Amanus from the south, and attacked Darius, encamped behind the river Pinarus ; *Fl*, are the flanking divisions of both armies on the hills to the right of the Macedonians : *J*, in these divisions means cavalry ; *K*, is the Persian king's position.

The reader will see that the tactics of this battle did not differ materially from those of the Granicus.

not doubtful, there was still a real and legitimate rival to the throne, commanding the sympathies of most of his subjects.

For the present, however, Alexander turned his attention to occupying the great capitals of the Persian empire—capitals of older kingdoms, embodied in the empire just as the King of Italy has embodied Florence, Naples, Rome, and Venice in his dominions. These great cities, Babylon in Mesopotamia, Susa (Shushan) in Elam, Persepolis in Persia proper, and Ecbatana in Media, were all full of ancient wealth and splendour, adorned with great palaces, and famed for monstrous treasures. The actual amount of gold and silver seized in these hoards (not less than £30,000,000 of English money, and perhaps a great deal more), had a far larger effect on the world than the discovery of gold and silver mines in recent times. Every adventurer in the army became suddenly rich; all the means and materials for luxury which the long civilization of the East had discovered and employed, were suddenly thrown into the hands of comparatively rude and even barbarous soldiers. It was a prey such as the Spaniards found in Mexico and Peru, but had a far stronger civilization, which must react upon the conquerors. And already Alexander showed clear signs that he regarded himself as no mere Macedonian or Greek king, but as the Emperor of the East, and successor in every sense of the unfortunate Darius.

He made superhuman efforts to overtake Darius in his retreat from Ecbatana through the Parthian passes to the northern provinces—Balkh and Samarcand. The narrative of this famous pursuit is as wonderful as anything in Alexander's campaign. He only reached the fleeing Persian as he was dying of the wounds dealt him by the traitor Bessus, his satrap in Bactria, who had aspired to the crown (B.C. 330). Alexander signally executed the regicide, and himself married the daughter of Darius—who had no son—thus assuming, as far as possible, the character of Darius' legitimate successor.

Darius Codomannus is one of those figures made tragic by great situations, and by their virtues, which are too small for their fortunes. Strange to say, this craven king who would never meet his Macedonian foe with a stout heart to conquer or to die, when an officer under Ochus, the only able and vigorous ruler whom the empire had possessed since Darius Hystaspes, had obtained his earliest reputation by accepting the challenge of a Cadusian Goliath, and slaying him hand to hand. Codomannus was handsome in person and strict in morals, evidently beloved by his people, and likely enough to make a good name in history had he not fallen upon so gigantic a crisis in human affairs. Like Louis XVI. of France,[1] his private virtues were of no avail to counteract his public incapacity, nor had his good example or honourable government time to undo the baleful effects of his predecessors' vices.

[1] See "The Story of Germany," by S. Baring-Gould, pp. 319-327, for an account of the sad career of Louis XVI.

IV.
BATTLE OF ARBELA.

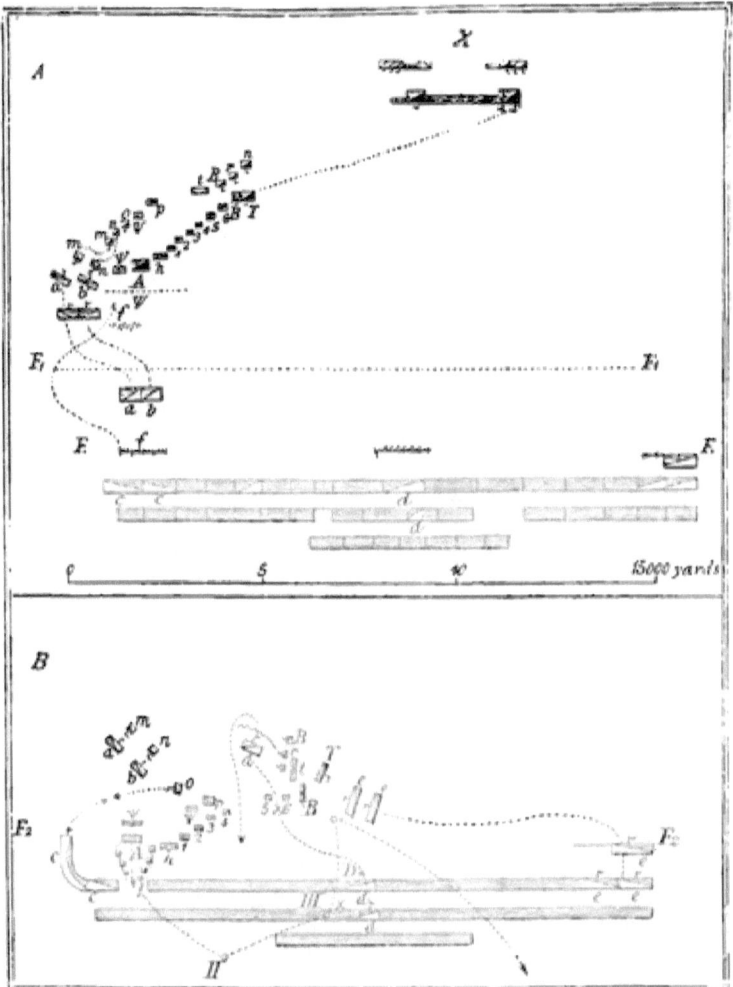

A, The preliminary actions; *B*, The battle; *X*, Alexander's camp. The same letters used for Alexander's divisions. *f*, The scythe chariots, sent to attack his advance by the Persians; *a, b*, The Bactrian and Scythian cavalry which attacked his advancing right wing; *c, c*, Arachosians and Dahae cavalry, forming left wing of the Persians; *d*, Persian and Indian cavalry, which broke Alexander's centre and separated his infantry; *e*, Cappadocian cavalry, which attacked the Macedonian left and rear; *D*, The position of Darius; *F, F¹, F²*, The successive fronts of the Persian army.

It is plain from these plans that Alexander was here in imminent danger of defeat; on Map B, his successive positions are marked *I, II, III*, showing how he had to wheel about to succour his defeated wing, when Darius fled.

IV.

THE MACEDONIAN EMPIRE, AND ITS LIMITS UP TO ALEXANDER'S DEATH.

(B.C. 323).

THE Persian Empire may be broadly divided into three parts, differing widely in their population, their produce, and their previous history. If we draw a line from the inmost corner of the Mediterranean near Issus to the Black Sea near Trebizond, we shut off all Asia Minor, a vast country which had many nationalities of various character; Greeks and Orientals, traders and pirates on the coast, shepherds and brigands in the mountains, mercenaries all, but in some general, not easily definable, way differing both from the Eastern peninsula of Europe, and from the great valley of Mesopotamia. This latter, the real centre of the Empire, has on one side the sea coast of Syria and Palestine, on the other the Alps of Media and Persia, in its centre the rich alluvial valley of the Euphrates and Tigris—a division endowed with all the requirements for sovranty, but in which, despite the domination of the Aryan mountaineers of Persia, the Semitic element was predominant. Here were the most faithful servants of the Great king, and here were his capitals. From Babylon and Nineveh had issued the commands which swayed Asia for centuries. If you draw a line from the mouth of the Persian Gulf to the foot of the Caspian, you cross a howling wilderness, the bed, perhaps, of a great salt lake like the Caspian, which gradually evaporated and left a salt steppe where no population can maintain itself, which caravans even cross with difficulty. The only highway from the West to the East of this tract is either by the narrow strip of mountain south of the Caspian, known of old as the Caspian passes, or by the sea coast of Gedrosia, a journey which cost Alexander a large part of his army; for he went into the East, in pursuit of Darius, by the former, and returned to Babylon by the latter. On the east then of this great Persian desert lay a quite distinct compartment of the empire—the upper provinces, of which the southern, Drangiana, Areia, Arachosia, and Gedrosia, have never taken any leading part in the world's history, except as the boundary land, which great conquerors have contested. The northern region, on the contrary, Bactria and Sogdiana, reaching to the country of the wild Tartars of the Steppes, have always maintained a warlike population, often recruited by immigrations from the wilder north, and here in Alexander's time were great independent barons, who served the great king as their suzerain, and lived not only in liberty, but in considerable state.

The story of the conquest of these three divisions by Alexander shows clearly their character. Asia Minor, so far as it was Greek, fell away willingly from Darius, if we except some coast cities held by the fleet; but two great battles and a triumphal procession through the country were enough to determine the question of master. When we come to the Semitic centre division, there is a curious contrast between the stubborn resistance of the coast—the sieges of Tyre and of Gaza—and the complete collapse of all further resistance after the battle of Arbela. There was, indeed, a stout attempt made by the generals of Darius to bar the great Persian passes leading from Susa to Ecbatana; but all the nations about Mesopotamia acquiesced at once in his victory. Egypt even hailed him as a deliverer.

The case was very different when Alexander attempted the conquest of the eastern or upper provinces. The southern, as I have said, were of little account. But Northern Areia, Bactria, and still more Sogdiana, revolted again and again; their chiefs, such as Spitamenes, won some victories over Macedonian detachments; they gave Alexander such trouble, and showed so keen a sense of liberty and of personal dignity, that he was obliged to have resort to the severest measures both of repression and conciliation. He almost exterminated the population in arms (and possibly the history of the world may have been affected by this destruction of the great barrier against Northern Turan), and he married the daughter of one of the proudest of the chiefs of Sogdiana. This queen, Roxane, was celebrated for her beauty, but we can hardly attribute the marriage to this cause. It was rather a political move to make the brave, rebellious province feel that it had succeeded to a large share in the empire. The new queen, of course, drew her personal retinue from her own people, and so it became the interest of these nobles to make the best of the new situation.

It is no part of a general sketch like this, to go into detail about the marches and counter marches, the "alarums and excursions" of these campaigns; we wish here merely to give the reader the kernel of the thing, the real outcome to the history of man. A study of the map of Alexander's march will show at once what marvellous distances he carried his army, and what wonderful novelties he opened to the astonished Europeans in these before unknown and fabulous regions. If any ordinary person now-a-days knows very little indeed about the Persian desert, about Herat, or Merv, or Candahar, and that only on the occasion of some British or Russian expedition, what must have been the absolute ignorance when there were no maps, no books of travel into these regions, no scientific inquiry into the distant parts of the world? Yet these provinces were then far richer and more populous than they now are; possibly the climate was more temperate; at all events, the Macedonians and Greeks found there, at least, a material civilization much superior to their own— that is to say, in gold and silver work, in embroideries, in tempered steel, in rich trees and flowers, in all the splendours which only a sustained and wealthy nobility gather round them. In all these things the Macedonian army began to feel its rudeness and vulgarity, along with its superiority in arms; and so we have the first step towards that fusion of the politics and intellect of Hellenedom with the refined manners and graceful luxury of the East.

No sooner had Alexander conquered all the realms ever claimed by the kings of Persia, than he felt that his main occupation was gone, and that he must find more kingdoms to subdue. Wild schemes of mastering, not only the habitable world, but of penetrating beyond the bounds of all that was known, were freely attributed to him in the popular romances still extant. They make him desire to reach the eastern portals of the sun, the fountain of life, and the hiding-place of the night. All these exaggerations are not pure fictions, but mark the general feeling of men that there was a vein of knight-errantry in him, that he courted adventure for its own sake, that he unduly surrendered the duty of organizing his vast dominions to the desire for new and amazing glory, to the longing for such territories as no human being, not even an Alexander, could control. His organization hitherto was merely that of military occupation, with a civil officer to control the taxing. His capital was not at Pella, at Alexandria, at Babylon, but in his camp, where he carried with him all the splendid appointments, all the pompous ceremony, all the complicated etiquette, which he had learned from his foes. We have no reason to think he would ever have ceased, if his troops had followed him, till he passed through India, Burmah, and China, to the Yellow Sea; for the itch of conquest was certainly growing upon him, and it became a passion which, after a time, he could not have controlled. But we must not anticipate.

When Alexander had conquered Sogdiana and Bactria, he found himself stopped by the lofty mountain chain of the Hindukush; and, to the south, he heard of the great waters of the Indus and the Deccan. Beyond were great peoples, with elephants and chariots, with a new culture and language, and a religion unknown even to report; but neither mountains nor rivers were able to resist him. He passed over the Hindukush with his whole army—a task that hardly any modern general would attempt; he forced the Koord-Kabul, and Khyber, passes; he crossed the Indus, the Hydaspes, in the face of a great hostile army; he conquered his new enemy and all his elephants with a skill not inferior to any yet shown; the whole Punjaub was in his hands; he was on the point of passing into India, when his troops—his Macedonian troops—refused to go further. They were worn out with battles and hardships; they had suffered terribly from the climate, especially from the heavy summer rains, as well as from the snow of the Asiatic Alps; they had more wealth than they could carry with them, and more than enough to fill their remaining years with splendour; above all, they saw that, as they were consumed by the chances of war, they would be replaced by Orientals; so that, when all the veterans were gone, Alexander would return from some land beyond the sun with a strange host to lord it over his old dominions.

The king was compelled to give way; but we may be sure he swore a great oath to himself that he would yet be lord over his rebellious troops, and carry out his own pleasure. His return by the south, his navigation of the Indus, and his march through Gedrosia, were rather geographical expeditions than campaigns, even though he had tough fighting on the Indus; and on one occasion, in attacking the town of the Malli, he not only scaled a ladder first, but leapt down by himself into the town, was desperately wounded, and all but killed, before his personal aides-de-camp and guards could succour him. But such perils were to him no more than hunting adventures with large game are to ordinary men.

In telling the story of Alexander's Empire we need not take any further account of his Indian provinces, except so far as we can trace Hellenistic[1] influences, and they are but few. Nay, even the Bactrian division breaks off very soon from any real solidarity with the West, and follows a policy and a history of its own. If Alexander had not permanently joined the Punjaub, or "Land of the Five Rivers," to the former Empire of Darius, he had at least let the Indians know of Western power and enterprise; he made them stand on the defensive, and fear invasion, and so he entered into that long and vast duel which

---

[1] Mr. Grote defines Hellenism as "the aggregate of habits, sentiments, energies, and intelligence manifested by the Greeks during their epoch of autonomy," or self-government, as opposed to the sense given it (he says) by Droysen—"the aggregate of kingdoms into which Alexander's conquests became distributed, having for their point of similarity the common use of Greek speech, a certain proportion of Greeks, both as inhabitants and as officers, and a partial streak of Hellenic culture"—a definition which Mr. Grote deems misleading, or at least not sufficiently strict. See the "History of Greece," chap. xciv., near the end. I prefer to use for the German Hellenenthum the word *Hellenedom*, as opposed to *Hellenism*, which includes the spread of Greek culture among nations not Hellenic in blood. The corresponding adjectives are *Hellenic* and *Hellenistic*. It is Mr. Grote's use of the word Hellenism which is really misleading.

subsists between the Oriental and the Frank to the present day.

At this point of our history it rather concerns us to consider what organization Alexander gave to his vast dominions, when he returned to Babylon, which he made for the moment his capital. Perhaps his first occupation was to reorganize his army, to introduce Orientals into it on a level with Macedonians, and no doubt, when disciplined, in far larger numbers. The Macedonians again revolted, but the king was now too strong for them. He dismissed them at once from his service, and so brought them to their knees. He then ordered the return to Europe of all the veterans, who were at once the least efficient for long and weary campaigns and the most dangerous for their discontent. With a new army and a new organization, apparently with a disposition of infantry looser and more manageable than the formidable but cumbrous phalanx, he meant to start on new conquests. We do not know whether he meant to subdue Arabia, and then start for Carthage and the Pillars of Hercules, or whether he had heard enough of the Romans, and their stubborn infantry, to think it his noblest path to further glory to attack Italy. The patriotic Livy thinks the Romans would even then have stopped his progress.[1] We, who look at things with clearer impartiality, feel sure that the conquest of Rome, though involving hard fighting and much loss, would have been quickly accomplished. If Hannibal easily defeated the far stronger Romans of his day by superior cavalry, how would the legions

[1] See "The Story of Rome," p. 111.

have withstood the charge of Alexander and his companions? Moreover, the Macedonians had siege trains and devices for attacking fortresses which Hannibal never possessed. We may regard it as certain that Rome would have succumbed; but as equally certain that upon the king's death she would have recovered her liberty, and resumed her natural history, with this difference, that Hellenistic culture would have invaded Rome four generations earlier, and her education would have been widely different.

We must confess it difficult to imagine that Alexander could have thought this campaign comparable to those in the far East, where the wonders of a splendid and unknown civilization had barely lifted the veil to his eager and astonished gaze. What were the Tiber and the Po compared to the Ganges and the Brahmaputra?

Yet one thing was clear. Before the king could adventure himself again into any of these knight-errant expeditions, he must insist upon order and method in his acknowledged conquests; and he found anything but order there. He found that the adventurous Greeks, and even Macedonian nobles, whom he had made governors over provinces, had not been proof against temptation. They heard of his continued triumphs in the East. They hardly expected that he would ever return; or at least they thought, like the servant in the Gospel: "Our Lord delayeth his coming." They rifled royal tombs, oppressed subjects, extorted treasure, and assumed royal power. Alexander made short work with these offenders. Of course, his various agents must have had large powers of control during his long absences. Antipater in Macedonia, and Antigonus in Phrygia, were old and tried servants, who kept for years quite a court for themselves, and many were the complaints of Olympias, the queen-mother, to her son of Antipater's arbitary conduct, and his replies, showing that he must carry out his trust without permitting the interference even of royal princesses. The king's treasurer at Babylon, Harpalus, embezzled money, and fled on the king's approach to Athens, where his advent with treasure, and his bribing of public men, caused that commotion at Athens which ended in the banishment of Demosthenes. So also we hear that in Egypt the Greek put in charge of the finances conducted himself badly, and was guilty of oppression and extortion. Everything showed that the whole system of the empire required reform, and that, besides military governors and fiscal agents, some settled method of control from the central point of the empire was absolutely necessary to prevent speedy dissolution.

Hitherto the king's capital had been his camp, moving with his campaigns, and often at the very extremity of his provinces. Here, indeed, there was always great state—pages, household officers, chamberlains, and all the ceremony of a royal residence. There were secretaries keeping a careful journal of every day's events; there was a staff office, with its adjutants and orderlies. There was a state dinner, to which the king sat down with fifty or sixty guests; and, as in the play,[1] when he pledged the gods in

[1] Hamlet, i. 4, vv. 859.

libations and draughts of wine, the bray of trumpets proclaimed to the whole army that the king drank. The excesses, too, of their revels were notorious, as they had been even in Philip's time; the king would tell his adventures and boast of his prowess in the chase and in war; they would spend the night in drinking, according to Macedonian and Thracian habits, and not as suited the hotter climate of the South. So the toils of the day and excesses of the night were such as must have exhausted many a sound constitution, and made many a young man grow old before his time. Our accounts of the great king at the age of thirty-two represent him as far advanced from the gaiety of youth, scarred with wounds, violent and often gloomy in temper, and shaking off his colossal cares only by the deep draughts and the noisy excitement of a long night revel. It required no solemn signs and strange portents to warn men that such a life could not last. Ominous events accompanied the king's advent to Babylon, and when after several nights of drinking, he was declared in fever, the public alarm must have been quickly aroused. We have the bulletins yet, which were issued to tell the army of their hero's illness; the anxious quest of oracles by his friends; the solemn march of the Macedonians past the bed-side of the speechless monarch. Then came the news that he was dead, and the world without a master.

A great terror seized upon the stoutest hearts. While the body of the great king lay alone, and deserted by the amazed household, stray shouts broke the anxious silence of the city, men hurried to and fro in the night, without lights and muffled in disguise, seeking in tumultuous council, or in random inquiry, to forecast what should happen on the morrow. There were confused sounds of mourning and woe, not round about the bier of the king, but for the disasters which each awaited in his home.

The Orientals had most to lose. Alexander had been their father and protector against the insolence and tyranny of Macedonians and Greeks. But even the Macedonians, who had revolted and complained of late, knew that the real secret of their supremacy over men had departed.

COIN OF PHILIP II. OF MACEDON.

V.

THE PROBLEM OF THE SUCCESSION.

THE conflict of various interests was not long in showing itself, and turned in the first instance on the succession to the throne. Alexander had left an illegitimate brother, the weak-minded Philip Arridaeus, son of a Thessalian dancer; he had an illegitimate son, Herakles, by Barsine, the widow of Darius's best Greek general, Memnon; his wife, Roxane, was expecting an heir. There was, moreover, Statira, daughter of the late king of Persia, to whom he had been recently married. All these claimants, or quasi claimants, found supporters either now or in the sequel. But all these supporters were advocating, not the interests of the royal house, but their own. There were also the queen-mother, Olympias, a woman of imperious character, beloved by the Macedonians as the mother of their hero, and Cleopatra (queen of Epirus), the full sister of Alexander; not to speak of Kynane, the daughter of Philip by a Thracian connection. It was the obvious misfortune of the king's early death, that he could not possibly have an adult heir, and so all these collateral claimants could make some case pending the birth of his child by the Queen Roxane.

At the very outset there were conflicts in the palace even while the king lay there unburied. Then it came out that the cavalry and horse-guards, headed for the moment by Perdiccas, the senior officer of the household, were in favour of a small council of lords, awaiting the expected birth of the king's heir, while the infantry, led by Meleager, a Greek, proclaimed Philip Arridæus king. After a dangerous crisis, a compromise was made, and the whole army, horse and foot, marched between the divided halves of a sacrificed dog, according to a quaint and barbarous survival of old Macedonian manners; and then came a sham fight, still in pursuance of precedent, in which the cavalry faced the infantry. In old days this may have been thought fair sides; but since Alexander's reforms in the army, and the acquisition of elephants, which counted as cavalry, infantry was perfectly helpless on open ground. The elephants could be used to break the phalanx, and then they could be cut to pieces by the cavalry; so the sham fight turned into terrible earnest. Perdiccas demanded the leaders of the party who had dared to anticipate his policy by setting up Philip Arridæus. Thirty of them, according to the lowest estimate, were surrendered, and forthwith trampled to death by the elephants—a horrible proof of the Oriental barbarism as to punishment which had infected the Macedonians, and which remains a blot on all the Hellenistic age.

According to the compromise, Philip Arridæus was to be titular king, until the birth and growth of the proper heir. Perdiccas was to be the regent, and to manage the central affairs, the main army, and the imperial interests. Various high offices of Court or of state were given to his rivals and friends, but the main thing was that the ablest and greatest of them were sent off to govern various provinces of the empire as satraps, and satraps with full military power in their province. The man who is said to have urged and carried this measure was Ptolemy, son of Lagus, an extremely active and trusted officer under Alexander, afterwards his historian, who preferred to leave the centre of affairs, and be exiled to a province, for the solid profit of making for himself a definite and defensible kingdom. He started at once for Egypt, which he never surrendered, but bequeathed, as we shall see, a prosperous and wealthy dominion to his posterity.

This short history need not concern itself with all the other divisions of provinces, which were upset and rearranged several times during the next few years, though a few, like the lot of Ptolemy, proved more permanent. Macedonia was given to Antipater, the old regent of that province, and he retained it all his life. He was so firm and loyal an adherent to the royal house, whose special guardian and protector he became, that he disinherited his son Casander, the bitter enemy of Alexander and his family; but that prince recovered what he regarded his patrimony, and though his weak and worthless children were set aside by Demetrius, it was the descendants of this king by Phila, daughter of Antipater and sister of Casander, who held the throne of Macedonia till it was swallowed up in the Roman Empire.

The other permanency, the kingdom of the Seleucids, does not yet appear, though Seleucus was already a distinguished officer, entrusted by the regent Perdiccas with the *Chiliarchy*, or next in command to the "Guardian Plenipotentiary" (ἐπιμελή- της αὐτοκράτωρ). But he was then only about thirty years of age, and stood below the veterans of the older generation, who naturally got the first choice. Of these, two of the most popular and important, Craterus and Leonnatus, were killed out of the way, the latter in battle with the Greeks, as shall presently be told, and at the moment when he and the royal Cleopatra, Alexander's sister, and widow of the king of Epirus, were about to marry, and set up claims to the whole Empire. A third, Lysimachus, disappears from prominence in his satrapy of Thrace, where he carried on war for years with the barbarians, with such varying success as to be once even taken captive, but who, before the end of his life, attained great power, and commanded not only Thrace, but a large part of Western Asia Minor. The princes of Perga- mum, called Attalids, were the successors to the Asiatic part of his kingdom. A fourth, Antigonus, who had already been satrap, under Alexander, of Phrygia for ten years, and was very popular there, was ordered by the Regent Perdiccas to leave his province and go with an army to assist in installing Eumenes in his lot of Paphlagonia, the country reaching from Sinope round to Trebizond and the Caucasus.

Here we come in contact with the two men who occupy all Asia for the next few years—Eumenes, the great king's private secretary, a clever boy of Cardia, who had made his own fortune, was promoted over the heads of many noble Macedonians, and consequently hated by them as an upstart Greekling; and Antigonus, the ablest of Alexander's generals, as it turned out, and the one who made far the best or the most dangerous attempt to wrest the whole empire into his own hands. Of these, Eumenes, from his position, was necessarily devoted to the interests of the royal family. As their minister and supporter he was great; as an independent sovereign he would not for an instant be recognized by the Macedonian armies. Hence he stood by Perdiccas the Regent, and was the only satrap who did so. All the rest sought to found independent sovranties at least, the more ambitious to seize the whole empire—some with the aid of a marriage connection with the royal family, some by the mere force of arms.

So began the struggles which lasted forty-five years, in which most of the companions and successors of Alexander lost their lives. To follow out the details of these varied conflicts is quite beyond the scope of any practical book. We need only concern ourselves with the campaigns which have gained a place in literature, and the main ideas which underlay the great conflict. Of the wars immediately following Alexander's death, only three phases are worthy of record here. First, the attack on Egypt by the Regent Perdiccas, who, when he had summoned the disobedient satraps before him, and Antigonus had fled to Europe, fell upon Ptolemy, and sought to crush him. The pretended cause of war was that Ptolemy had met the splendid funeral *cortège* of Alexander, on its way to the tomb assigned by the Regent (probably a shrine of Jupiter Ammon at Aegae, the mausoleum of the Macedonians), and from Syria brought it to Memphis, pending its establishment in Alexandria. All men thought the presence of the hero, even dead, would bring no ordinary honour and blessing to the resting-place chosen for him, and when we hear that several years later Eumenes was able, by the fiction of a royal tent, and the spiritual presence of the king, to appease the jealousy of the Macedonians, we see that the great king was already becoming that kind of fetish, which filled the imagination of all the romances for centuries.

Ptolemy met the invasion, defeated it, and in the confusion and anger of the defeat, insurgent soldiers killed Perdiccas. Here we may once for all note the extraordinary difficulty of invading Egypt, except by means of a superior fleet, and even then along a coast which contained no harbours for hundreds of miles. Antigonus at the zenith of his power tried the same thing, and miserably failed. This was the secret of Ptolemy's choice, and the secret of his singular success. Even the Romans were exceedingly afraid of this peculiar and isolated position, owing to the power it conferred on its ruler, and so they took special care to let no ambitious or distinguished person assume so unchecked an authority.

Meanwhile Antipater had been waging a dangerous contest with the Greeks, known as the Lamian War, in which the confederated Greeks attempted to assert their liberty. They were under the command of the gallant Leosthenes, and besieged the veteran general at Lamia in Thessaly. He was in great straits, even after the death of Leosthenes, who was killed in a skirmish.[1] With the help of troops from Asia, and of Leonnatus, who was however killed in a battle, but still more with the help of time, which disintegrates all confederations when opposed to a despotic enemy, he won the substantial victory at Crannon, and dictated his terms to the Greeks. More stern, and perhaps more practical, than Philip after Chæronea (B.C. 338) and Alexander after the destruction of Thebes (B.C. 335), he insisted on the death of the political leaders who had led the republican opposition. So Demosthenes and Hypereides met their fate (323), and this in itself has made the war of Antipater famous. Otherwise his settlement of Greece was not severe; he raised the franchise, excluding paupers from political rights, and by means of Macedonian garrisons sought to keep order throughout the country.

The last moments of the orator have been made immortal by the narrative of Plutarch. He has done nearly as much for Eumenes, so far as a stirring biography can do it.[2] When the Successors, Diadochi,[3] as they are designated, assembled to make a new division at Triparadeisus (321), Antipater and Ptolemy were confirmed; so was Antigonus in his kingdom of Phrygia, and Seleucus was assigned Babylon; but Eumenes

[1] The virtues of Leosthenes are celebrated in the splendid funeral oration of Hypereides, recovered to us some years ago on an Egyptian papyrus.
[2] See his "Life of Demosthenes," and "Life of Eumenes."
[3] The word *diadochi* means successors, and is used to include Antigonus, Ptolemy, Seleucus, Lysimachus, etc.—the actual companions of Alexander.

(who had been the close ally of Perdiccas, and who moreover had meanwhile slain in battle Craterus, the most popular of all the generals, and Neoptolemus), was declared by the Macedonians a public enemy. His ability and tried loyalty to the royal house, now given in charge to Antipater, gave him such power in his province, that he was not easy to conquer, and the next years are filled with widely extended and elaborate campaigns, sieges, victories, and defeats, sustained by either side in the great war between Antigonus and Eumenes. They at times even met as friendly rivals, and endeavoured to make a settlement; but their interests never agreed, they were each too ambitious to play a second part, and too suspicious to trust themselves to any agreement without retaining their armaments. In the end, Antigonus won by seducing Eumenes' Macedonian veterans, and put his adversary to death (B.C. 315). This was in Persia, and it gave him command of the eastern provinces and their enormous wealth. The coalition kept together against him by Eumenes was dissolved; and he proceeded to settle all Asia according to his desire.

The only important obstacle was Seleucus, the popular satrap of Babylon. Antigonus endeavoured to summon him to a trial, of which the issue could not be doubtful; but Seleucus escaped with the greatest difficulty into Egypt, to await better times. So far Antigonus, however, was master, and was plainly no earnest supporter of the royal house; he sought universal sovranty for himself, and then for his splendid son Demetrius, who seemed more likely than any one else to succeed to the position of Alexander.

Meanwhile the European provinces had gone through a series of battles of their own. So long as Antipater lived, there was some peace; but when not only his death supervened, but he was found to have left the regency entrusted to him to Polysperchon, one of his brothers in arms, and not to his son Casander, all manner of seeds were sown for future wars. Casander, who from the beginning discarded the theory of submitting to Alexander's children, set up in opposition to Polysperchon. The latter, finding himself in difficulties, issued one of those many absurd proclamations, *giving liberty to all the Greeks*, which were made in after years by every ruler ambitious of their support—by Antigonus and by his son, by Ptolemy, but always with the intent of securing a more permanent dominion over them.

These party struggles do not concern us. On the whole, Casander was successful; he re-introduced peace and order into Athens, after the disgraceful scenes countenanced by Polysperchon, and with him by the silly phantom of a king, Philip Arridæus. Plutarch has again given us a picture of the times which no one that reads it can forget, in the closing scenes of his "Life of Phocion," when we see what use the Athenian rabble made of their so-called liberty. All this was stopped by Casander, so far as his power reached. At Athens, a pupil of Aristotle, Demetrius of Phaleron, a philosopher, man of letters, and man of pleasure, kept things quiet and orderly.

with the help of a Macedonian garrison close at hand in the Piræus.

Casander never gained complete control of Greece. He was always contending with the representatives of the royal house, and it was only with the aid of their internal quarrels that he was able to plan their destruction. Olympias, the queen-mother, who was devoted to her son and his heir, got hold of Macedonia for a while, and forthwith ordered the murder of the titular king Arridæus, and of his wife Eurydike, the grand-daughter of Philip, whose masculine ambition made her dangerous, and likely to oust the proper heir, now a growing child. But Olympias did not confine her vengeance to these pretenders. She raged among the partisans of Casander, and made herself so odious, that her great prestige could only delay her murderers and make them hesitate. She died a splendid old savage queen, devoting all her energies to the protection of her grandson, but encumbered with perplexities, with varying factions, with cross-purposes in policy, which no woman that ever lived could have overcome.

By a settlement made between the contending satraps in the year 311, after a struggle of four years on the part of a coalition to overcome Antigonus, or perhaps rather of Antigonus to subdue all these his rivals, Casander was secured in the possession of Macedonia, and the royal widow Roxane and her son, whom the death of Olympias had left in his hands as prisoners, were placed in his charge till the prince should be of age. No one dared to question the boy's rights, and every ambitious leader pretended to assert them against the encroachments of his rivals; but Casander, of all the Successors, was the most coldly and cruelly determined to abolish the whole house of Alexander, and to assert himself as king of Macedonia. He had married a daughter of Philip (Alexander's father), and had reconquered the authority of Antipater, bequeathed to a stranger, Polysperchon. He determined to keep the boy and his mother in close ward at Amphipolis, and when voices were heard among the people, commiserating the fate of the unfortunate prince, he had both mother and son privily murdered.

Nothing in history is more tragic than the fate of this child of thirteen, for whom all the world waited in anxious expectation; born with no father to protect him, and carried about even as an infant from camp to camp, from province to province, the watchword of parties, the cloak for ambitions, the excuse for murders, in charge of two homicidal princesses, his mother and grandmother. Then he was gradually neglected, confined, imprisoned, and while titular lord of all the Eastern world, was the captive of a cruel and relentless despot. At last he disappears like the English Princes in the Tower, with a fate like that of Louis XVII. and of the *Roi de Rome*, but without leaving us a trace of his person or of his character. He gives the date and authority to coins; he is named in pompous hieroglyphics as the king Alexander, the Great Lord, Blessed, that liveth for ever. To us, as to the men that made the inscription, the imperial child is but a name, and yet so tragic from his every fortune that few of the greatest sufferers, whose heroic sorrows are known to us all, can claim a higher place in the hierarchy of human martyrdom.

With the death of this prince and his mother, following on that of Olympias, and her opponents Philip Arridæus and Eurydike, all pretence of sustaining the dynasty of Alexander was abandoned. The great king's sister Cleopatra, lived indeed a royal widow at Sardis, wooed by all the world; but those whom she would have chosen, Leonnatus and Perdiccas, died before the event, and she spurned the rest as unworthy consorts. Still Antigonus kept her in his power, and when at last she consented to marry Ptolemy, to escape from his control, Antigonus had her murdered, lest the Egyptian chief should get this title to supremacy. So disappears the last legitimate claimant to the empire. The bastard Herakles was indeed set up for a moment, as every possible puppet was, to strengthen the case of adventurous freebooters in their search after royalty; but he was thrust aside and murdered (B.C. 309) like the rest, and the details of his life need not trouble us here.

COIN OF DEMETRIUS I.

VI.

THE LATER WARS OF THE DIADOCHI DOWN TO THE BATTLE OF IPSUS.
(B.C. 313–301.)

THE CAREER OF DEMETRIUS.

WE come now to an epoch when all the satraps, who had pretended to hold their sway in the interest of the royal house, became independent princes, and presently assumed the title of kings. Beginning in the year 306 B.C., monarchy became the popular title and the accepted form of government all through the great empire of Alexander. It was not hereditary; but in those days, it must be repeated, no claim was dreamt of older than the division after Alexander's death. He was conceded by all to have conquered the world by lawful conquest and to own it by an indefeasible right. All succeeding monarchs traced back their legitimacy to his title, and so a perfectly new epoch in Hellenic and Eastern history begins. This is called the epoch of Hellenism. Such little antiquated hole-and-corner affairs as the kingdom of Sparta were no longer looked upon as of the least importance, or as models for any one to copy. We notice that none of these satraps, however powerful, or well established in their kingdoms, ventured to assume the name of king till the royal family was extinct; we notice that then they assume it almost simultaneously; Antigonus and Ptolemy first, then Casander, Lysimachus; by and by, Demetrius the Besieger. Nor do we hear of one word of objection to the title on the part of nations whose whole watchword had been, not only liberty, but democracy. It was the Athenians who led the way in hailing Demetrius as king.

This remarkable state of feeling throughout the nations requires a moment's explanation. It was no doubt induced, in the first instance, by the enormous figure Alexander had made in the world. He had shown that an absolute monarch—for he was practically such—could protect and enrich his friends, and overcome his enemies, as no republic had ever yet done up to that time. His nation, of whom the dominant class took up the reins of empire from his hand, were all brought up under monarchical principles; the great Republic of Italy was still in obscurity; the Greek philosophers, now an important element in public opinion, were recommending monarchy in all their writings; they argued that the public was an ass, the majority fools, and that the rule of a few select men, or of one pre-eminent person was the only form of government fit for civilized men. We may add, that if ever a state of nature appeared to be a state of war, it was in these dreadful times, when no one could see an end to the conflict among the various kings, and when the only safety possible was the protection of a powerful and victorious monarch.

Neutrality meant the certainty of being conquered or plundered by each of the warring sides in turn. Moreover, these belligerent kings were too busy and too vagrant to weigh heavily on the local liberties of any small city state. In general, a contribution of men and money for war was all that was demanded, and they were profuse in their declarations of liberating the Greek cities in this particular sense, of *communal autonomy*, or the right of managing their own local affairs as they pleased. The occasional violation of this privilege by armed interference, which was not unfrequent under these sovrans, was thought a lesser evil than the perpetual tyranny of the needy classes, who, in the case of manhood suffrage, turned their political power into a daily source of plunder.

There was indeed one expedient, which would naturally occur to any American reader, by which small free states might secure their independence without submitting to a foreign monarch—I mean the principle of Federation. And, as might be expected, this principle was adopted as a means of escape from Monarchy, and with some success. The present crisis, about the year 306 B.C. when kings sprang up all over Alexander's empire, suddenly shows us the first of these Federations in growth, that of the maritime and island cities in the Levant, reaching from Heraclea in Pontus, and Byzantium, down to Rhodes, the chief organizer of this system. These cities had the peculiar advantage, that they were so defended and supplied by the sea, as to render their conquest impossible without a blockade by a superior fleet, and this arm of war the Federation could itself supply in such strength as to checkmate kings who had large land armies. So this Federation of free coast and island cities obtained for itself respect and attention from the neighbouring kings, and performed the duty of looking after maritime commerce by keeping the seas free of pirates, and by establishing a sound system of marine law. The Rhodian code was in use up to the days of the Roman Empire.

These remarks will explain the situation of the world, which lasted from 311 to 301 B.C. when the lesser aspirants to empire had been cleared away, and five remained as masters of the spoil—first, *Seleucus*, now returned from Egypt and popular in Babylon, with a control, though not very absolute, of the eastern provinces. Then came *Antigonus*, whose kingdom included the main body of Asia Minor, but who was far from being content with this, and hoped to subdue Seleucus in the East, which he had already conquered in former years, and had only lost owing to his head being full of trouble in warring with *Ptolemy* for the possession of Syria, and if possible Egypt, as well as the coast cities of Asia, which Ptolemy helped with his fleet and money. The ambition of Antigonus was also checked to the north-west by *Lysimachus*, whose power, not yet consolidated in Thrace, was yet growing stronger and stronger, and, after the foundation of his new capital Lysimacheia, on the sea of Marmora, was to extend into Asia Minor. This coalition of Seleucus, Ptolemy, and Lysimachus, was strengthened in Europe by Casander, who had always followed consistently the policy of separate kingdoms, whereas Antigonus

plainly aspired to ruling the conquests of Alexander
alone. His power was so great, that he was all but a
match for the rest, especially with the assistance of
his brilliant son *Demetrius*, who was a general and
admiral of the first order, and whom he sent to detach
Greece from Casander, and so produce a diversion
against his foes in the west. The wars of Demetrius
have been told us by Plutarch in a *Life* of no less
interest than any of his famous series, and which is
only less read because the historical period in which
it lies is so complicated and little understood, that

COIN OF DEMETRIUS I.

his deeds do not fall into any particular frame. This
it is which the present book strives to make known
to the reader. Demetrius' successes at Athens and
throughout Greece were very brilliant; he was
received at Athens as the Deliverer and Defender.
He was worshipped in the temple of the Virgin
Goddess, the Parthenon, though his habits of life
were those of a Don Juan, and not of a companion of
Athene. Having thus paralyzed Casander, he also
sought in a great campaign to subdue Rhodes, and
compel its powerful fleet to join the force of Antigonus.
If he had succeeded, Ptolemy would have been ruined,

for a more powerful fleet would have enabled Antigonus to land his superior land forces in Egypt, and thus avoid the disasters which he, like all the other invaders of that country at this period, suffered by attempting the attack by way of Palestine and the Arabian desert.

So all the world's attention was fixed on the great struggle at Rhodes (B.C. 305 ?), where Demetrius exhausted all known means of attack, while the Rhodians, actively helped by Ptolemy's money, supplies, and men, were no less zealous in the defence. Fortunately he was not able to invest the town, which was open to help, and so the siege resembled that of Sebastopol, which the assailants tried to reduce by bombardment and assault, while the defenders were constantly being reinforced from without. Demetrius bombarded the place literally, for since Alexander's day the power of engines to throw darts and great stones was so developed, that not only was their range increased to 300 yards, but they were able to shake walls and batter down defences without actually coming within the close range of the battering ram. The great machine used by Demetrius, and called the *City Taker* (ἑλέπολις), can be compared to nothing but the broadside of one of our old line-of-battle ships, which poured out destruction from the port-holes of several decks. It was constructed in several stories, protected with raw hides and penthouses from fire and from darts, and carrying an immense number of men and engines, so as to sweep the opposing battlements of its defenders, as well as to shake the walls themselves. Yet all this and many assaults were unavailing against the Rhodians, who kept communication open with Egypt by sea, constantly intercepted Demetrius' supplies, and defended every point with the greatest bravery.

All the time empty courtesies were passing between the combatants, which show how war had become the every-day occupation of the better classes, and was carried on as a matter of policy, not of principle or of passion. The Rhodians had made every effort to remain neutral, in fact, they had ceded every point demanded except to take part in active warfare against Egypt, and to give one hundred hostages of their magnates as security to Demetrius. When hostilities commenced, it was agreed by both sides to surrender prisoners made in battle at the rate of five minæ for a slave, and ten for a free man—a very high rate, by the way, as compared with the two minæ (about £8) customary in Herodotus' day or before it, throughout the Peloponnesus. When the Rhodians complained that a celebrated picture of the mythical Ialysos would be burnt in the painter's studio, if the suburbs were cleared for the siege, Demetrius answered that he would rather defile the tombs of his ancestors than molest the artist and his work. Perpetually embassies were arriving from neutral states throughout the Greek world, offering mediation, and truces were held, during which terms of agreement were discussed. When at last the prince saw that the siege was not progressing and might last long enough to ruin his interests elsewhere, he agreed to a peace very much on the basis originally offered by the Rhodians, except that they ceded the point about hostages, with the proviso that they should not be office-bearers. This, we may presume, saved the principal magnates from the compulsory residence, though doubtless in luxury and comfort, at Ephesus, the town appointed for them.

The great siege confirmed the public opinion of the power and determination, as well as of the moderation and good sense, of the Rhodian Republic, and greatly strengthened their power to lead in a Federation of mercantile cities, not unlike the Hanseatic League. It was doubtless the success of this league of maritime cities, which suggested to the smaller and obscurer states of Greece, which had no imperial record, and no capital with insurmountable claims or jealousies, to form similar confederations, or to strengthen and extend those which already existed. Among the neutral powers offering mediation at the siege of Rhodes were the Ætolians, afterwards almost the leaders in the Greek world. The Achæan League was also in existence, but in obscurity. It was not for another generation or two that the importance of these Alpine Federations, for such they were, became manifest; though even now they were accumulating one necessary condition of power, and that was wealth. As the trade of the Levant, after the destruction of Tyre, had fallen into the hands of the Greek maritime cities of the Asiatic coasts and islands, and so enriched them as to make their fleet and finance indispensable elements in estimating the powers of the day, so the fortunes gained by Ætolians, Achæans, and Arcadians, who had an old habit of leaving their mountain glens and serving as mercenaries, were now so large, that

THE NIKE OF SAMOTHRACE, A MONUMENT SET UP BY DEMETRIUS I.

A, Actual remains ; *B*, Restoration ; *C*, Coin of Demetrius ; *D*, Restoration (from the coin), of the whole monument.

they outran in comforts and luxuries the life of the older and more settled cities, which were visibly declining, both in men and money.

For the present the world's interest was elsewhere—in the renewed attempt of Antigonus to gain universal mastery, and in the renewed coalition of Seleucus, Lysimachus, Ptolemy, and Casander to crush his power. He was still apparently a match for them, his central position in Syria (he had a capital, called after himself Antigoneia, on the Orontes) enabled him to fight them separately, so that their junction was difficult. He had sent Demetrius to Greece, who was gradually pushing back Casander northwards, and promised soon to subdue him altogether. But the hopes of Antigonus, which were high, shipwrecked upon two unexpected difficulties—the strategic powers of Lysimachus, and the enormous forces of Seleucus. This latter prince had disappeared from our view for the last ten years, during which we know that he was engaged in campaigns on his eastern frontier, and among those nations which Alexander had rather terrified into submission by a great battle or two, than systematically subdued. Porus, his faithful subject, had been murdered, and other claimants arose. In Seleucus' day a great Oriental, Chandragupta, whom the Greeks called Sandracottus, had developed such power beyond the Indus, that Seleucus was glad to come to terms with him, purchasing his hearty alliance and support by the cession of those eastern provinces which lie beyond the great Persian desert—Gedrosia, Arachosia, and Paropamisus; but he obtained five hundred elephants, and treasure so large that he from this time rises to the first rank among the Diadochi.

His support, however, was tardy. He could not come by way of Mesopotamia and Syria, without conquering Antigonus single handed, and there seem to have been great difficulties in the route by way of Armenia, which he was obliged to follow. Meanwhile, Lysimachus, expecting earlier aid, had invaded Asia Minor from the north, and carried all before him down to the mountains which bound Phrygia on the south; but as Antigonus' hands were free, and Ptolemy was timid and lukewarm in making a diversion by way of Palestine, Lysimachus found himself in presence of a superior force, far from his base of operations—the Hellespont. On this occasion he showed his great qualities as a general. By fortifying lines, refusing battle, and compelling Antigonus to undertake regular siege-approaches, he occupied the precious time. No sooner was the assault upon his defences imminent than he retired suddenly northwards, and repeated the same tactics with great success. This occupied the whole summer of 302 B.C.

Meanwhile, Ptolemy had advanced as far as Tyre, but stopped and retired at the false news of a defeat of Lysimachus. About Seleucus' approach nothing was known. Everybody was in expectation, but the allies were separated, as has been said, and had no communication. At last Seleucus appeared, just when Lysimachus in his fortified camp in Mysia was in great difficulties. Not only was he opposed to Antigonus; but that king had sent for his son Demetrius, just when he stood ready over against Casander to win a decisive battle. The lesser war was obscured by the greater, and both combatants agreed that there should be peace in Greece while they sent their forces to the great scene of the world's conflict. Demetrius was superior in fleet; and he also intercepted and harassed the supports sent from Macedonia by way of land to help Lysimachus. Had the campaign been protracted; had Antigonus avoided a decisive conflict, the empire would probably have come into his hands; but he was old, impatient, and obstinate. He and his son Demetrius met on the field of Ipsus, in Phrygia (B.C. 301), the combined forces of Lysimachus, with Casander's contingent, and that of Seleucus with four hundred and eighty elephants, and a vast cavalry commanded by the crown prince Antiochus. The conflict was bloody, and Demetrius with his cavalry performed the part of Prince Rupert in pursuing while the battle was still in the balance. Ultimately Antigonus fell, aged eighty-one; his forces were scattered and surrendered, and his son became a fugitive with a few thousand men, but with a fleet which was still able to withstand his enemies.

So ended the last serious attempt to reconquer the whole empire of Alexander. Demetrius, indeed, never abandoned the dream. After many adventures as a fugitive, as a pirate almost, then as a pretender to the throne of Macedon, then (when Casander was dead) as king of Macedon, he that had kept the world in turmoil was taken by Seleucus, and as a state captive eat away his heart in fretful idleness and despairing dissipation. The "Life" by Plutarch gives us a curious picture of this wonderful personage, so attractive to the end that countless cities begged his release from Seleucus (a release which old Lysimachus so dreaded that he offered 2000 talents to Seleucus to make away with him)—so attractive that his noble wife Phila, Casander's sister, stood by him through all his infidelities and political marriages, and took her own life when she despaired of his success; so attractive that his noble and serious son Antigonus, the founder of a new line of kings in Macedonia, offered to surrender his own liberty, and was even ready to sacrifice his life for his knight-errant father.

When the sons of Casander were set aside—the one murdered by his brother, the other by Demetrius—there was no home claimant for the throne so strong as the husband of Phila; but his struggles were with Pyrrhus, the adventurous king of Epirus, on the one hand, and with Lysimachus on the other. These princes were more than a match for him, if not in strategy, at least in prestige and popularity. Lysimachus was one of the Companions of Alexander, a title in that day surpassing every other honour; Pyrrhus was singularly genial and kindly, as well as chivalrous, and in these taking qualities Demetrius seems to have failed when he was actually king; but his adventures and fortunes in these later years are among the complications of history which serve to perplex and not to instruct the reader.

VII.

FROM THE BATTLE OF IPSUS TO THE INVASION OF THE CELTS.
(B.C. 301-278.)

WITH the battle of Ipsus there began a new epoch for the Diadochi. Lysimachus and Seleucus had borne the brunt of the fight, and took the lion's share of the spoil. Ptolemy had been lukewarm, and had even left them in the lurch, so Seleucus took the cities of Phœnicia and Syria, which the other had bargained for, or even occupied with garrisons, and henceforth this western point of his great empire gives it its title in history. All the East was in his power. He ruled up to the line from Trebizond to Issus, and was here separated from the power of Lysimachus by a sort of neutral zone of smaller states—Pontus, Armenia, and Cappadocia—which, though insignificant, pursued a policy of their own, had their own dynasties, which they derived from the Persian kings, and were the last remnants of the empire of Alexander subdued by the Romans. Mithridates of Pontus and the kings of Armenia figure as enemies or allies of Rome, long after the greater members of the empire were gone. Lysimachus, on the other hand, got valuable possessions in Asia Minor, one of which, Pergamum, became itself an important kingdom. He was the second king in the world then, and but for the unmanageable Demetrius, would doubtless have occupied Macedonia permanently after Casander's death. This latter was left in possession of what European possessions he could assert, possibly he was assigned the kingdom of Pyrrhus, if he could take it. Casander died of disease (a rare end among this seed of dragon's teeth) in 297 B.C., and so the Greeks were left to assert their liberty, and Demetrius to machinate and effect his establishment on the throne of Macedonia, as well as to keep the world in fear and suspense by his naval forces, and his preparations to reconquer his father's position. Lysimachus, Seleucus, and Ptolemy were watching one another, and alternating in alliance and in war.

All these princes, as well as Demetrius and Pyrrhus, king of Epirus, were connected in marriage; they all married as many wives as they pleased, apparently without remonstrance from their previous consorts. So the whole complex of the warring kings were in close family relations, reaching from the daughter of the Indian Sandracottus, married to Seleucus, to Lanassa, the daughter of the Sicilian tyrant, Agathocles, who married Pyrrhus of Epirus, and then proposed to change him for the more romantic Demetrius. Pyrrhus was now a very rising and ambitious prince; if not in alliance with Demetrius, he was striving to extend his kingdom of Epirus into Macedonia, and would doubtless have succeeded, but for the superior power of Lysimachus. This Thracian monarch, in spite of serious reverses against the barbarians of the North, who took both him and his son prisoners, and released them very chivalrously, about this time possessed a solid and secure kingdom, and moreover an able and righteous son, Agathocles, so that his dynasty might have been established, but for the poisonous influence of Arsinoe, the daughter of Ptolemy, whom he, an old man, had married in token of an alliance after the battle of Ipsus.

The reader can hardly understand the complicated family quarrel which brought about, first, the death of Agathocles, then of his father Lysimachus, then of Seleucus, and the consequent rearrangement of the whole Eastern world, without the following table. It will start for convenience' sake from Ptolemy, and will only mention those of his wives and of his children which concern us in the present matter.

Ptolemy I. (Soter) born 367, king 306, died 283.

married—
Eurydike, sister of *Casander*.
Her children—
1. Ptolemy Keraunos.
2. Ptolemais, married king Demetrius.
3. Lysandra, married—(1) Alexander (son of *Casander*); (2) Agathocles (son of *Lysimachus*).

married—
Berenice, daughter of Magas (prince of Cyrene).
Her children.—
4. Arsinoe, married—(1) King *Lysimachus*; (2) her half brother (Ptolemy Ker.); (3) her full brother (Ptolemy Phil.).
5. Ptolemy II. (Philadelphus) born 309, king 285, d. 246) married—(1) Arsinoe (daughter of *Lysimachus*); (2) *Arsinoe*, his own full sister.

Every one who studies this table will see the main cause of the confusion which envelopes the history of the period. Every prince is father-in-law, or son-in-law, or brother-in-law to every other. Moreover the names are limited in number, and Arsinoe, Alexander, Agathocles, Ptolemy are repeated with puzzling frequency.[1]

The family quarrel which upset the world arose in this wise. To seal the alliance after Ipsus, old king Ptolemy sent his daughter Arsinoe, to marry his rival and friend Lysimachus, who on his side had sent his daughter, another Arsinoe, in marriage to the younger Ptolemy (Philadelphus). This was the second son of the great Ptolemy, who had chosen him for the throne in preference to his eldest son, Keraunos, a man of violent and reckless character, who accordingly left the country, and went to seek his fortune at foreign courts. Meanwhile the old Ptolemy, for safety's sake, installed his second son as king of Egypt during his own life, and abdicated at the age of eighty-three, full of honours, nor did he leave the court, where he appeared as a subject before his son as king. Keraunos naturally visited, in the first instance, the Thracian court, where he not only had a half sister (Arsinoe) queen, but where his full sister Lysandra, was married to the crown prince, the gallant and popular Agathocles; but Keraunos and the queen conspired against this prince; they persuaded old Lysimachus that he was a traitor, and so Keraunos was directed to put him to death. This crime caused unusual excitement and odium all through the country, and the relations and party of

[1] These recurring names are tabulated and their relations made plain at the end of the present volume.

the murdered prince called on Seleucus to avenge him. He did so, and advanced with an army against Lysimachus, whom he defeated and slew in a great battle, somewhere not far from the field of Ipsus. It was called the plain of Coron (B.C. 281). Thus died the last but one of Alexander's Companions, at the age of eighty, he, too, in battle. Ptolemy was already laid in his peaceful grave (B.C. 283).

There remained the last and greatest, the king of Asia, Seleucus. He, however, gave up all his Asiatic possessions from the Hellespont to the Indus to his son Antiochus, and meant to spend his last years in the home of his fathers, Macedonia; but as he was entering that kingdom, he was murdered by Keraunos, whom he brought with him in his train. This bloodthirsty adventurer was thus left with an army which had no leader, in a kingdom which had no king, for Demetrius' son, Antigonus, the strongest claimant, had not yet made his good position. All the other kings, whose heads were full with their newly acquired sovranties, viz., Antiochus in Asia and Ptolemy II. in Egypt, joined with Keraunos in buying off the dangerous Pyrrhus, by bribes of men, money, and elephants, to make his expedition to Italy, and leave them to settle their affairs.[1] The Greek cities, as usual, when there was a change of sovran in Macedonia, rose and asserted what they were pleased to call their liberty, so preventing Antigonus from recovering his father's dominions. Meanwhile Keraunos established himself in Macedonia; he even, like

[1] For an outline of the career of Pyrrhus in Italy, see "The Story of Rome," pp. 119-128.

our Richard, induced the queen, his step-sister, his old accomplice against Agathocles, to marry him! but it was only to murder her children by Lysimachus, the only dangerous claimants to the Thracian provinces. The wretched queen fled to Samothrace, and thence to Egypt, where she ended her guilty and chequered career as queen of her full brother Ptolemy II. (Philadephus) and was deified during her life!

Such then was the state of Alexander's Empire in 280 B.C. All the first Diadochi were dead, and so were even the sons of two of them, Demetrius and Agathocles. The son of the former was a claimant

COIN OF PTOLEMY II.

for the throne of Macedonia, which he acquired after long and doubtful struggles. Antiochus, who had long been regent of the Eastern provinces beyond Mesopotamia, had come suddenly, by his father's murder, into possession of so vast a kingdom, that he could not control the coast of Asia Minor, where sundry free cities and dynasts sought to establish themselves. Ptolemy II. was already king of Egypt, including the suzerainty of Cyrene, and had claims on Palestine and Syria. Ptolemy Keraunos, the double-dyed villain and murderer, was in possession of the throne of Macedonia, but at war with the claimant Antigonus. Pyrrhus of Epirus was gone to conquer a new kingdom in the West. Such was the state of things when a terrible new scourge broke over the world.

VIII.

THE INVASION OF THE CELTS (GALATIANS) AND ITS CONSEQUENCES.

IT is said that the invasion of the Celts or Gauls, who destroyed the Roman army at the Allia and captured the city,[1] destroyed also all the ancient archives of the Republic, so that there was a complete break in the annals, which could only be filled up from memory and from oral tradition. In like manner the huge inroad of the Celts into Macedonia and Thrace (B.C. 278) makes the end of a period and the beginning of a new epoch. It nearly coincides with the death of the last great Diadochi; it sweeps away the claims of the worst of the Epigoni, or second generation, inasmuch as the first defender of Hellenism who met them in battle was Keraunos, whom they slew and annihilated his army. Their inroads into Greece and Asia Minor filled men's hearts with a new sort of terror, and not only breathed new heroism into them, but gave new inspiration to the sculptor and the poet, so that the art of Greece undergoes, if not a transformation, at least a revival from the "storm and stress" of the times. The Apollo Belvidere, the

[1] See "the Story of Rome," p. 101, for some account of "tearful Allia," B.C. 390.

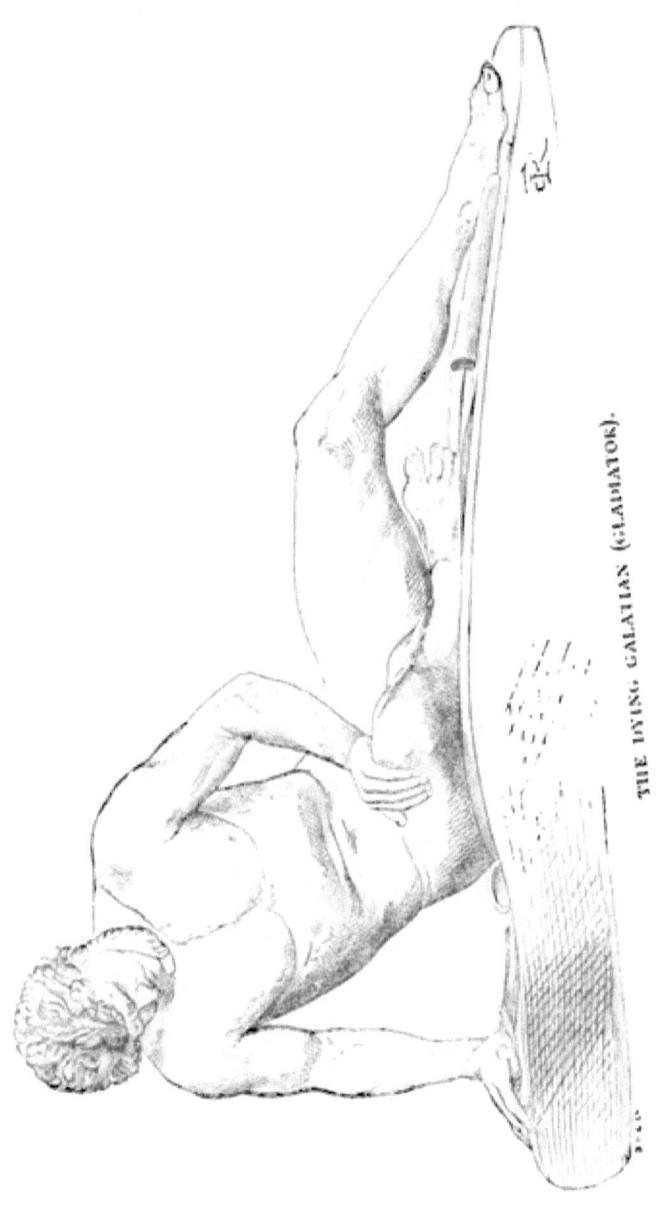

THE DYING GALATIAN (GLADIATOR).

Dying Gladiator (really a Gaul), the Great Altar lately exhumed at Pergamum, these and other masterpieces still tell us of the enthusiasm which inspired a splendid revival of sculpture. The tame and prosy Pausanias [1] becomes quite poetical, when he tells the horrors of the invasion into Macedonia and Greece. He evidently used some poem, which described these thrilling events, in which there is a curious repetition of the details of the Persian invasion as told by Herodotus, the fight at Thermopylæ, and defeat of the barbarians, the turning of the pass by treachery, the diversion to reach the treasures of Delphi, the great miracles with which the god protected his temple and brought dismay and ruin on the invaders. There are the most frightful narratives of the savage cruelty of the Galatæ, their disregard of all the laws of civilized warfare—leaving their dead unburied, rifling every ancient tomb, slaying and ravishing, eating the children of the Greeks. Not Polyphemus or the Læstrygones in Homer were so terrible. There was the same attempt at confederation among the Greeks, the same selfishness and separatism to destroy it. But this time the important factors of the Greek army are no longer Athens and Sparta, though Athens still had the command from her old reputation, but Ætolia, which sent some ten thousand warriors to the fray, bore the brunt of the fighting, and carried off the chief share in the glory. The Galatæ, as had been the case in Italy, could conquer in battle, but knew no other use of victory than aimless plunder and rapine; after devastating all Macedonia and Thrace, they went

[1] Pausaunias x. 20, 59.

over to Asia, each state being anxious to pass them on
to its neighbour, and moreover they were so ready to
serve as mercenaries, that no army appears in those
days without its contingent of Celtic troops, long
regarded as almost invincible, had they not been ready
to fight on both sides, and thus neutralize their power.

It may be as well to sum up the remaining effects
of their invasion, and their settlement in Galatia here,
and so wind up one thread of the tangled skein which
we are essaying to unravel. After the check at
Delphi, which only destroyed a detachment, they
fought a battle with Antigonus at Lysimacheia (277)
in which the king was completely victorious, and
raised his character so much as to open the way for
his return to Macedonia. Strange to say, he forthwith
hired a division of the barbarians to help him in this
enterprise. Then Nicomedes, king of Bithynia, and
the Greek cities of the Propontis, hired them to protect themselves against their enemies, and so they
came to settle in Galatia, under promise to occupy a
fixed territory, but like all other barbarians, making
constant raids for plunder, and becoming the terror of
all Asia. Hence it was that both Antiochus I., son of
Seleucus, made his mark, and obtained his title of
Soter (Saviour) by a great victory over them, of which
both date and place are unknown—after which they
were surrounded by a series of Macedonian forts, and
confined within their province. This victory was
commemorated, like that of Assaye, on the colours of
the English regiments engaged, by the figure of an
elephant which we find on medals of Antiochus. A
generation later (about 237) the same story is repeated

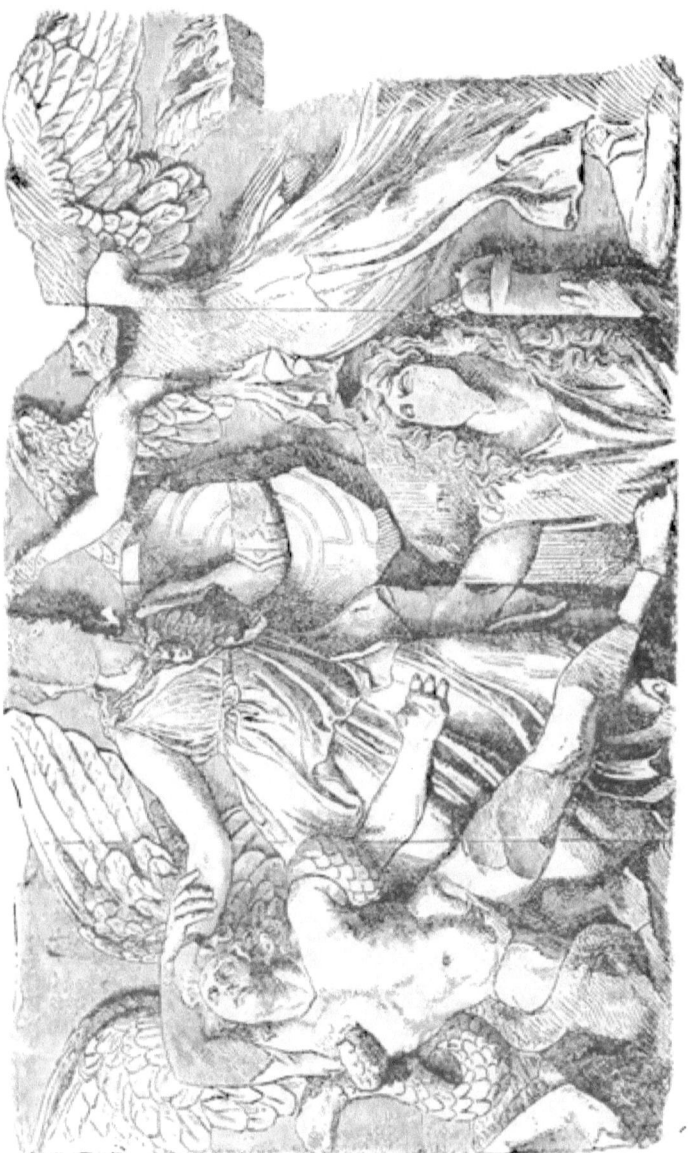

FROM THE FRIEZE ON THE GREAT ALTAR AT PERGAMUM.

in the case of Attalus of Pergamum, who defeats the
Galatæ, and is hailed with the title of king. The
great outburst of artistic work at his capital is directly
connected with this victory. Every great shrine in
Greece was adorned with memorials of these victories

The barbarians thus checked at intervals did not
however change their nature, and they were still the
terror of surrounding peoples, till the Romans, under
the Consul Manlius Vulso, immediately after the defeat
of Antiochus the Great (B.C. 190) made a most wanton
attack upon them, though they strove hard to avoid
all cause of quarrel. Being then completely defeated

COIN OF ANTIOCHUS IV.

by Roman arms, they became quiet members of the
Roman Empire, and it is at Ancyra (Angora), their
principal town, that the famous copy of Augustus' will
known as the *Monument of Ancyra* has been found.
When St. Paul preached among them, they seem fused
into the Hellenistic world, speaking Greek like the rest
of Asia ; yet the Celtic language long lingered among
them, and St. Jerome says he found the country people
still using it in his day (fourth cent. A.D.)

Such, then, is the brief history of this violent foreign
element, intruding itself into the Empire of Alexander,
and at first threatening to overthrow all its civilization.

Though causing frightful disorder and destruction, and introducing a certain savagery into warfare, which disgraced Hellenism down to the days of the last Philip, we cannot but feel that this invasion of outer barbarians, strange in features, in language, in religion, in customs, had a powerful influence in welding together the feelings and interests of all the Hellenistic world. People thought that even an Indian or an Ethiopian, if he spoke Greek and belonged to a civilized kingdom, was something radically different from these northern savages, who were held to have regard for neither gods nor men, neither age nor sex, neither oath nor promise, neither honour nor helplessness. It is no doubt to their conduct as mercenaries of the various petty tyrants who sprang up in those days, that we must ascribe the terrible reputation for cruelty which the tyrants acquired—a feature exhibited in a popular tragedy about Apollodorus, tyrant of Cassandreia in Thessaly, that Lycophron brought out at Alexandria, and which afforded a type for succeeding writers.

IX.

KING PYRRHUS OF EPIRUS.

AMONG those who claimed to succeed to Alexander's Empire, and who were at some moments thought to have no mean chance, was the Epirot king, Pyrrhus. He is one of the most interesting figures of the times, playing his part as well in Hellenistic history as in Roman, where to most of us he is familiar. We are fortunate in having from the inimitable pen of Plutarch a charming "Life" of the adventurous and chivalrous monarch. His marvellous escape from the enemies of his house when a mere infant forms the opening of Plutarch's narrative. He was brought to Glaucias the Ætolian, who set him up on his throne a boy of twelve years old. The marriage of his elder sister Deidamia to the brilliant Demetrius brought him into relation to that prince, who seems to have formed his notions, and trained him in splendour and culture. So he came as a hostage for Demetrius to the court of Ptolemy, where he so ingratiated himself with the queen, that she gave the youth of doubtful claims and fortunes her daughter Antigone in marriage. Thus he took rank among the great royal houses of the East, to which he added an alliance with the Sicilian Agathocles, the adventurer-king who sought to attain the same social position, by marrying his daughter Lanassa.

The early years of his reign were spent alternately in putting down revolutions among his own ill-cemented states, and in struggling with both Demetrius and Lysimachus, presently with young Antigonus, for the sovereignty of Macedonia. All his wars with Demetrius did not destroy their old friendship, and he was one of those who begged hardest for the release of that king, when he fell at last into the hands of Seleucus, and into the captivity which brought on his death. At the time of the invasion of the Celts it suited all parties to get rid of this dangerous and impressible claimant for empire. He had become a general whom no one but old Lysimachus was able to defeat. The art of war was his absorbing study, and he rated all else as of no interest. So, then, he was furnished with supplies of men, elephants, and money by all his rivals and enemies, and invited to make himself an empire in the West.

His adventures in Italy and Sicily belong to Roman history. His battles with the Romans opened his eyes to the real dangers to which the Empire of Alexander was exposed, and he called in vain to his supporters and relations to send him more aid for this struggle. Had he been adequately supported he would doubtless have checked the advance of Rome for a generation or two, perhaps for centuries; but the Eastern kings were too busy with their own quarrels, and so he returned defeated, and burning with revenge for what he considered a betrayal. He had been seduced from conquering a kingdom in

Greece and Macedonia by the promise of sufficient help to make a kingdom in Magna Græcia. He threw himself upon king Antigonus, who was, after the "Celtic fury," laboriously reconstructing Macedonia and Greece into a kingdom. Always victor in battle against this king, whom he drove out a mere fugitive, he tried to conquer Sparta, and to subdue the Peloponnesus. No doubt his dreams were like those of Demetrius, to start again from Macedon and to conquer the whole Empire of Alexander. But his attack on the fortifications of Sparta was unsuccessful; Antigonus, who ever recovered himself after defeat, like his grandfather Antigonus, collected an army, and they met at Argos. In the battle for the possession of that town, the Achilles of the day was killed by a tile thrown from a house-top by an old woman. So disappeared the last great obstacle to the settlement of the Hellenistic world. Pyrrhus, with all his kingly qualities, was really fit only for a captain of condottieri. He loved fighting for its own sake, and even in the art of war sacrificed larger aims for battles; he was the greatest tactician of his day, but no strategist. He was opposed the first to the stubborn force of a nation determined to withstand to the uttermost, and on whom the loss of battles had little effect. Many defeats did not subdue them, while one defeat at Beneventum was his ruin in Italy. He then encountered a similar antagonist in Antigonus. Though defeated in almost every battle, this wily and able statesman recovered himself, and stood ready for the fray when he ought to have been a homeless exile or a subject.

Pyrrhus was a meteor flashing through the sky of Hellenism—of baleful portent, but of no real influence; but he had discovered for himself, and shown to the whole world of Hellenism, that beyond all their petty quarrels for the balance of power lay another far greater problem—the question of supremacy between the East and the West. Fortunately for Hellenism, Carthage stept in, and with her great naval resources, her stubborn character, and the genius of the Barcide family stopped the decision of that question on the field of battle for a century—the century in which the successors of Alexander did for the world all that the genius of Hellenism was able to accomplish. This, the final stage of Alexander's Empire, we shall now attempt to describe.

COIN OF ACHÆUS, SYRIAN PRETENDER.

X.

THE GOLDEN AGE OF HELLENISM.

There were three great kingdoms—Macedonia, Egypt, Syria—which lasted, each under its own dynasty, till Rome swallowed them up. The first of these, which was the poorest, and the smallest, but historically the most important, included the ancestral possessions of Philip and Alexander—Macedonia, most of Thrace, Thessaly, the mountainous centre of the peninsula, as well as a protectorate more or less definite and absolute over Greece proper, the Cyclades, and certain tracts of Caria. Its strength lay in the fine timber forests it possessed, in its gold mines; but far more in the martial character of its population, who were as superior as the modern English are to southern or Oriental peoples.

Next came Egypt, including Cyrene and Cyprus, and a general protectorate over the sea-coast cities of Asia Minor up to the Black Sea, together with claims often asserted with success on Syria, and on the coast lands of Southern Asia Minor. Its strength lay in the compactness and unity, as well as the immense fertility of Egypt, its world traffic through Alexandria, and its consequent supremacy in the finances of the world.

Thirdly came what was now called Syria, on account of the policy of the house of Seleucus, who built there its capital, and determined to make the Greek or Hellenistic end of its vast dominions its political centre of gravity. The kingdom of Syria owned the south and south-east of Asia Minor, Syria, and generally Palestine, Mesopotamia, and the mountain provinces adjoining it on the East, with vague claims further east when there was no king like Sandracottus to hold India and the Punjaub with a strong hand. There was still a large element of Hellenism in these remote parts. The kingdom of Bactria was ruled by a dynasty of kings with Greek names—Euthydemus is the chief—who coined in Greek style, and must therefore have regarded themselves as successors to Alexander.

There are many exceptions and limitations to this general description, and many secondary and semi-independent kingdoms, which make the picture of Hellenism infinitely various and complicated. There was, in fact, a chain of independent kingdoms reaching from Media to Sparta, all of which asserted their complete freedom, and generally attained it by balancing the great powers one against the other. Here they are in their order. Atropatene was the kingdom formed in the northern and western parts of the province of Media, by Atropates, the satrap of Alexander, who claimed descent from the seven Persian chiefs who put Darius I. on the throne. Next came Armenia, hardly conquered by Alexander, and now established under a dynasty of its own. Then Cappadocia, the land in the heart of Asia Minor, where it narrows between Cilicia and Pontus, ruled by sovereigns also claiming royal Persian descent, and with Armenia, barring out all Asia Minor from the Seleucids except by way of the southern coast. Fourthly, Pontus, under its equally Persian dynast Mithridates—a kingdom which makes a great figure in Eastern nistory under the later Roman Republic. There was moreover a dynast of Bithynia, set up and supported by the robber state of the Celtic Galatians, which had just been founded, and was a source of strength and of danger to all its neighbours. Then Pergamum, just being founded and strengthened by the first Attalid, Philetærus, an officer of Lysimachus, and presently to become one of the leading exponents of Hellenism. Its principal danger lay from the Galatians, not only of Asia, but from those settled in Thrace, in what was called the kingdom of Tylis, their mountain fortress. This dominion reached as far as the Strymon. Almost all these second-rate states (and with them the free Greek cities of Heracleia, Cyzicus, Byzantium, &c.) were fragments of the shattered kingdom of Lysimachus, whom Seleucus had killed in battle, but whose possessions he was unable to organize before his own murder by Keraunos, who again had neither the genius nor the leisure to undertake it.

Let us proceed with our list of fragments. If Thessaly, Bœotia, Attica, all sought to assert their freedom from Macedonia, and were consequently to be handled either with repression or persuasion by Antigonus, the Alpine confederation of the mountaineer Ætolians was distinctly independent, and a power to be reckoned with. So was the kingdom of Epirus after its sudden rise of glory under Pyrrhus. In Peloponnesus, the Achæan League was beginning to assert itself, but Sparta was still really independent, though poor and insignificant, and depending on Egyptian money and fleets to make any active opposition to the encroachments of Macedon. The other cities or tribes, Argos, Arcadia, Elis, Messenia, are far too insignificant to count in this enumeration of the world's array, but they were like all other Greek cities and states, poor, proud, and pretentious, and very perilous to depend upon for loyal support.

So far we have taken no account of a very peculiar feature extending all through even the Greek kingdoms, especially that of the Selucids—the number of large Hellenistic cities founded as special centres of culture, or points of defence, and organized as such with a certain local independence. These cities, most of which we only know by name, were the real backbone of Hellenism in the world. Alexander had founded seventy of them, all called by his name. Many were upon great trade lines, like the Alexandria which still exists. Many were intended as garrison towns in the centre of remote provinces, like Candahar—a corruption of Iskanderieh, Iskendar being the Oriental form for Alexander. Some were mere outposts, where Macedonian soldier were forced to settle, and guard the frontiers against the barbarians, like the Alexandria on the Iaxartes. His immediate successors, the Diadochi or $\delta\iota\alpha\delta\varepsilon\xi\acute{a}\mu\varepsilon\nu o\iota$, as Greek historians call them, followed his example closely, even to the puzzling practice of calling numbers of towns by the same name. There were a number of Antigoncias, of Antiochs, of Ptolemaises, besides a Cassandreia, a Lysimacheia, a Demetrias or two, and a number of Seleuceias.¹ As regards Seleucus indeed we have a remarkable statement from Appian that he founded cities through the length and breadth of his kingdom, viz., sixteen Antiochs called after his father, five Laodiceas after his mother, nine Seleucias after himself, three Apameias and one Stratoniceia after his wives. Other towns he called after Greek and Macedonian towns, or after some deed of his own, or named it in Alexander's honour. Hence all through Syria, and Upper Asia there are many towns bearing Greek and Macedonian names—Berea, Edessa, Perinthos, Achæa, Pella, &c.

The number of these, which have been enumerated in a special catalogue by Droysen,² the learned historian of Hellenism, is enormous, and the first question which arises in our minds is this: where were Greek-speaking people found to fill them? It is indeed true that Greece proper about this time became depopulated, and that it never has recovered from this decay—it is only in our own day that the population is increasing again, and promising to become consider-

---

¹ These towns were all written with *eia*, viz., Alexándreia, Seleúceia, Antiocheia, &c.; but as they were pronounced with the accent on the antepenult, the Romans wrote Alexandria, Seleúcia, which really represents the pronunciation, provided we read the c as k, and pronounce the *ei* as ee. Antioch is known in that form since our English Bible so rendered it.

² It is true that Grote refuses his faith in this long list, for reasons given in a note to the xcivth chapter of his history, though he still believes the number to have been not inconsiderable.

able. A great deal of this depopulation was caused by what may be called internal causes, constant wars, pestilence, and the habit among young men of living abroad as mercenaries. Yet even if all this had not been the case, the whole population of Greece would never have sufficed for one tithe of the cities—the great cities—founded all over Asia by the Diadochi. We are therefore driven to the conclusion that but a small fraction, the soldiers and officials of the new cities, were Greeks—Macedonians, when founded by Alexander himself—generally broken down veterans, mutinous and discontented troops, and camp followers. To these were associated people from the surrounding country, it being Alexander's fixed idea to discountenance sporadic country life in villages and encourage town communities. The towns accordingly received considerable privileges, not only territory, but the right of meeting in assembly, of managing their own courts, taxes, &c., subject to certain military and fiscal dues to the Empire. The Greek language and political habits were thus the one bond of union among them, and the extraordinary colonizing genius of the Greek once more proved itself. It was not Alexander's notion, or that of his successors, to found colonies of this kind for the relief of, or the profit of, any mother-country; these people, though some of them in Bactria essayed it, when they heard of Alexander's death, were not to return home to Macedonia or Greece when they had realized some money; they were to become the population of the Empire, one in language, and to some extent in habits, but only gradually becoming uniform by intermarriage, by the same military system and by the spread of Greek letters and culture. The cities were all built—at least all the important ones—on a fixed plan, with two great thoroughfares at right angles, intersecting in the centre of the town, the lesser streets being all parallel to these thoroughfares, as is somewhat the case in Philadelphia (U.S.A.). They all had special shrines or memorials of the founder. Most of them had no doubt, like Alexandria, low quarters for the Aborigines and a fashionable or strong quarter for the " Macedonians," as they liked to call themselves, or Greeks, as the subjects generally called them.

Whenever a monarch had his residence in one of them, there was the state and luxury of a royal court, with all its etiquette, its lords-in-waiting, pages, chamberlains, uniforms, and whatever other circumstance could be copied from the court of the great model Alexander, or of his wealthiest successors. There was also a display of art, statues set up in bronze or marble; pictures exhibited, much handsome building in the way of temples, halls, and porticoes. We may be sure that theatres and games were universal, and so Euripides and Menander attained an audience and an influence extending all over the empire. We shall return to the critical estimate of this literature and this art in due time, when we have reached further into the history of the century of its greatness, but this is the place to describe the deeper thoughts which occupied the men who had lived through the wars and tumults, the distresses and disillusions, the splendour and miseries of the Forty-five Years' War.

XI.

THE NEW LINES ADOPTED BY PHILOSOPHY UNDER THE DIADOCHI.

THERE had been a long and noble stream of philosophers in the Greek world ever since the sixth century B.C. They flourished in Asia Minor first, where the wealth and culture were the greatest, then in Sicily, Italy, all over the Greek world, as itinerant sophists, in a monastic association under Pythagoras at Croton, finally, when Athens became the centre of the civilized world, in the schools of that city. Plato, in the earlier half of the fourth century, had summed up in his famous *dialogues* all that had been thought out by his masters, and left behind him suggestions of almost all the systems which have succeeded him to the present day. His *conversations* on philosophy did not form a clear or easily-grasped system, and were interpenetrated with a mystical element, as the vulgar would call it,—not mystical in the religious, so much as in the speculative sense, making the unseen and imperceptible the eternal and most real, and substituting for the facts given to the senses the speculation of the intellect. His philosophy was transcendental, as being above the crowd, incomprehensible to the vulgar, and therefore not applicable to the wants of ordinary life. It was a theory for the cloister and the schools, not for the highways and thoroughfares of life. The school or *Academy* which Plato founded at Athens, thus giving a word for that kind of thing to all modern languages, was essentially a place of retirement, like an Oxford College, from which people went into the world as theorists, not as practical men.

Very much the same criticism may be made, for somewhat different reasons, on the rival school of Aristotle. He saw indeed, that we must not substitute speculation for experience, that we must first collect all the facts of life before we can venture upon a theory, but his training in speculation was too strong to allow him to become a mere empiric. Not only did his philosophy require encyclopædic research, and an amount of study quite incompatible with life duties, but when all this is done, and we come to his *Metaphysics*, we find him just as transcendental and difficult as Plato. He is not the least like Locke or Mill, a mere analyser and observer of our experience. He was no man of the world. Though he had extended his collection of facts to the cataloguing of all the known political constitutions of the civilized nations—he had found, at least, one hundred and fifty of them—not one word in his famous *Politics*, where he gives the analysis of this experience, leads us to think that he foresaw, or understood, the great problem of Hellenism solved by his pupil Alexander. To him, barbarians, however civilized, were a thing distinct from Greeks, however rude.

In one point only, perhaps, he and Plato had led the way to the new state of things. Without venturing to claim openly for monarchy its pre-eminence, both of them distinctly preached against democracy in the form known to the Greeks—that is to say, a manhood suffrage of free men, in small states, where this minority ruled over an immense number of slaves and strangers. The smaller such a democracy is, the more open and brutal will be the jobs, the injustices, the insolences it will commit as regards the minority of the rich, and the unprivileged. Schemes of ambition and of plunder are not brought before the large tribunal of a nation, but settled with the bitterness of personal hatreds, and the incitement of personal profit by those immediately interested. All this the philosophers saw, but the only remedy which their pupils adopted, when they entered into politics, was that of a self-assumed monarchy based on superior knowledge; and this form of government, known as *tyranny* among the Greeks, was so violently opposed to Hellenic feeling that whoever adopted or supported it was considered a public enemy, and the killing of him the greatest public duty. So then the philosophers were out of tune with the public; Plato and Aristotle, kings of thought, had no influence on the politics of their day. Moreover, they and their followers were either religious sceptics, or held religious views not reconcilable by ordinary men with the current creeds. They, and the lesser teachers who tried to rival and imitate them, taught *free-thinking* in its strictest sense, and what religion as ever been able to accept such a mental attitude as conformable to orthodoxy?

Then came the great commotion of the world by

Alexander, the extension of Greek manners and culture, the superseding of Greek democracies by a large and tolerant monarchy, based upon such superior force as made its justice, in those days, indisputable. The great single man had indeed arisen, of whom the philosophers had dreamt, and said that if the most worthy could be found, he should by natural right rule over mankind. But this king was not a pupil of Aristotle in the technical sense, though he was so actually. He never could be claimed by any of the Athenian schools, as a Platonist, an Aristotelian, or the like, for he was not a student from an academy, but a great practical thinker, brought up in contact with courts and kings and public affairs. We may be sure that he despised the analysis of the one hundred and fifty petty polities by his master. We know that he rejected his advice as antiquated, of treating barbarians—that is to say, long civilized Orientals—on a different footing from Greeks.

Alexander then justified, but completely modified, the idea of monarchy. To the Greek cities it was monarchy from without, not the assumption of that authority from within each state. So it obviated the resistance of that ingrained feeling of jealousy in the Greek mind, which would even now protest with equal vehemence against any native Greek being made ruler over his fellows.

But then came the desolating Forty-five Years' War when men were made keenly alive to the miseries of this mortal life. No care, no prudence, no diligence, no policy could save men from the catastrophes which accompany the shock of empires. Theories were of no avail. Force, or astuteness in meeting force with some counteracting force, that is diplomacy, opportunism, these were the springs of action, and the elements which determined ordinary life and happiness. How is it, then, that under these terrible circumstances, when all theories of life seemed to break down, the once despised and suspected philosophers come into strange public importance? If an important embassy is to be sent to a hostile monarch threatening invasion, it is to Xenocrates of the Academy, a man never seen in the assembly, that they entrust it. If Antigonus wants a safe officer to hold the Acrocorinthus, the key of the Peloponnesus, he chooses Persæus the Stoic. When Alexander, in his despair at the murder of Clitus, sits in dust and ashes, and will not eat or drink, they send two philosophers to bring him to reason. All over Greece the men whose lives are devoted to speculation are now regarded as venerable and influential advisers, as peace-makers and politicians above the ordinary level, as the honour and pride of the cities where they choose to dwell. Kings and satraps court their company. Pupils note down and publish their table-talk. How did this revolution come about?

The Forty-five Years War saw the birth of three new systems of philosophy, which were intended, not only for the closet and the market-place, but for the comfort of men and women removed from public affairs and concerned only with private life. Two of them, possessing a positive body of doctrine, and being taught by very eminent men, have very distinct titles—Epicureanism and Stoicism. The third was

EPICURUS.

Scepticism, not so general, not so satisfying to the public mind, but still of the last importance in destroying the remains of old creeds, and in leading the way to something deeper and better. But its teachers— Pyrrho of Elis, Aristo of Chios, and Timon of Phlius —founded no fixed or permanent school. It was only after two or three generations that the successors of Plato, the so-called New Academy, arrived at similar conclusions, and taught them through Arcesilaus and Carneades, even at Rome.[1] The Philosophies of Epicurus, and of Zeno, the founder of the Stoics, were essentially practical systems; not that they refused speculation, but that they set forth ethics and the laws of moral action as the main end, and their speculation was of the dogmatic kind, the master stating his views on higher philosophy, and the pupil adopting them as the decision of a greater man. Happiness, not knowledge, was the object of these schools. Happiness, too, they were agreed, must be within reach of the sage, by reason of himself, and independent of catastrophes from without. The only question between them was the proper method of obtaining it.

Epicurus, a native Athenian, who settled in middle life at Athens, where he left his house and gardens as an heirloom and foundation for his followers, held that as every man must pursue happiness, *as an end*, he is always in the pursuit of pleasure. How can most pleasure be obtained? Is it by gratifying the passions? by disregarding the pleasure of others? by satisfying every desire as it arises? By no means. There are pleasures and pleasures—some of the body,

[1] See "The Story of Rome," page 319.

violent, short-lived, productive of after pain; others of the mind, quieter but lasting, with no sting behind. The sage will balance these carefully, he will postpone the worse for the better, he will cultivate love and friendship for his own sake; philosophy, therefore, and virtue consists in this long-sighted prudence, which contents itself with moderate and safe enjoyment, and finds happiness in contemplation, in memory, in friendship, even when physical pain and poverty cloud the latter days. Above all, it removes the fear of hereafter by abolishing anything like Providence. Epicurus believed only in what was given by the senses. Dreams and visions, speculations, transcendental theories are all nonsense. If there are gods, they care not in the least for mortal men, and never interfere in their affairs. Death is the end of all things, and the only immortality consists in the memory of friends and followers, who treasure the wise man and commemorate his virtues.

If the reader will enter more fully into this system, let him refer either to the great poem of Lucretius, on the *Nature of things*, or to Mr. Walter Pater's *Marius the Epicurean*, where all the higher side of this system, as understood by refined minds, is presented with rare grace and eloquence. It is a delicate and studied science of living, and has found response in all advanced and thoughtful human societies.

If there are in every age Epicureans, who despise high speculation, and pursue culture from a utilitarian point of view, there are also in every age people of sterner stuff, who take a different line of thinking, and lead apparently the same life from very different principles. These are the Stoics. Zeno, and his followers, Cleanthes and Chrysippus, taught in the frescoed colonnade called the coloured Stoa at Athens, and though the school were at first called *Zenonians*, the importance of the other two masters was so great, that the title, Men of the Porch, or Portico—Stoics—prevailed. These men, far from being mere Empirists, believing only in the data of the senses, believed in the gods as manifestations of one great Divine Providence, ordering human affairs, and prescribing to man the part he should play in the world, by conforming his conduct to that of the world's Ruler. If happiness was indeed his object, it was to be obtained, not by direct pursuit, but by performing duty, by doing what was right, as such, without regard to consequences, by asserting the dignity and royalty of the wise man over all the buffets of fortune. He who thus co-operated with Divine Providence might be a slave, a prisoner, in misery, in torture, yet he was really free, wealthy, royal, supreme. His judgment was infallible, his happiness secure. To use a modern phrase for the same kind of theory, he had *found peace*.

Both schools held that there was no longer Jew or Gentile, Greek or Barbarian, bond or free; they were essentially cosmopolitan, and were thus, unlike the earlier systems of Plato or Aristotle, fit for all the world that spoke Greek, beyond the pure descendants of Hellen. Still there were shades of difference in that respect. The teaching of Epicurus, as it was that of a pure Athenian, so it was essentially one suited to the pleasure-loving, refined, selfish Greek intellect.

while the sterner school of Zeno, taught by a stranger from Cyprus, and continued by foreigners, chiefly from the South-eastern Levant, was of a severe, semi-Oriental aspect, which found disciples among those outside Hellenists, who had gloomier views of human life and prospects. It is remarkable that very few pure Greeks were noted as Stoics. They came mostly from Cilicia, where Tarsus had long a pre-eminence in that way of thinking, as any one may know who studies the Stoic colour of St. Paul's mind; they were the fashion in Pergamum, in Macedonia with King Antigonus, by and by came their conquest of Rome, where that philosophy at last ascended the imperial throne with M. Aurelius; and it is remarkable that though they taught the wise man's complete independence of all the world, and his contempt for human politics, carried on by *fools*, as they called the unregenerate, they were quite ready to theorize for the vulgar, to direct public affairs, when the occasion arose; and as they acted upon pure principle, apart from love, or hate, or personal interest, they became at times the most dangerous and desperate of irreconcileables. Such were the advisers of King Cleomenes of Sparta, whom we shall meet again, of the Gracchi, at Rome, and such was the Brutus who figures so sadly in the tragedy of Julius Cæsar.

If the Stoics were not always Quietists, this was strictly the case with the Epicureans and the Sceptics, who taught that all meddling in politics was only the cause of disturbance and annoyance to the wise man, and should be avoided as an evil. Thus they withdrew from public life, and brought with them many able and thoughtful men, who ought to have produced their effect in moderating party struggles, and in advising forbearance and humanity. Accordingly, the active effects of philosophy were to start theorists upon the world, theorists who believed in, and justified, the rule of the one superior man, and so vindicated the claims of absolute monarchy; the passive effects were to draw away from public affairs the timid, the cautious, the sensitive, and turn them to the pursuit of private happiness.

I have said nothing as yet of the schools of Plato and Aristotle, both of which subsisted at Athens beside the Stoics and Epicureans, and which were known as the Academy and the Peripatetic School (so called, as has been hinted, from the περίπατος, or public garden, where Aristotle taught). They were still represented by eminently learned and worthy men, and in the earlier part of the period we have reviewed, when Demetrius Phalereus was governor of Athens (B.C. 317-307), Theophrastus, the Peripatetic Chief, was in the highest fashion. We find, too, the heads of both schools holding a position like the Christian bishops in the Middle Ages, devoted to their special work, and summoned from it to lead the city when some great danger or crisis was at hand, as ambassadors or as advisers of peace. All the heads of schools, except the Epicureans, attained this position, if they had long and honourably presided over their followers —Xenocrates, Menedemus of Eretria, Zeno, and others; and so we have the spectacle oft-repeated of ordinary and vulgar people, swayed by ignoble and selfish motives, yet honouring from afar those who lived a purer and more austere life. If the Epicureans never attained this position, it was not only because their systematic Quietism would have refused to interfere in public affairs on any conditions, but because their doctrine suffered from the obvious travesty to which the *pursuit of pleasure*, as a principle of human life, is exposed. Cooks and courtesans, gluttons and debauchees, could profess, not without some show of reason, that they were disciples of Epicurus.

This, then, was the serious side of Hellenistic life at the opening of its golden age; this was its established clergy, its higher teaching; this was the spiritual outcome of that generation of aimless and immoral wars, which exhausted the whole life of the Diadochi. But, here, as in after days, when philosophy became a religion among the Greeks, and established itself with what I will venture to call a professional clergy, there comes the wide rift between laity and clergy, and much greed, sensuality, and cruelty, among the former, combined with a profound respect for the opposite qualities in the latter. The philosophic ideas which dominated it were all born at the very opening of the great wars: while ambitious satraps were disputing the possession of the empire, and men's hearts were wasting with the weariness of endless and aimless wars, great minds had found peace and comfort where alone it can be found— in the calm of a good conscience, and the contentment of a quiet and sober life. As a curious contrast to this serious development of philosophic life, of which Athens was the first home and centre, we find at Athens, too, a curiously frivolous and shallow society, manifested, not only in the shameful public flatteries and political degradations which we see reflected in Plutarch's *Lives* of Phocion and Demetrius, but in the fashionable comedy of the day. This, the so-called New Comedy of Diphilus, Philemon, Menander, and many other poets, outlasted other forms of poetry, and was even transferred to Alexandria, as the amusement of the higher classes. As regards style, Menander and his fellows deserve all the praise they have received, but when the ancient critics go into ecstasies at the perfect pictures of life and character upon his stage, we can only say that it is well we have the Stoics and their rivals in the schools to give the lie to any such pictures as an honests account of all Attic life. The society of the New Comedy is uniformly a shallow, idle, mostly immoral society, in which strictness and honesty are often ridiculed as country virtues, and immoral characters represented as the people who understand life. The young scapegrace, who lives in debauchery and dishonour, cheating his father, and squandering his substance in riotous living, has the sympathy of the poet. The lady of easy virtue, who upsets the peace of homes, is often the heroine, and sometimes even (as we may see in Plautus) the guardian angel, who sets things right in the end of the play. Worse even than immoral young men are immoral old men, who are not ashamed to be seen by their own sons joining in the disgraces for which youth is the only palliation. Respectable women, if heiresses, are always disagreeable, trusty slaves almost always dishonest; no one has one thought for the nobler side of life, for the great interests which then engrossed courts and cloisters. The only virtues admired in these plays are good temper, forbearance, gentle scepticism, and readiness to forgive the sins and follies of youth. These are the general features we find reiterated with wearisome sameness in our Latin copies of the New Comedy—inferior, no doubt, to the originals in grace and style, omitting, no doubt, many delicate traits, but giving us, in Terence at least, an adequate notion of the social and moral aspects in which the poets found it desirable to represent good society at Athens. The composition of these plays, and the performance of them, lasted for some generations after the literary decay of Athens, and yet we do not find that even the growth of the great schools, and the importance of the great ethical teachers afforded them a single character or a single scene. They never pourtrayed a great man; they were bound to their wretched commonplaces about the shallowest and meanest Athenian life.

SYRIA, AND THE ADJACENT LANDS.

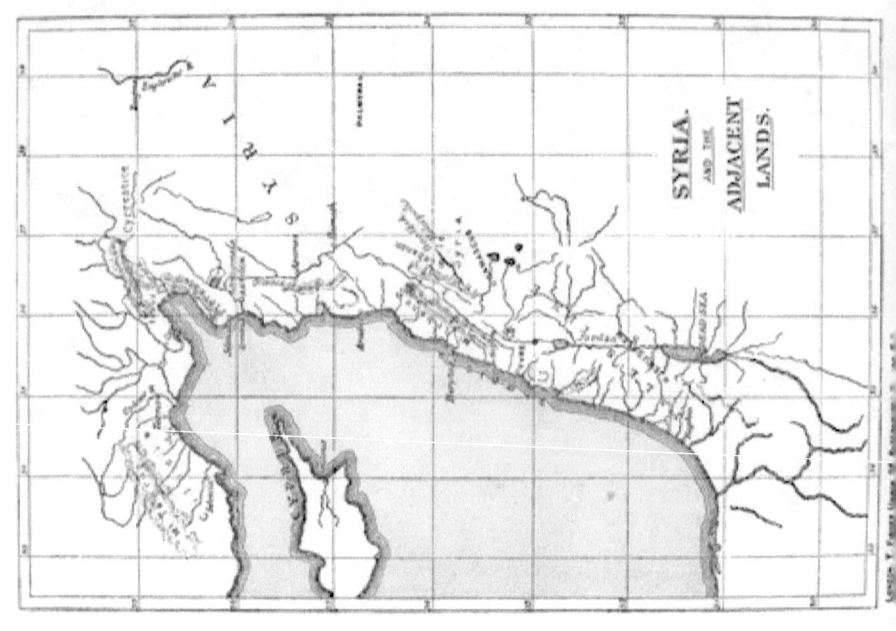

XII.

THE STAGES OF HELLENISM IN THE THIRD CENTURY B.C.

THE third century B.C., the golden age of Hellenism, is marked out in stages curiously distinct, considering the number of empires and of sovereigns concerned Nay, even Roman affairs, which now come to exercise their influence on the East, conform to the same curious coincidence of coincidences. The deaths of the last Companions of Alexander—Ptolemy, Lysimachus, Seleucus, the invasion of the Galatæ—and the

COINS OF ANTIOCHUS III. AND PTOLEMY IV.

outbreak of the conflict between the Greeks of the West and Rome—all these things happening close around B.C. 280 make at the moment of a great crisis, not settled by war or succession till near B.C. 270, at which time the age of Hellenism has well begun. From this time for half a century, the relations of the East, and indeed of the West, are fully determined.

A short chronological table will best illustrate what this means:

PERGAMUM.	MACEDONIA.	EGYPT.	SYRIA.
Philetaerus ... acc. 283 B.C.	Antigonus Gonatas I. acc. 279 B.C.	Ptolemy Phil. II. acc. 282 B.C.	Antiochus Soter I. acc. 281 B.C.
Eumenes ... acc. 263 B.C.	Demetrius II. acc. 239 B.C.	Ptolemy Euergetes III. acc. 246 B.C.	Antiochus Theos II. acc. 261 B.C.
Attalus I. ... acc. 241 B.C.	Antigonus (Doson) III. acc. 229 B.C.	Ptolemy Philopator IV. acc. 221 B.C.	Seleucus Callin II. acc. 246 B.C.
	Philip V. ... acc. 220 B.C.		Seleucus Soter III. acc. 226 B.C.
			Antiochus the Great III. acc. 222 B.C.

ROME.

War with Pyrrhus	278–4 B.C.
Punic War I	263–241 B.C.
Relations with Illyria and West of Greece	235–28 B.C.
Opening of Punic War II	220 B.C.

At this last momentous time 222-220 B.C., three boys all of them under twenty, succeeded to the three thrones of the East. They lived to be conquered by the Romans, as were Philip and Antiochus, or to solicit their suzerainty, as did Ptolemy. But this is the subsequent stage of Hellenism, which Polybius describes. We are now concerned with the two epochs: 279-245, during which time the three thrones were in possession of great monarchs, Syria supplying two for one in each of the rest; and then the period 245-220, when again, Egypt is under one vigorous king, while Macedonia and Syria are each represented by two. Even the lesser, but very important kingdom of Pergamum changes hands almost simultaneously with Syria (263, 241), then comes the long reign of Attalus I., which outlasts the crisis of 221, and reaches into the following century.

This general correspondence naturally brings some kind of system into the otherwise most complicated history of the time, for all these kingdoms, from the very causes of their origin, were perpetually connected by commerce, diplomacy, alliance, if not locked in still closer embrace by struggles for the supremacy, or for a redressing of the balance of power. These struggles were not only carried on directly, as for example, in the so-called *Syrian Wars*, or campaigns of the Ptolemies against the Seleucidæ, generally fought out in Palestine, but indirectly, by setting on Greece against Macedonia, Cyrene against Egypt, the lesser states of Asia Minor against Syria—every king having constant trouble with these insurrections fomented by his rivals. The policy of the island cities under Rhodes, and of the king of Pergamum, was that of a strongly armed neutrality. All this time the Romans were so occupied with the alarm, the strain, the exhaustion of their great struggles with Carthage, that they were unable to do more than secure their supremacy over Hellenism in Italy and Sicily. It was not till they had come successfully out of the great crisis with Hannibal that they awoke to vast ideas of universal empire, and took the occasion of Philip's interference in the second Punic War, to stretch out their hands, not for safety, but for dominion across the Adriatic. This opens the last act of independent Hellenism.

It is plain enough from this sketch, that in a short book it would be very confusing, nay impossible, to give all the facts, the lesser wars, the conflicts of diplomacy, among these many kingdoms. The reader must permit a selection to be made for him of what was really important, as showing the character of the age, or in its effects upon the general tide of human history.

XIII.

THE THREE YOUNG KINGS.

A SKETCH OF ANTIGONUS GONATAS, HIS ACTS AND CHARACTER.

ANTIGONUS GONATAS[1] was king from B.C. 277–239, but claiming the sovereignty of Macedonia both through his father, Demetrius Poliorcetes, and his mother, Phila, daughter of Antipater. He had made every effort since the death of his father, imprisoned by Seleucus in Syria, to obtain what he considered his lawful heritage. During his youth he had not only had the advantage of a noble and spirited mother, to whom he owed, no doubt, the deeper traits of his character, but he had spent much time in Athens among the philosophers, while his father was wandering in wars and adventures through the Hellenistic world. Hence many anecdotes, preserved in the lives of the philosophers, attest his devotion to serious study, and his friendship with men of learning and character, especially Stoics. His devotion to his father was absolute. He offered himself as a prisoner in his father's stead, and when the latter died, brought him with

---

[1] He is said to have been so called because he was brought up at an obscure place called Goni, in Thessaly.

great grief and pomp to Corinth, to be buried in the City of Demetrias. Then he claimed the throne of Macedonia, but with little effect against Lysimachus and Pyrrhus, both superior generals. Italy relieved him for a time of Pyrrhus, whom he even helped with ships; the battle of Corupedon of Lysimachus; but against old Seleucus he had no chance. When the veteran was murdered, Antigonus was at war with Ptolemy Keraunos, the murderer, who had the advantage of a great army ready at hand, when he succeeded to the place of his victim. But the invasion of the Galatæ overshadowed all other differences, and when Keraunos was killed by them, it was Antigonus' chief anxiety to defeat them, and so earn the throne of Macedon.

This was his first great victory. Then, in settling Macedon, he came in contact with the hideous tyrant Apollodorus, of Cassandreia (in Thessaly), whom he subdued with trouble and by strategem. This gave him a new claim on the gratitude of the northern Greeks; but presently Pyrrhus, who had in vain begged him for help against the Romans, when his first successes had shown him the arduous nature of the enterprise, came back from the west to assert a kingdom in Hellas and Macedonia, which he had been unable to conquer in Italy. Antigonus now lost his kingdom again, and was driven out by Pyrrhus, but with the aid of a fleet and of many Greek friends, kept up the struggle, till Pyrrhus was killed by an old woman with a tile from the roof of a house, while he was fighting in the streets of Argos. This time Antigonus became finally master of Macedonia, for though we hear that once again, while he was at war with Athens, he lost his kingdom to Alexander, king of Epirus, his son recovered it so quickly by a second battle, that this strange and obscure episode need hardly been taken into account.

For more than thirty years then, he was one of the leading sovereigns of the empire, keeping a learned and refined court at Pella, cultivating Stoic philosophy and science, but at the same time having his hands full of complex policy. After a preliminary war with Antiochus, he made with this king a permanent peace, not only owing to the alliance with him by marrying his sister Phila—Antiochus' wife Stratonice was already a bond of that kind, being Antigonus' sister—but because Antiochus was obliged to permit several intermediate kingdoms, as well as the coast and island Greeks, to assert their liberty. Of this anon. Antigonus' main struggles were with Ptolemy, and were carried on by each in the country of the other, by fomenting revolts, and supporting them with money and with ships. Thus Ptolemy was always urging the Greeks to claim their liberty; he even figures in inscriptions of the times as their generalissimo, and he produced at least one great coalition against Antigonus, headed by Athens—the so called Chremonidean war. On the other hand, Antigonus had a hold upon Caria, from which he could threaten Egypt directly; and he sent his brother Demetrius (the Fair) to Cyrene, producing an important and effectual revolt against Egypt. The Chremonidean war he seems to have settled, first by defeating the Spartans, whose king, Areus, fell in the battle at Corinth, to which they had advanced in the hope of raising the siege of Athens; next by a great naval victory at Cos, in which the Egyptian fleet of relief was destroyed, and owing to which Athens was obliged to surrender (B.C. 266).

From that time onward, Antigonus had to contend with no further active interference from Philadelphus; though the relations of the two kingdoms were always strained, and their interests at variance.

The difficulties he had with Greece were more serious, because the intrigues of Ptolemy fell in with the spirit of the nation, and even with its noblest aspirations. The grave and solid system of the Stoics did not serve Antigonus only, as a rule of life, it seems to have affected the tone of Athens just as the eloquence of Demosthenes affected it towards the close of the struggle with Philip. Men became serious about politics and fought for conscience' sake. These stoical people often opposed Antigonus on principle, and were not the least satisfied with the result of a battle; their opposition was irreconcilable. Still more serious was the rise of the Federal principle in Ætolia and Achaia, which brought together democracies of towns into democracies of states, and so created powers able to contend with the power of Macedonia. Antigonus strove all his life against these difficulties by establishing garrisons in strong places, such as Corinth, by isolating the petty states, and hence, by putting into them tyrants, devoted to his interests. These tyrants were not all high-minded Stoics, like their master, and committed many injustices and outrages. Hence the popular sentiment could easily be roused against the king.

Thus the theory that Macedonia should lead Greece while each state was left free to manage its own affairs, was met by the theory that a Federal Council of the states themselves could do it better. There was also towards the close of Antigonus' life that remarkable revival of Sparta under Agis, on the theory that a reformed royalty at Sparta was the natural head of the Peloponnesians. These things will be considered presently.

All together they tended to weaken the king's position, and render it very difficult. His first duty was to make in Macedonia a strong bulwark against northern barbarism, and this he did effectually; but whether his action on Greece was equally good may be fairly doubted. As things turned out, we feel that the Greeks were unfit to manage their own affairs, and yet the history of the Achæan League is among the most honourable passages in Greek history. Antigonus was fain in the end to recognize its power, and made peace with Aratus. The diversion he had produced in Cyrene had also turned out badly. Demetrius the Fair, who had been sent out as future bridegroom of the youthful heiress Berenice, intrigued with her widowed mother, and was finally put to death with her almost in the presence of the insulted girl. Then her marriage with the young king Ptolemy (Euergetes) was arranged, and this king also defeated Antigonus' fleet at Andros; but Eastern affairs called away Euergetes' attention, and so the western empire was at peace, just when the Romans began to rest after their first Punic War, and the old king died full of years and of glory (B.C. 239).

Ptolemy Philadelphus, the second of these kings, ruled from 282 to 246 B.C., and unlike Antigonus, who had to fight over and over again for his crown, succeeded at the age of twenty-four peacefully, in his wise father's lifetime, and without trouble from his desperate elder brother, who set all the rest of the empire aflame. Indeed he took advantage of the confusion caused by Seleucus' murder to seize Coele-Syria and Phœnicia, which Antiochus did not recover for ten years, and during most of his life he was striving, with considerable success, to grasp the coasts of Lycia and Caria, to control the Greek cities of Asia Minor, and to extend his influence over the Black Sea, so as to close the northern trade-route from the East to Europe. He fought all his wars rather by political combinations and subsidies from his great wealth, than by actual campaigns, for he was no general, and never took the field. So he raised up enemies against Antigonus, as we have just seen, in Greece. He set the dynasts of Bithynia and Pontus against their suzerain Antiochus. He even sought the friendship of the Romans, to whom he sent a friendly embassy (B.C. 273), just after their defeat of Pyrrhus—an embassy received with great enthusiasm and every distinction by the Romans, for he was then the most powerful monarch in the world.

Let us first turn our attention to his capital. Alexandria, founded by the great conqueror, increased and beautified by Ptolemy Soter, was now far the greatest city of Alexander's Empire. It was the first of those new foundations which are a marked feature in Hellenism; there were many others of great size and importance—above all, Antioch, then Seleucia on the

Tigris, then Nicomedia, Nicæa, Apamea, which lasted ; besides such as Lysimacheia, Antigoneia, and others, which early disappeared. In fact, Macedonia was the only great power in those days content with a modest capital, for the Antigonids had not taken up Cassander's foundation, Cassandreia, nor would they leave their old seat at Pella. Alexandria was the model for all the rest. The intersection of two great principal thoroughfares, adorned with colonnades for the footways, formed the centre point, the *omphalos* of the city. The other streets were at right angles with these thoroughfares, so that the whole place was quite regular. Counting its old part, Rhakotis, which was still the habitation of native Egyptians, Alexandria had five quarters, one at least devoted to Jews who had originally settled there in great numbers. The mixed population there of Macedonians, Greeks, Jews, and Egyptians gave a peculiarly complex and variable character to the population.

Let us not forget the vast number of strangers from all parts of the world whom trade and politics brought there. It was the great mart where the wealth of Europe and of Asia changed hands. Alexander had opened the sea-way by exploring the coasts of Media and Persia. Caravans from the head of the Persian Gulf, and ships on the Red Sea, brought all the wonders of Ceylon and China, as well as of Further India, to Alexandria. There, too, the wealth of Spain and Gaul, the produce of Italy and Macedonia, the amber of the Baltic and the salt fish of Pontus, the silver of Spain and the copper of Cyprus, the timber of Macedonia and Crete, the pottery and oil of Greece—a thousand imports from all the Mediterranean—came to be exchanged for the spices of Arabia, the splendid birds and embroideries of India and Ceylon, the gold and ivory of Africa, the antelopes, the apes, the leopards, the elephants of tropical climes. Hence the enormous wealth of the Lagidæ, for in addition to the marvellous fertility and great population—it is said to have been seven millions—of Egypt, they made all the profits of this enormous carrying trade.

We gain a good idea of what the splendours of the capital were by the very full account preserved to us by Athenæus of the great feast which inaugurated the reign of Philadelphus. The enumeration of what went in the state procession is veritably tedious to read, but must have been astonishing to behold. It took the whole day to defile through the streets, at which we need not wonder, when we find that the troops alone, all dressed in splendid uniforms, numbered nearly 60,000. Not only was there gold and silver in infinite display, but every kind of exotic flower, forced out of its natural season, and troops of all the wild animals in the world, from the white polar bear, to the rhinoceros of Ethiopia—gazelles, zebras, wild asses, elephants, bisons. There were, moreover, great mummeries with mythological and allegorical figures, just like those of the Middle Ages; hunting scenes too and vintage scenes, with satyrs treading the wine-press, and the streets flowing with the foaming juice. There were negroes and Indians, mock prisoners in the triumph of Dionysus, and personification of all the cities, and the seasons of the year, and a great deal more with which it is not necessary to delay the reader.

124 SPECIMENS OF THE GREEK ARCHITECTURE

AN IONIC CAPITAL.

A CORINTHIAN CAPITAL.

CORINTHIAN PILASTER.

A CORINTHIAN CAPITAL.

PYLON (PORTAL) OF A TEMPLE, EDFU.

A TEMPLE AT PHILÆ.

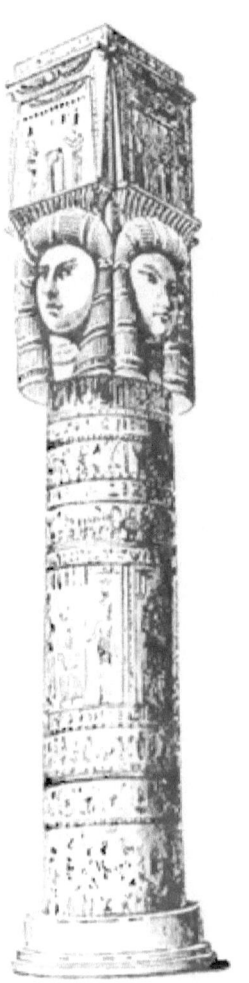 

PILLAR FROM PHILÆ.   STATUE OF OSIRIS.

All this seems idle pomp, and the doing of an idle sybarite. Philadelphus was anything but that. He was determined to drain life to the uttermost, and for that end he essayed every sort of enjoyment, except that of military glory, which his weak frame and delicate health precluded. After his accession he cleared away the possible claimants or disturbers of his throne with the quick and bloody ruthlessness of an Oriental despot, but from that time on his sway was that of gentleness, mildness, subtlety. Diplomacy was evidently one of his main pursuits, and he embraced in his practice of it all the known world. At every court he had his emissaries, and in every kingdom his supporters. He fought all his wars by raising up enemies to his opponents in their own land. He enjoyed the support and friendship of many potentates. It was he who opened up the Egyptian trade with Italy, and made Puteoli the great port for ships from Alexandria, which it remained for centuries. It was he who explored Æthiopia and the southern parts of Africa, and brought back not only the curious fauna to his zoological gardens, but the first knowledge of the Troglodytes for men of science. The cultivation of science and of letters too was so remarkably one of his pursuits that the progress of the Alexandria of his day forms an epoch in the world's history, and we must separate his University and its professors from this summary, and devote to them a separate section.

Nor was he content with pure intellectual pleasures, or the pleasures of diplomatic intrigue. Like Augustus of Saxony and Louis I. of Bavaria, he varied his pursuits of art or politics with galant adventures, and his amours were the talk of the capital. He had married his full sister Arsinoe,[1] when she was near forty years of age, and had already passed through a gale of fortunes, which may have made her weary of ordinary love and jealousy. She was deified by her husband, and associated with him in all his public acts. We do not hear that they ever quarrelled; but she left her husband full liberty to follow his wild search for some new pleasure—perhaps on condition of his forming no other royal alliance. So the king's favourites lived, like the Princess Dolgorouki the other day, in the Royal Palace, and their portraits were as common as are now the photographs of professional beauties—one in particular, in a single tunic without sleeves, as she had just caught his fancy drawing water with a pitcher. All this life was so full, with its diplomacy, its art, its science, its letters, its loves, that we do not wonder to hear that the king longed to enjoy it beyond the span of ordinary men, and sought in mystic rites for the elixir of immortality. Nevertheless he had his griefs too, especially from his feeble health, and when tortured with gout, he would look out upon the Fellahs at work in the broiling sun, or resting at their frugal noonday meal, and long that he could enjoy life as they did; and yet he and his sister-wife were gods, worshipped as the *Philadelphi;* and the priestess (Canephorus) of Arsinoe the murderess, the adulteress, the traitoress, now queen of Egypt, was

---

[1] Hence his title of Philadelphus, sister-loving; such an union was very offensive to Greek ideas, where marriages of uncle and niece, and even of half-brothers and sisters were tolerated.

PERSONIFICATION OF THE CITY ANTIOCH, WITH THE RIVER ORONTES.

like the great priestesses of Argos and elsewhere, used to fix the date of all public events.

We are not astonished that Philadelphus, with all his physicians and his magic draughts, failed to reach the advanced age of his great rival Antigonus. He died about the age of sixty-three, worn out no doubt by the enjoyments and labours of his wonderful life. But he left a splendid empire and a full treasury to a brilliant son, and might justly boast that as he had handed on the torch of empire unquenched to his successor, so perfectly had he attained and perfected all that was great and good in Hellenism. Rhodes, Pergamum, Antioch, were all great and splendid in the peculiar style of this period, but none of them ever equalled Alexandria in their effects on the civilization of the world. We shall return presently to the literary side of Alexandria, when we have given, for completeness' sake, a short sketch of the third monarch of the empire —Antiochus, who was established in the rival capital of Antioch, and sought to emulate both the commerce and the culture of Alexandria.

Antiochus Soter is the last of these kings. The Syrian monarchs had shorter reigns than those of the rival kingdoms. Antiochus I. had fought at the battle of Ipsus, when the cavalry under him was defeated by Demetrius Poliorketes; he did not succeed till the age of forty-four, after having long governed the "Upper provinces" of Seleucus' great empire with his wife Stratonice, sister of Antigonus Gonatas, who had been married to his father Seleucus, but whom the old king gave up to his son, when he found that he was dying of love for his step-mother. These Diadochi were indeed very lax about their marriage relations! Succeeding upon the sudden murder of his father by Keraunos, then finding his realm invaded in the north-west by the Galatæ, in the south-west by Ptolemy, the valiant king was unable to hold all that was bequeathed to him. He made peace with Antigonus, ceding to him Macedonia, which he had never possessed, and giving him his sister Phila in marriage. Then he was obliged to give up his sovranty over Pontus, Bithynia, and the Greek cities in the north of Asia Minor. His victory over the Galatæ earned him the name of Soter (Saviour), and gave him a sort of suzerainty over the lesser kingdoms which the barbarians threatened. Even Armenia maintained its independence, and in the south he was unable to wrest Cœle-Syria and Palestine from Ptolemy.

Nevertheless he kept great state at his mighty capital Antioch, which from its lovely situation, its splendid water-supply from the overhanging mountains, its fairy suburbs, especially Daphne on the higher slopes, its fine seaport (Seleucia on the Orontes), and its proximity to many other cities and rich plains of Inner Syria, became one of the world's resting-places. The city was built on the plan of Alexandria, but stretched along the Orontes, as the overhanging mountains forbade extension in breadth. Every private house had its own water-supply, all the public places their fountains; people of all nations came there together, to enjoy the fruits of Greek culture, and to commune in the Greek tongue. Antiochus was fond of letters also. Aratus the astronomer was at his court as well as at that of Antigonus; it was Antiochus who began that remarkable fashion of having the books of other nations translated into Greek. Berosus, the Chaldean, published the mythology and history of Babylon from the cuneiform records, by order of the king, and then settled in Cos, where he taught astrology. It was doubtless at his suggestion that Manetho translated a similar work from the hieroglyphics on the history of Egypt for Philadelphus. Nay, it is more than probable that the early Greek version of the Pentateuch, with which our *Septuagint* version began, was made at the same time, and with the same object—to acquaint Greek-speaking people with the wisdom and the mysteries of all ancient and cultivated races; for true Hellenism was, like Christianity, no respecter of persons or of races. All peoples who showed culture, who could contribute to human learning or happiness, and who could do it in Greek, were welcome to take their place within the sphere of great civilization. Hellenism was then an expression such as " European culture " is now.

Though we know little personally of Antiochus Soter, we can feel that he was a worthy and useful promoter of the great spirit of his time, and when he died at the age of sixty-four, just after a defeated endeavour to subdue Eumenes, the new prince of Pergamum, who refused him submission, the world must have felt a serious loss.

He was succeeded by his son, called Theos (the god) by the Greek cities (Miletus, &c.), which he declared free when he found he could no longer control them. About this king we know even less than we do about his father. We are informed that he made conquests as far as Thrace—endeavouring to make good some of his father's losses; that he was unable to subdue Pergamum, but liberated the neighbouring great cities, probably to set them against the new dynast; also that he had a long and tedious war with Ptolemy Philadelphus, which so wearied that monarch that he settled it on the basis of a new alliance, whereby Antiochus was to give up his previous wife Laodice, banish her and her children, and marry Berenice, daughter of the Egyptian king. By this means the old diplomatist expected to secure a practical supremacy in Syria; but Philadelphus just lived long enough to hear of the fearful catastrophe which upset all his plans. The discarded queen and her party managed to entice Antiochus to visit them at Sardis. There he was poisoned, and forthwith the young Egyptian queen was pursued through Antioch to her retreat at Daphne and murdered. This tragedy gave rise to a great war, which will naturally be related under the reign of the next Ptolemy, who undertook it immediately after his accession (B.C. 246).

Such were the events which agitated the East in the last years of the veteran Antigonus; but the reign of Antiochus Theos is far more deeply interesting, from another cause. It gives us the date when a series of revolts in the "Upper provinces" not only severed them for a time from the heritage of the empire, but brought a great Oriental reaction to bear upon Hellenism. The reader has already been told how the empire of Chandragupta had invaded the Eastern provinces of Seleucus, and how Seleucus had made a cession of what he could not hold. For the building of his capital Antioch and his whole policy, showed that his eye was set on the West, on the Mediterranean as the true home of Hellenism, and therefore of real culture and progress. Doubtless this fixing of his residence near the western extreme of his kingdom was one chief cause why the " Upper provinces" fell away. In the reign of the king now before us, it seems that Atropatene, named in honour of the satrap Atropates, who had declared himself king after Alexander's death, took the lead. It was practically Northern Media, and its independence stopped the way from the East along the foot of the Caspian—the Seleucian Sea it had been called—and so the great northern highway of traffic to the Black Sea. No doubt Ptolemy's far-seeing diplomacy promoted this revolt, though the facts are lost to us. Then we find that the provinces of Bactria and Sogdiana, separated from the empire by this revolt, set up kings of their own, but marvellous to relate, kings with Greek names (Euthydemus, Diodotus), who gave them a thoroughly Greek coinage, which has recently been discovered. The scanty remains of their architecture also show that the kings of this far remote Asiatic realm bordering upon the Tartars were Hellenistic in culture, and are still to be regarded as distinct descendants of Alexander. So far, then, Hellenism was still triumphant, but of course with many compromises and concessions as to religion and language. Above all the kingdom of Chandragupta was now in the hands of his pious grandson Açoka, whose adoption of the creed of Buddha was probably as great an event as the adoption of Christianity by Constantine. This great king's influence gave free scope to the strong missionary spirit of the Buddhist priests, and we are told in his inscriptions that their apostles reached into the kingdoms of the Hellenistic world. Antiochus, Antigonus, Magas, Ptolemy, Alexander of Epirus, are all named. So, then, an influence strongly antagonistic to Hellenism was at work in the Eastern provinces, and we may take it as probable that Buddhist missionaries preached in Syria two centuries before the teaching of Christ (which has so many moral points in common) was heard in Northern Palestine. So true is it that every great historical change has had its forerunner, and that people's minds must be gradually led to the great new truths, which are indeed the gift of Divine inspiration.[1] The tolerance of Hellenism, nay, the curiosity which ordered the translation of the sacred books of Jews, Egyptians, and Babylonians into Greek, must have allowed free play to the dissemination of these deeper moral systems. How far even later Stoicism may not have been affected by them it is hard to say. The Stoics were certainly in contact with Cilicia and Syria, and may well have been struck with the doctrine which, along with its Pantheism, preached humility, abstinence, charity, benevolence in

---

[1] This is true even of teachings that are not divinely inspired. Witness those Hanifs who, just before the appearance of Mohammed, were eagerly looking for some religion more satisfactory than the Arabian fetishism and idol-worship. See "The Story of the Saracens," chap. vi.

a way far more complete than any Hellene could ever have conceived. If the creed of Buddha had been translated into Greek, and so circulated, there can be little doubt that it would have had its missionaries and monks all over the Mediterranean, and perhaps even at Rome. But without that step it was totally foreign to Hellenism. And this step it was, the producing of its gospels in Greek, which gave Christianity at once a passport to all the civilization of the West.

But we must leave these deeply attractive considerations which reach far away into subsequent history, and return to tamer problems. We have postponed till now some account of the literature, of Alexandria, and hence of the Hellenistic world in the days of Philadelphus.

COIN OF SELEUCUS III. OF SYRIA.

XIV.

SCIENCE AND LETTERS AT ALEXANDRIA IN THE DAYS OF PHILADELPHUS.

It is the bane of history that we are obliged to set down so much about wars and alliances, about the follies and prowesses of princes and generals, and so the better part—the development of ideas, the progress of culture and of letters, the advance of political and moral knowledge—in fact, the life of peoples and not that of their accidental governors is left out, or pushed into a corner. It is a pleasant escape, therefore, from the tortuous and complicated diplomacies, the cross-purposes, the labyrinths of alliances among the royal houses of the day, to a consideration of the import of what they have left us in science and literature. It is, alas, but very little! Five Alexandrian poets are preserved. We have in the earlier books of the Septuagint a specimen of what sort of Greek was current in prose at that time. We have some information as to the pursuit of science; but the history of the organization of the University and its staff is covered with almost impenetrable mist. For the Museum and Library were in the strictest sense what we should now call an University, and one, too, of the

Oxford type, where learned men were invited to take Fellowships, and spend their learned leisure close to observatories in science, and a great library of books. Like the mediæval universities, this endowment of research naturally turned into an engine for teaching, as all who desired knowledge flocked to such a centre, and persuaded the Fellow to become a Tutor.

The model came from Athens. There the schools, beginning with the *Academy* of Plato, had a fixed property—a home with its surrounding garden, and in order to make this foundation sure, it was made a shrine where the Muses were worshipped, and where the head of the school, or a priest appointed, performed stated sacrifices. This, then, being held in trust by the successors of the donor, who bequeathed it to them, was a property which it would have been sacrilegious to invade, and so the title *Museum* arose for a school of learning. Demetrius the Phalerean, the friend and protector of Theophrastus, brought this idea with him to Alexandria, when his namesake drove him into exile (see p. 59), and it was no doubt his advice to the first Ptolemy which originated the great foundation, though Philadelphus, who again exiled Demetrius, gets the credit of it. The pupil of Aristotle moreover impressed on the king the necessity of storing up in one central repository all that the world knew or could produce, in order to ascertain the laws of things from a proper analysis of detail. Hence was founded not only the great library, which in those days had a thousand times the value a great library has now, but also observatories, zoological gardens, collections of exotic plants, and of other new and strange things brought by exploring expeditions from the furthest regions of Arabia and Africa.

This library and museum proved indeed a home for the Muses, and about it a most brilliant group of students in literature and science was formed. The successive librarians were Zenodotus, the grammarian or critic; Callimachus, to whose poems we shall presently return; Eratosthenes, the astronomer, who originated the process by which the size of the earth is determined to-day; Apollonius the Rhodian, disciple and enemy of Callimachus; Aristophanes of Byzantium, founder of a school of philological criticism; and Aristarchus of Samos, reputed to have been the greatest critic of ancient times. The study of the text of Homer was the chief labour of Zenodotus, Aristophanes, and Aristarchus, and it was Aristarchus who mainly fixed the form in which the Iliad and the Odyssey remain to this day.

In this time of mental activity, Eratosthenes devoted himself, among other things, to chronology, endeavouring to establish it upon a scientific basis. He made an effort to verify the Trojan era, fixing it at 1183 or 1184, which, though now considered conjectural and only approximate, is still acknowledged to be entitled to consideration. The varied accomplishments of this remarkable man led Strabo, in contrasting him with Callimachus, who alone is deemed worthy of comparison with him for versatility, to remark that Eratosthenes was not only a poet and a grammarian, as Callimachus was, but that he had also reached the highest excellence as a philosopher and a mathematician. He was the first person who bore the title of philologer. His reputation rests mainly upon his discoveries, for his literary labours have perished, with the exception of a few fragments. Such were some of the men who, under the patronage of the Ptolemies, preserved for us all the best specimens of Greek literature that have been spared from the ravages of time. Their unwearied learning, extraordinary talents, and unbounded ambition for contemporary praise, made the city of Alexandria a hotbed of literary activity.

The vast collections of the library and museum actually determined the whole character of the literature of Alexandria. One word sums it all up—*erudition*, whether in philosophy, in criticism, in science, even in poetry. Strange to say, they neglected not only oratory, for which there was no scope, but history, and this we may attribute to the fact that history before Alexander had no charms for Hellenism. Mythical lore, on the other hand, strange uses and curious words, were departments of research dear to them. In science they did great things, so did they in geography, and their systematic translation from foreign sacred books have been already mentioned.

But were they original in nothing? Did they add nothing of their own to the splendid record of Greek literature?

In the next generation came the art of criticism, which Aristarchus developed into a real science, and of that we may speak in its place; but even in this generation we may claim for them the credit of three original, or nearly original, developments in literature

—the pastoral idyll, as we have it in Theocritus; the elegy, as we have it in the Roman imitators of Philetas and Callimachus; and the romance, or love story, the parent of our modern novels. All these had early prototypes in the folk songs of Sicily, in the love songs of Mimnermus and of Antimachus, in the tales of Miletus, but still the revival was fairly to be called original.

Of these the pastoral idyll was far the most remarkable, and laid hold upon the world for ever. To the pedants in their cloisters, to the fashionable world living in the hot streets, and surrounded by the sand hills of Alexandria, nothing could be more delightful than the freshness of the cool uplands, the shade beside the fern-plumed well, the whispering of leaves and music of falling water, the bleating of sheep and the lowing of kine, the bubbling of the pail,

> "The moan of doves in immemorial elms,
> And murmuring of innumerable bees."

They delighted to hear of the shepherds' rivalry in song, and of the pipe sounding through the vales, which was silenced in hot mid-day when angry Pan took his siesta, and would brook no disturbance save the soothing pertinacity of the sunburnt cicada.

All this poetry was as artificial as the "Arcadia" of Sannazaro,[1] the pictures of Watteau, or the *Trianon*

---

[1] See "Rambles and Studies in Greece," third edition, chap. xiii., where the history of the Arcadia of poetry is given for the first time. If the reader wants a famous English example of this artificial poetry, let him turn to the "Lycidas" of Milton, where he and his friend King appear as shepherds, and their college tutor as "old Damoetas,"

of the hapless Marie Antoinette. Even the pedants were dressed up as shepherds in these idylls, and addressed in feigned names; but artificial nature has always been popular among very civilized people. The limits of this book do not permit extensive quotations, but a few lines must be admitted from the admirable version of Theocritus by C. S. Calverley.

Idyll IX.

PASTORALS.

DAPHNIS. MENALCAS. A SHEPHERD.

Shepherd.

A song from Daphnis! Open he the lay,
He open: and Menalcas follow next:
While the calves suck, and with the barren kine
The young bulls graze, or roam knee-deep in leaves,
And ne'er play truant. But a song from thee,
Daphnis—anon Menalcas will reply.

Daphnis.

Sweet is the chorus of the calves and kine,
   And sweet the herdsman's pipe. But none may vie
With Daphnis; and a rush-strown bed is mine
   Near a cool rill, where capeted I lie

---

a Sicilian hind. The influence of Theocritus, without his artificiality, is seen in Tennyson, and it has been more marked in the Laureate than that in any other modern poet.

On fair white goatskins. From a hill-top high
The westwind swept me down the hard entire,
  Cropping the strawberries; whence it comes that I
No more heed summer, with his breath of fire,
Then lovers heed the words of mother and of sire.

Thus Daphnis; and Menalcas answered thus :—

Menalcas.

O Ætna, mother mine! A grotto fair,
  Scooped in the rocks have I : and there I keep
All that in dreams men picture! Treasured there
  Are multitudes of she-goats and of sheep,
  Swathed in whose wool from top to toe I sleep.
The fire that boils my pot, with oak or beech
  Is piled—dry beech-logs when the snow lies deep;
And storm and sunshine, I disdain them each
As toothless sires a nut, when broth is in their reach.

I clapped applause, and straight produced my gifts:
A staff for Daphnis—'twas the handiwork
Of nature, in my father's acres grown :
Yet might a turner find no fault therewith.
I gave his mate a goodly spiral-shell :
We stalked its inmate on the Icarian rocks,
And ate him, parted fivefold among five.

        There we lay
Half-buried in a couch of fragrant reed
And fresh-cut vine leaves, who so glad as we?
A wealth of elm and poplar shook o'erhead;
Hard by, a sacred spring flowed gurgling on
From the Nymphs' grot, and in the sombre boughs
The sweet cicada chirped laboriously.
Hid in the thick thorn-bushes far away
The tree-frog's note was heard; the crested lark
Sang with the goldfinch, turtles made their moan,
And o'er the fountain hung the gilded bee.

All of rich summer smacked, of autumn all :

Pears at our feet, and apples at our side
Rolled in luxuriance; branches on the ground
Sprawled, overweighed with damsons; while we brushed
From the cask's head the crust of four long years.
Say, ye who dwell upon Parnassian peaks,
Nymphs of Castalia, did old Chiron e'er
Set before Heracles a cup so brave
In Pholus' cavern—did as nectarous draughts
Cause the Anapian shepherd, in whose hand
Rocks were as pebbles, Polypheme the strong,
Featly to foot it o'er the cottage lawns:
As, ladies, ye bid flow that day for us
All by Demeter's shrine at harvest-home?
Beside whose cornstacks may I oft again
Plant my broad fan: while she stands by and smiles,
Poppies and corn-sheaves on each laden arm.

THE PRAISE OF PTOLEMY.

"Land and sea alike
And sounding rivers hail King Ptolemy.
Many are his horsemen, many his targeteers,
Whose burdened breast is bright with clashing steel;
Light are all royal treasuries, weighed with his;
For wealth from all climes travels day by day
To his rich realm—a hive of prosperous peace.
No foeman's tramp scares monster-peopled Nile,
Waking to war her far-off villages:
No armèd robber from his war-ship leaps
To spoil the herds of Egypt. Such a prince
Sits throned in her broad plains, in whose right arm
Quivers the spear—the bright-haired Ptolemy.
Like a true king, he guards with might and main
The wealth his sires' arms have won him and his own.
Nor strown all idly o'er his sumptuous halls
Lie piles that seem the work of labouring ants. . . .
None entered e'er the sacred lists of song,
Whose lips could breathe sweet music, but he gained

Fair guerdon at the hand of Ptolemy.
And Ptolemy do muses votaries hymn
For his good gifts—hath man a fairer lot
Than to have earned such fame among mankind? . . .
Ptolemy, he only, treads a path whose dust
Burns with the footprints of his ancestors,
And overlays those footprints with his own.'

THE SERENADE.

" I pipe to Amaryllis; while my goats,
  Tityrus their guardian, browse along the fell. . . .
    Ah, winsome Amaryllis! why no more
Greet'st thou thy darling, from the caverned rock,
Peeping all coyly? Think'st thou scorn of him?
Hath a near view revealed him satyr-shaped
Of chin and nostril? I shall hang me soon.
See here ten apples: from thy favourite tree
I plucked them; I shall bring ten more anon.
Ah, witness my heart-anguish! Oh, were I
A booming bee, to waft me to thy lair,
Threading the fern and ivy in whose depths
Thou nestlest! I have learned what love is now."

The other poets we still possess from the days of Philadelphus are far inferior, but still by no means despicable. They are Callimachus, who has left us " Hymns to the Gods," on the model of the Homeric hymns; Apollonius Rhodius, who has left us the

---

[1] The reader who prefers prose to verse will like to consult the excellent version of Theocritus by Andrew Lang, which is valuable for the essay which precedes the translations; but a poetical translation of a poet is greatly to be preferred, and this is now-a-days no truism, as it ought to be.

epic of the Argonauts; Aratus, who has given us a treatise on astronomy in hexametres, and Lycophron, whose "Alexandra" has become famous for its obscurity. All these poets were spoilt by their erudition. They are always seeking out obscure myths, and dealing in recondite allusions. The vocabulary they use is not the living speech of any Greeks, but a pedantic collection from the curiosities in older poets. This is their general character, and the same may be said of the epigrams, which all that school cultivated, and which became as fashionable at Alexandria as double acrostics are now. In these it was not only neat points, and general smartness, which were successfully studied, but the words employed are often such as puzzle any classical scholar trained upon pure models.

Callimachus, who was also librarian of the great Library, and so had the highest literary post at Alexandria, was the most celebrated of these poets in his day; Apollonius Rhodius is certainly, so far as we know, the best next to Theocritus. His epic on the adventures of the Argonauts contains not only the usual amount of erudition, of recondite myth and mythical geography, but it has the story of a great passion, the love of Medea for Jason, which has inspired the noblest of all Roman poets, Virgil, with his matchless episode of Dido.

This painting of the passion of love, which led ultimately to the prose novels of the Greeks, such as the "Daphnis and Chloe" of Longus, was perhaps the most important new feature in Alexandrian literature. It is not the painting of revenge, or of a fatal passion, like Euripides' Medea and Phædra, but simply the analysis of the process of falling in love, which was so new and attractive to the Hellenistic Greeks. Its earliest type was Callimachus' metrical story of Acontius and Cydippe, of which we know that it merely related how two young people, whose beauty was very fully described, fell in love, were thwarted by their parents, went through the usual perturbations on such occasions, and finally, with the aid of sickness and the advice of friendly oracles, overcame the resistance of father and mother, and were happily married. It seems almost grotesque to speak of such a plot as a novelty in literature, and yet such it was. It was combined, presently, with another vein of romance, that of wonderful travels in remote lands, and adventures therein, such as are told of Alexander in the curious romance ascribed to Callisthenes, but really composed at Alexandria somewhat later than the generation before us. Nevertheless, we may be sure the materials were already accumulating in the folklore of the Alexandrians.

The works of Aratus, who is really a scientific man who wrote in metre, and the obscure prophecies of Alexandra (Cassandra) given in hardly intelligible Greek by Lycophron, are not literature that any one will take up now for either pleasure or profit; and still Aratus was closely copied by Virgil in describing the signs of weather in his *Georgics*, a passage of great beauty in the Latin version.

The seven tragic poets, called the Pleiad, are to us only names; and the comic poets, who transferred the genteel comedy of Athens to Alexandria, have only left us a few fragments showing how closely they adhered to the Attic models. But let us not forget that these second-rate Alexandrian poets were the first models adopted by the Romans, when this people were admitted to Hellenistic culture. Callimachus and his rivals were the source from which Catullus, Propertius, and even Virgil and Ovid, drew their inspiration. It was not till Horace that we find the Romans discovering purer and higher poetry in Alcæus and Sappho, and rejecting Hellenistic for truly Hellenic art.

We have yet to say a word on the most important and remarkable, though not the most artistic, of the literary remains left us by the Alexandria of Philadelphus. We have in the Septuagint, a Greek version of the Hebrew Old Testament, the first great essay in translation into Greek, a solitary specimen of the ordinary language spoken and understood in those days. There is a famous legend of the origin of the work by order of the Egyptian king, and of the perfect agreement of all the versions produced by the learned men who had been sent at his request from Judæa. Laying aside these fables, it appears that the books were gradually rendered for the benefit of the many Jews settled in Egypt, who seem to have been actually forgetting their old language. Perhaps Philadelphus gave an impulse to the thing by requiring a copy for his library, which seems to have admitted none but Greek books. Probably, too, the Pentateuch was translated first, and about this time, the rest following, till the days when the translator of "Ecclesiasticus" (about 140 B.C.) speaks of the main body of books as clearly before the Greek public.

We can see from the Septuagint what sort of Greek was spoken in Hellenistic capitals—very coarse and rude as compared with Attic refinement, interlarded with local words, which would differ according to the province and its older tongue, but a practical and handy common language, such as Latin was in the Europe of the Middle Ages, and such as we hope English will one day become, when we make our spelling as simple as our grammar, and give up the absurd fashion of writing one sound and speaking another.

No great common culture is possible without a common language, and what unity there now is in European civilization was created by the Church with its Latin ritual, and its constant teaching of Latin as the tongue of educated intercourse. Had this not been the case, the great nations of Europe would now stand asunder to an extent almost inconceivable. So Syria and Macedonia, Egypt and Greece, were perfectly isolated in culture until the common bond of language united them. Açoka (the Indian king) speaks of them all as kings of the Yavanas (Ionians or Greeks), and rightly. The Egyptian papyri of the time speak of the invaders as Greeks, and yet it was only in language that they were Greeks, and perhaps in the most superficial elements of their culture. But it was the great connecting link which helped to advance the world with a rapidity that can only be compared to the effects of steam on modern intercourse.

To describe the developments of science, of which the leading production was the great book of Euclid which still infests our schools, of geography, developed by Eratosthenes, and of medicine and natural history—all of which were studied with great success at the Museum of Alexandria—would take us beyond our limits.

XV.

THE THIRD GENERATION OF HELLENISM.—THE THREE GREAT KINGDOMS.

LET us take another look at chronology, and give a table of the third generation of Hellenism in the three great kingdoms of the empire:

SPARTA.[1]	MACEDONIA.
Agis IV. ... ... acc. about 244, put to death 240	Demetrius II. ... ... acc. 239
	Antigonus (Doson) ... acc. 229
Cleomenes III... ... acc. 236, died in Egypt, 220	Philip V. ... acc. 220, at the age of 17.

EGYPT.	SYRIA.
Ptolemy III. (Euergetes) acc. 246	Seleucus II. (Callinicus) acc. 246
Ptolemy IV. (Philopator) acc. 221, not more than 24 years old.	Seleucus III. (Soter) ... acc. 226
	Antiochus III. (the Great) acc. 222, at the age of 20.

[1] Of course there were two lines of kings (Agidæ and Proclidæ) of Sparta. The second king, Leonidas, was deposed by Agis, and Cleombrotus put in his stead. Then Leonidas returned, drove out Cleombrotus, and succeeded in putting Agis to death. The son of Agis, being an infant, and his mother married to Cleomenes, Leonidas's son, there was practically only one king, and this was more strictly the case when Agis's son died—his brother was in exile—and Cleomenes succeeded his father Leonidas. For our purpose, then, the above table is sufficient, if we remember that Cleomenes represented the Proclid kings; Agis, the Agidæ.

During the whole of this generation, and far into the next, Attalus I. reigned at Pergamum.

The history revives again from its obscurity by the fact that we have three important and picturesque *Lives* of Plutarch which cover it: those of Agis, Cleomenes, and Aratus; but we must resume the thread of the Eastern kingdoms, which entered into a great and momentous conflict while old Antigonus was still alive. This was the war undertaken in all haste by Ptolemy Euergetes either to save his sister Berenice's life, or to avenge her murder. The new king of Syria, Seleucus II., a mere youth, was in Asia Minor. Ptolemy was before him at the mouth of the Orontes, seized Seleucia, then Antioch, all Syria, and with his great army conquered all he desired of his rival's kingdom. He even penetrated the East as far as Bactria, and brought home from Persia, Media, Susiana, such treasures as astonished the Egyptians. It was from this cause that he was called Euergetes, the benefactor, especially as some Egyptian gods were among the spoil he recovered.[1] If he had had

---

[1] The history of this king has received much light, not only from the Adulitan inscription, but from the famous stone found at San (Tanis) in 1865, giving in hieroglyphics and Greek (the demotic version is on the edge) a decree of the priests assembled at Canopus for their yearly salutation of the king. When they were so assembled, in his ninth year, his infant daughter, Berenice, fell sick and died, and there was great lamentation over her. The decree first recounts the generous conduct and prowess of the king, who had conquered all his enemies abroad, and had brought back from Persia all the statues of the gods carried off in old time from Egypt by foreign kings. He had also, in a great threatening of famine, when the Nile had failed to rise to its full amount, imported vast quantities of corn from Cyprus, Phœnicia, &c., and fed his people. Consequently divine honours are to be paid

the ambition of Alexander, he would have aspired to a complete conquest of the East; but he was recalled by trouble westward, apparently a revolt in Cyrene; also an uprising of the Greek towns of Asia Minor in favour of Antiochus's heir, who had met so hard a fate at the very opening of his career. So, with Egyptian astuteness, Euergetes set up Seleucus's younger brother Antiochus Hierax, a boy of fourteen, as his rival; and the war of the brothers occupied and weakened Syria for years. Thus Egypt was able to assert a just supremacy in the East. She owned considerable portions of Southern Asia Minor, swayed many of the Greek cities as far as the Propontis, possessed territory in Thrace up to the Macedonian frontier, and held all Palestine and Syria, along with Seleucia on the Orontes, by way of muzzling Syria as effectually as Germany in our day has muzzled France by holding the fortress of Metz.

For the time, the Seleucid kingdom, distracted by rival claims and ravaged by enemies, lost its position in the empire. It is interesting to note that Euer-

---

to him and his queen as *Benefactor-Gods* in all the temples of Egypt, and feasts to be held in their honour; one especially on the day of the rising of the Dog-star, which is not to vary with the day of the month, seeing that the common Egyptian year was only 365 days, and so the summer feasts had gradually moved into winter, and *vice versâ*.

This attempted reform of the calendar, by introducing the Sothiac year of 365 days and a quarter, is very interesting.

These divine honours, and a special statue, with a special crown to distinguish her from her queen mother, are decreed to the child Berenice. The details of the crown are quite heraldic in their accuracy. This great inscription, far more perfect and considerably older than the Rosetta stone, can now be cited as the clearest proof of Champollion's reading of the hieroglyphics. It presented no difficulty to those who already understood Egyptology.

getes left as satrap of his most eastern conquests, Persia and India, the famous soldier of fortune Xanthippus, who had just returned from his victorious campaign against Regulus in Africa, full of rewards and honours, but either distrusting, or distrusted by the merchants of Carthage.[1]

It was quite natural that this predominance of Egypt should call forth first the apprehensions, and then the resistance of the second-rate powers immediately concerned with it. Moreover the wars of the Seleucid brothers had so disturbed Asia Minor that the Galatians, who fought on all sides as mercenaries, were again let loose upon their neighbours, and plundered almost at will. It was to meet these dangers that we hear specially of Pergamum and Rhodes, as the leaders of Hellenism. Now it is that these two powers, one a monarchy, the other a republic, begin to take an active part in politics, and a leading place in art; and they are the cities that we shall consider, when we pause again in our chronicle of facts to consider the social life and culture of this agitated period.

We must say a few words more on the character and achievements of Euergetes, and the Egypt of his day, as that famous kingdom and dynasty, which he brought to its highest pitch of greatness and glory, almost collapses after his death from the incompetence or the vices of its rulers. With the third Ptolemy all the virtues of that great race, except, perhaps, the taste for patronizing learning, seem to take their departure. We have, unfortunately, no con-

[1] See "The Story of Rome," p. 132.

nected history of this king; what we know of his brilliant acts is derived from inscriptions, which are pompous panegyrics, and, moreover, fragmentary and incomplete. The small temple of Esne, which he built, was covered with the record of his wars, but these valuable inscriptions, seen and understood by Rosellini and Champollion in 1829, have since either been covered up, or were destroyed with the temple— at least, they are not accessible to the historian; but the remains of other temples show how nobly the Ptolemies carried on the architectural traditions of the old kings of Egypt. We have, moreover, in the *Coma Berenices* of Catullus, a translation of the poem written by Callimachus, the poet laureate, to celebrate the vow of the young Cyrenæan queen, Berenice, to devote her hair to the gods upon the safe return of her youthful husband from his great expedition to avenge the death of his sister Berenice, the queen of Syria.

It appears to have been this king who first carried out the scheme of Alexander, and effected the circumnavigation of Arabia, so as to open its coasts to Hellenistic traffic. We have, too, the remarkable inscription of Adula, on the East Coast of Africa, not far from the present Suakim, which an Egyptian monk, Cosmas Indicopleustes, saw in the fifth century A.D. on a marble throne set up by Euergetes to commemorate his visit, at the very end of his reign. Luckily the monk copied the inscription, which not only details the king's Eastern campaigns, but also his explorations and expeditions to Southern Arabia, Abyssinia, and Ethiopia, where he made highways, swept the seas of pirates, and brought back elephants to be trained for the purposes of war. It is possible that these southern campaigns and voyages may account for his apparent indifference to Hellenistic politics.

The strides of science at this time were not less remarkable. Geographical exploration was not left without theory to gather and explain the facts. Eratosthenes, the father of the scientific study of the earth, having learned that at the summer solstice the sun cast no shadow at Syene (Aswân), in Upper Egypt, noted the shadows at Alexandria, and at intervening places, having measured the distance. He thus, by his "Science of Shadows," discovered or proved that the earth was round, and estimated the way from Syene to Alexandria was one-fiftieth of the circumference of the globe. At the same time Apollonius was making those researches into the properties of the section of a cone, which led ultimately to the pure science of astronomy, and the practical science of systematic navigation. The true method of criticism was at the same time being applied by Aristophanes of Byzantium, who was afterwards chief librarian, to the poems of Homer, and so he founded the great school of men who have taught us moderns how to understand the literary history of the early books of all nations.

If Egypt overshadowed Syria completely at this time, it likewise overshadowed Macedonia, whose king Demetrius is strangely unknown to us. He was engaged in fierce struggles against the Illyrian and Dardanian barbarians, who were then threatening Greece with their invasions, and whose depredations on the coast of Italy were stopped, as all readers of Roman history know,[1] by the active

[1] See "Story of Rome."

interference of the Romans, who then for the first time brought an armed force across the Adriatic. The northern barbarians of this period are like the northern heathen in the legends of Arthur, and the first duty of every Macedonian king, on his accession, was to secure that frontier of his dominions. On they came, again and again, helped by the jealous divisions of Achæans, Spartans, and Ætolians, on the south of Macedonia, and so King Demetrius II. spent his life first in conquering the barbarians, then in conquering the Greeks, who had advanced as far as Thessaly against him, then again returning in haste to protect his northern frontier, where, after nine years of a glorious and successful reign, he fell in battle against the Dardanian hordes.

Such were the external events of his life. Of his character, appearance, or of his court, we know absolutely nothing. But I have here anticipated events up to his death, in order that we may turn back at leisure, and consider from the *Lives* of Plutarch, the social and political movements in Greece since the rise of the Achæan League to power. These movements began in the days of Antigonus Gonatas, and they proceed in development down to the absorption of the empire by the Romans. But in ordering so complicated a subject, it has been thought better to follow the history of the three main kingdoms of the empire till the secondary become of such importance as to make a capital figure in the world. This was the case with Greece after the middle of the third century B.C., and with Pergamum and Rhodes about the same time.

XVI.

THE RISE OF THE ACHÆAN LEAGUE UNDER ARATUS. HIS POLICY.

No reader of this history should omit to have beside him Plutarch's *Lives*, and there study the picturesque details of the life of the men of this age, for which there is no space in this short book. Nowhere is Plutarch more picturesque than in the opening chapters of his sketch of Aratus, drawn, no doubt, from that politician's once well-known "Memoirs." The habit of keeping notes of one's own life, and leaving them as memoirs to posterity, was already fashionable, so that instead of the severe political history of Thucydides, which scorns personal details, most of our authorities now give us plenty of piquant anecdotes, witty sayings, and clever stratagems. The course of serious history is often obscured by these sallies; great national movements come to be attributed to the accident of this or that man's action; for people are always glad to find some definite personal cause for a great vague movement, the growth of which they cannot grasp. If, however, we lose in political insight by this biographical way of treating history, we gain immensely in our knowledge of social and moral phases, in our appreciation of human nature, in the colour and richness of our picture, even when it varies considerably from the reality which it professes to copy.

Aratus, like Pyrrhus, narrowly escaped death in his infancy at the hands of one of the many tyrants who in succession seized the rule of Sicyon. We see this kind of thing happening all through Greece, where any ambitious man, who could by a massacre or otherwise make himself ruler, could count on the support of Antigonus Gonatas, or of Ptolemy, as these kings found it far easier to deal with Greek cities when represented by one man, than by the changing humour of a public assembly. When this particular tyrant Abantidas murdered Cleinias, father of Aratus, and sought to slay the child, he escaped and wandered in terror and alone till he came to the house of his uncle, who was married to a sister of the tyrant. This good woman hid him, and sent him away safely to Argos.

Though an exile he grew up among rich friends, and apparently with ample means, and it was noted that instead of being educated in philosophy or in the science of strategy, he devoted himself to athletics, so as to compete in the Pentathlum or five events [1] of the public games. It is characteristic of the time to note that this was thought an inferior training, for not only was he no polished writer or speaker, but he had no nerve in regular warfare; his whole appearance in his statues savoured of the coarse athletic habit, and he was eminently successful only in night surprises, or in equally surreptitious devices of a tortuous dip-

[1] Running, jumping, wrestling, boxing, and hurling quoits.

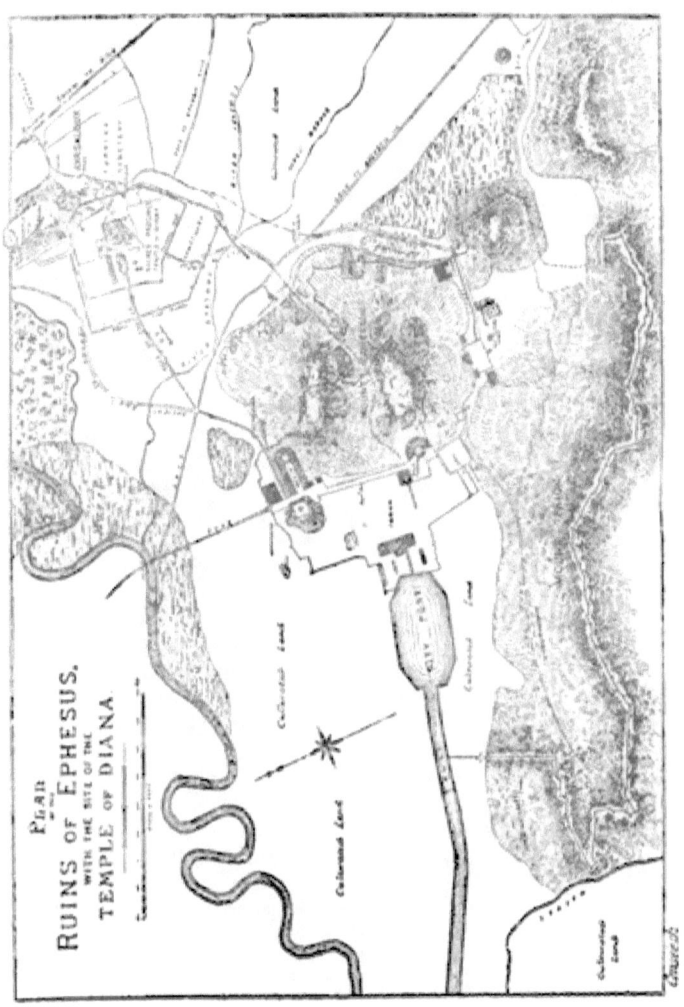

lomacy. This, too, is remarkable, that while he was noted as the bitterest enemy of local tyrants, he always valued the favour of great kings, Ptolemy and Antigonus, and was eminently a courtier. For these sovrans were now conceded to have a lawful and even a divine right, while the upstart tyrants were fellow citizens, whom the inborn Greek jealousy could not tolerate over them, however just or enlightened was their rule.

His great ambition was to free his native town, where one tyrant had succeeded another, and Plutarch has told us, evidently from the autobiography of Aratus, the thrilling narrative of the successful adventure, which he did not undertake till he had in vain solicited the help of the kings. First the tyrant's spies at Argos had their suspicions disarmed by seeing him among his companions in youthful revelry. When they saw garlands and wreaths of flowers, and singing girls being sent to his house for a feast, they laughed at their master's fears from such a youth as this. And yet the rumours about his designs were correct. Then comes the preparation of scaling-ladders, the attempt to secure the dogs of the gardener, who dwelt beside the easiest spot of the walls of Sicyon. The party arrive before dawn, and set up their ladders in spite of the barking of the two little dogs, which had escaped when their master was seized and were very "pugnacious and uncompromising." The party had to lie down while the night watch passed along the wall, and now the cocks began to crow about the country, and they feared the early people would be coming in to market; but the barking of the gardener's dogs, and the sullen answer of a large sporting dog, kept as a watch in one of the towers on the wall, were taken to be a response to the bell of the night watch, and so at last the conspirators got in, and without any massacre seized the town, and burned the tyrant's house, while he escaped for his life.

Aratus's next and most politic act was to put Sicyon (B.C. 250) under the Achæan League, which was still small and obscure, so that it seemed great condescension for a Doric city to join them. Even then he saw that without large funds, the return of exiles would be ruinous, for when they reclaimed their property it was impossible to satisfy them without banishment of the new occupiers. It was then that he undertook his adventurous[1] journey to Egypt, and begged from Philadelphus one hundred and fifty talents, wherewith he satisfied all the rival claims, before a court of fifteen arbitrators. We are told that he gained the favour of Ptolemy by presents of artistic value — statues and pictures, for which Sicyon was then very remarkable, and of which he was an excellent judge. His policy was to play the part of Egypt against Macedonia, his nearer enemy. His capture of Corinth, in 243 B.C., is a story no less romantic than that of Sicyon, and was a great blow to Antigonus in his old age. This strengthened the League, and gave it a claim to extend itself all over

---

[1] Adventurous, because the fleet of Antigonus held the islands, and he was already recognized by the king as an enemy, who, by abolishing tyrants, took away Greek cities from Macedonian control. Aratus was all but captured on his way.

Northern Peloponnesus. The extreme old age and death of Antigonus no doubt weakened the activity of Macedonia at this juncture, and gave Aratus time for the prosecution of his plans. Still they depended on foreign help for sufficient funds, and Ptolemy Euergetes was appointed the head of the League in war both by sea and land. This, of course, threw Antigonus necessarily into alliance with the Ætolians, the rival federation in the north of Greece. As the obscurest province of the Peloponnesus now took the lead under Aratus, so the obscurest and most uncultivated part of Northern Greece also took the lead. These Ætolians were only a great combination for mutual defence; their League was not a true political system, though a very serious military power, and their influence on Greek history was very disastrous; but we shall not describe the principles and constitution of these federations, so interesting especially for Americans, till we have noticed another new departure in the Peloponnesus—the revolutionary attempt of King Agis of Sparta.

XVII.

KING AGIS OF SPARTA.—THE POLITICAL THEORISTS OF THE DAY.

WE have noticed that Aratus was not a philosopher or a theorist, but a practical man, often a mere diplomatist, carrying out a peculiar policy perhaps from ambition, perhaps from a higher principle, but as we shall see, never without jealousy and selfishness. He lived in an age when practical philosophy had taken deep hold of the nobler minds, and such men were eager to carry their theories into life. Some philosophers, like those at Sicyon who were friends of Abantidas, and enticed him to a discussion in their garden where he was murdered, were determined opponents of monarchy, and still held by the old Greek instinct of Republican liberty. So strong was this feeling in Epirus, that when the daughter of Pyrrhus, Queen Deidamia, lost her two sons, the heirs to the throne of Pyrrhus, th people insisted on abolishing the royalty (about 234 B.C.), though an old and hereditary one, with a glorious past, and established a federation of towns, no doubt on the model of Achæa. On the other hand, earnest thinkers, especially Stoics, saw in the rule of one superior man the only safeguard from socialism and the violences of the mob. Some wrote tracts in favour of it; others even grasped at such power themselves in order that they might carry their theories into practice. This must have been the case with the gallant Lydiades, the tyrant of Megalopolis, who (about the same time 235 B.C.), when he found that the risks and danger to the public weal exceeded the advantages he had hoped to confer, voluntarily surrendered his rule, and became with his city a loyal and valuable member of the Achæan League.

There was one state in Greece, Sparta, where monarchy was indeed so ancient and respectable, that there if anywhere the name of king could excite no malevolence; but then the divided throne and the power of the ephors had long since reduced the kingship to a position not unlike that of the sovran of England, who has all the prestige of royalty, and a great influence in a political crisis, but no control of the ordinary government of the country. It was an attractive idea, to recover again the reality of this ancient and hereditary power, and to try the experiment of real monarchy in Greece, not with an upstart tyrant, but with the high title and recognized homage frankly accorded to the lineal descendants of Herakles.

The account given by Plutarch of the Sparta of that day is most curious. While the old forms of the Constitution remained, the social conditions of the country were so changed, that of the full-blooded Spartans seven hundred only remained, and one hundred houses held all the property; the rest being paupers, and therefore of unequal civil rights. Moreover a great part of the property lay in the hands of women—evidently from the habit of making daughters heiresses by will, to the exclusion of sons. We may suppose that the Spartan of that day thought that his sons might quite well earn an independence and even wealth as mercenaries, and that they were better away from Sparta, while his daughters were helpless and despised without a good fortune, influential in society if they possessed it. But as always happens, this or any other precaution did not get rid of the pauper-nobles or gentry of Sparta; and so was formed a large and dangerous class of the needy or encumbered, who idled about, envying and cursing the rich minority, and longing for the old half-mythical, over-praised, sentimental, Lycurgean life, which most of the theoretical lawgivers like Plato had made the model for their ideal Republics. Here then we meet the land question, in its most aggravated form; and with it crops up the larger question of Socialism—the right of the poor to equality with the rich in every respect—as if the very essence of society, without which it never has existed and never will exist, did not lie in natural inequalities among men.

Agis, a generous enthusiast, young and full of hope, did not see so far as this. He merely desired to apply over again the supposed arrangements of Lycurgus—the division of the land in the vale of Sparta, the richest and best, in equal lots to 4,500 Spartans, the rest among 15,000 Perioeki, as the subject population had been long entitled, "dwellers around" the Spartan land, and that these should be made up of strong men, fit to bear arms—strangers even if the population did not suffice. With it came the usual proposal for the abolition of all debts. This was brought by a friendly ephor before the assembly in 243 B.C., and of course excited a most furious opposition. Agis was quite in earnest ; he had persuaded his mother, grandmother, and other friends to follow his example, and gave all their private property to the State. All the young and the needy were with him, and so were those of the rich who had great debts, and whose policy it was to carry out the repudiation of their liabilities, but by no means to give up their large properties. Moreover, as the king had not touched the old Constitution, the annual election of ephors could be used to upset his reforms. This was in effect done with the aid of King Leonidas, who had been brought back from exile by the Conservative party. The young king, whose military achievements were perhaps not remarkable, and who took no care to protect himself from legal persecution, was cited before the ephors, and took refuge in the temple of Artemis. Thence he was treacherously ensnared by some of his own companions, and murdered in jail (B.C. 241) by order of the ephors, together with his noble mother and grandmother who hurried to save him. The reader must look for a full account of this most pathetic tragedy in Plutarch's *Life*. His brother was exiled, and King Leonidas remained sole master of the situation.

What were the relations of Aratus and of Antigonus to this youthful hero ? To both he was a grave danger. For if Sparta reasserted its old primacy in the Peloponnesus, it was all up with the new-fangled federation which was the life-project of Aratus. The prestige of Sparta was such, that no Greek city would range itself under Achæa, so long as the same advantages, or even far less of the same kind, could be obtained from Sparta. Aratus had no ostensible ground for quarrel. Nay rather he was obliged to court Agis's alliance against the common enemy which Antigonus, their rival for supremacy in the Peloponnesus, had sent against them. In a great invasion of the Ætolians, which reached up to Sparta itself, enormous plunder in men and property was carried off, doubtless with the deeper object of making the young king unpopular. To resist a threatened renewal of this invasion, Aratus and Agis agreed to unite their forces near the Isthmus, and fight the Ætolian robbers; but when the armies were encamped together, Aratus soon decided that the Spartan king was more dangerous to him than the foe. Wherever Agis appeared, crowds followed him; he inspired enthusiasm by his frank and martial air, as well as by the high breeding he showed, in comparison with the prize-fighter of Sicyon.[1] Above all, the needy and discontented who had heard of his land schemes and of the abolition of debts, hailed him as the reformer of the day, the exponent of the new ideas in political economy and in law. Nothing could be more distasteful to Aratus. Quite apart from the jealousy which a smaller nature feels for the hero, apart from the contempt which the practical man feels for the visionary, Aratus was himself rich, and associated with rich people. As we shall see presently, the constitution of the Achæan League was intended to give

[1] Plutarch specially notes that Aratus's statues had this aspect.

preponderance to the wealthy. He hoped, moreover, to keep his pre-eminence, as much with the foreign gold of Egypt, as with his federal army; and thus paupers, and plenty of them, would increase his influence. Accordingly he politely declined any further aid from Agis, and submitted to defeat and loss in his campaign in preference to the dangerous rivalry of the more attractive and picturesque revolutionary king. Antigonus, too, in his last days was relieved of this danger, though the loss of Corinth, which he had seized and now lost, by stratagem, was serious; but the king was too old to undertake more wars, and settled his kingdom in peace, before he died. Let us then also pause to describe the constitution of this Achæan League, which now begins to figure so prominently in our history.

XVIII.

THE RISE AND SPREAD OF FEDERATIONS IN THE HELLENISTIC WORLD.—THE ACHÆAN AND OTHER LEAGUES.

UNION BECOMES POPULAR.

As everybody knows, the configuration of the soil of Greece—small valleys or plains separated by sea and mountains—isolated the people into small sections. The town in each of these cantons became a distinct state, so much so that state and city are the same word, πόλις, in Greek. The whole of Greece was therefore separated into small city-states, embracing a little territory and some villages. These towns strove to be independent and self-supporting, and dealt with their petty neighbours as with foreign states, so that the treaties between neighbouring Greek towns, such as Tegea and Mantinea, Sicyon and Corinth, would be distinctly international treaties, however small the scale upon which these treaties could be applied. What Mr. Grote calls the instinct of *autonomy*, of managing their own affairs, was so deep-set in the Greek mind, that all the mischiefs which it produced could not wean them from it, till it ruined the whole complex of towns called the Greek nation.

Professor Freeman, in his admirable "History of Federal Government," has shown how foreign to these

people was even the notion of representative government, because each man held it his indelible right to go in person to vote and speak when the affairs of his town were being discussed. Hence it was only in religious matters, such as the sending of delegates to the half-yearly religious meetings at Delphi and Thermopylæ, that such a principle was admitted.

The rise of great powers like those of Egypt and Macedonia, the prevalence of piracy and plunder in the terrible Forty-five Years' War, these things first taught most of the Greeks that the independence of single cities was no longer possible: there remained only two practical possibilities. They might put the town directly under the control of a power like Macedon, which required the presence of a garrison of its own, or a faithful local tyrant with his troops, who would repress any republican feelings, or the defection by means of a public vote to another power. Secondly, they might combine into a Federation, in which no city should have the pre-eminence, but in which each should still have liberty to manage its internal or communal affairs; while as to external policy, war and peace, the election of federal officers, and the like, all the cities could send their citizens to a common centre, and there decide in a joint assembly. This latter model, which has ever since commanded the admiration of the world, was only to be found in one obscure corner of Greece, where four little towns early in the century before us, either invented or renewed this form of political combination.[1]

[1] Let us caution the reader not to confuse with this idea those confederacies under a leading state, such as had existed long before under

Those who have visited the beautiful northern slopes of Mount Erymanthus, where these great serrated tops bar all access from the south, and when the eye ranges freely over the sapphire-blue gulf of Corinth, with all the islands lying seaward at its mouth, and with the huge mountains of Ætolia lowering on the opposite coast—those who have seen from Patras, the site of one of the old members of the League, how the land lies, will at once conclude that it was against pirates the League was formed; for attack from land is very difficult, if not impossible, whereas the deep recesses of the bay are eminently suited for pirates' nests, though on the other hand there is time from the commanding slopes to see and guard against invasion by the hastening of all the neighbours to the threatened point.

Now that the hardy mountaineers had made their fortunes in mercenary service, and had moreover learned the luxuries of life, we may be sure that their homes were not only more exposed, but more tempting to plunder, and so we may see special reasons for the strengthening of the League. They thought fit, about 255 B.C., to abolish the practice of having two chief officers, and elected but one, Margos of Keryneia, a name more honourable than celebrated in the history of the time.

Athens and Sparta, or under Philip and Alexander. For there the whole policy was dictated by a master, and even the internal affairs of the subject confederates were only safe from interference so long as the dominant state was otherwise occupied. Thus Alexander ordered the reception of all the exiles into their old homes in Greece, though he had guaranteed autonomy to the single states which entered his League against Persia.

Mr. Freeman notes that they avoided the mistake of making a large city their place of meeting, which might easily become a capital, and outbalance its neighbours; nor had they thought of the American device of making a political capital apart from all the leading cities. Fortunately Ægion, the most important or central town of the original League, which long remained their ordinary meeting-place, answered the purpose exactly, for though respectable it was insignificant. Ultimately they decided to meet in the cities in turns; but as they did not send representatives to their general-assembly, and every citizen from each town had a right to be present, it was necessary on the one hand to prevent the city where the meeting was held from outvoting the small numbers who came from distant cities, and also to make the meetings as few and short as was convenient. This was done in the following way.

The ordinary Congress was held at Ægion twice a year, and could only last for three days, nor could the assembly discuss any topics except those prepared for it by the Council, and brought before it as Government proposals. Extraordinary meetings could be summoned at other places, and this was not unfrequently done, but only on urgent cause existing. At the assemblies the people voted by cities, each city casting one vote, by which means thirty or forty men coming from the most distant town had their influence, and the crowd who were at home had not too much. During the rest of the year the Government business was carried on by a *Strategos*, the President or Commander of the League, a Lieutenant-General, a Master of the Horse, a Chief Secretary, and a Cabinet Council of ten, who brought bills before the assembly, and practically decided on the policy of the League. There was also a Senate of one hundred and twenty, which seems to have been a committee of the whole assembly to discuss and prepare bills for the Congress.

This whole Constitution was clearly intended to give preponderance to the wealthy. It is plain that however the Council was elected, it must have been from men who had means as well as leisure, for we hear later on of an offer of money from Attalus to be invested that the interest might supply salaries. So, also, no obscure or poor man could rise to the chief posts, nor could he even hope to live on the indirect profits which all Greek politicians had always derived from office; for he could not hold the office of Commander two years running, but at most every second year—as was the case with Aratus during the brilliant period of his life. Whenever the tyrant of some city, from principle or from fear, surrendered his power and made his city join the League—such as Lydiades of Megalopolis or Aristomachus of Argos—it was usual out of compliment to make him commander. Some of these men, especially Lydiades, had large notions of reform, and of giving the poorer people more power in the League; some may have been of doubtful loyalty.

At all events, we find Aratus's policy divided between conspiracies and threats to new tyrants to join the League, and tortuous diplomatic devices to neutralize their influence when they did join it. He was either a wholly selfish politician, or so antique a Conservative, that he could tolerate no change whatever in the League, except its extension; and even here there are reasons to suspect that he avoided including Athens when it was possible to do so, merely because the literary and philosophical renown of that city, and the existence of many philosophical Radicals in it, made him apprehend its influence. He knew that his first and ablest enemy, Antigonus Gonatas, could not last long, and he was only waiting for his death to take advantage of the change of rulers, and enlarge his League by military force. The rise of Agis in Sparta must have greatly terrified him; but Agis passed through the political sky like a meteor, and when Antigonus died Aratus at once entered into league with the Ætolians to attack Macedonia in Northern Greece.

These Ætolians have only been described to us by their enemies. We are told that their League was merely an association for plunder, that there was no Constitution beyond a half-festive, half-military meeting at the capital of the League, Thermus, where they kept great state and splendour, and elected a commander for coming expeditions, with a salary of one-third of the plunder. We find cities as far as the Black Sea joining the League, which only means that by this act, and the payment of a certain tax, they were not indeed saved from all the raids of the rest of the League, but allowed to lay their complaint before the Government and obtain restitution. Moreover, if attacked by any foreign power, they could appeal for aid, which was sent them; and this was a great gain, for the Ætolians were a very powerful military nation at this time, and kept all the Greek coasts and islands in alarm.

The worst and most immoral point, however, about this League was that it shared with Illyrians, Dardanians, and other northern barbarians, the principle that each member of the League had a right to go to war when it liked; that if any neighbouring state was attacked, any Ætolian city might join the assailants; as they expressed it—that they would as soon take Ætolia out of Ætolia as abandon the right to "plunder when plunder was going." These Ætolians came to power long before the Achæans; they were a prominent power in Greece at the death of Alexander, and stood out as I have described for the cause of freedom. So they did in the Lamian War; still more in the terrible invasion of the Gauls, they may be said to have saved Greece. But if they did so then, they ruined it afterwards; for they it was who, for their own selfish ends, brought the first Roman fleets and armies into Greece.

In his brilliant chapter on the Constitution of these Leagues Mr. Freeman compares them to the American and older Swiss confederations respectively. He shows that the Achæan and American Federations were as like as possible for them to be, seeing that the one was a union on equal terms of small independent cities, the other of large provinces originally dependent on a distant crown. He shows that while the Achæan League was more democratic in theory, as every citizen was entitled to go and vote at the Congress, it became more aristocratic in practice, being altogether in the hands of the rich. Though the Achæan President was called a General, his symbol of office was the Public Seal ; nor was he addressed, as was the President of the Lycian League, by any such title as Right Honourable ($ἀξιολογώτατος$). In other points the likenesses to our Prime Minister and his Cabinet are no less striking. The Ætolian League, on the contrary, is to be compared to the Swiss Confederacy, consisting not of towns but of the cantons of mountaineers, combining for defence, and finding their prowess sufficient to acquire subjects or new members among Germans and Italians united to them in various relations often far from that of equality.

We have delayed too long upon this question of Constitutions. It is important in the remaining history of the Empire of Alexander, because it was imitated in all directions by all Greek tribes who desired to protect themselves from home tyrants or foreign masters. Epirus and Acarnania in particular adopted it, and we find in Lycia a curious, perhaps old reproduction of the principle, differing, however, from all the Greek Leagues or Federations in this, that the towns composing it had votes differing in number according to their population, the largest having three, the smallest one vote.[1] Thus they corrected the flaw in the Achæan League, that if Corinth or Megalopolis joined it, these large and populous towns only had one vote like the little original ten Achæan towns, which had combined on equal terms without any anomaly.

[1] This idea was reproduced by the Emperor Augustus, when he renewed and reformed the Amphictyonic Council, and gave all the states of Greece votes in it according to his royal favour.

XIX.

THE EVENTS OF KING DEMETRIUS II.'S REIGN.—THE FIRST INTERFERENCE OF THE ROMANS IN THE EMPIRE OF ALEXANDER.

WE are now in a position to resume briefly the acts and position of Demetrius II., and define the importance of his reign (B.C. 239-229) for the history of the empire. Like every new king of Macedonia since Philip, he found all his kingdom shattered—revolt, invasion, and treason everywhere. He was set upon by the Dardanians on the north, by the combined Ætolians and Achæans on the south. He succeeded at first in defeating both, but when hard pressed a second time hit upon a terrible device. His allies the Acarnanians had been so worried by the Ætolians, that in despair of help from Demetrius they applied for help to Rome, now recovered from the exhaustion of the first Punic War, which had closed B.C. 241, leaving them with a vast increase of naval power, and a position of serious importance to all surrounding nations. The Senate was long ambitious to be recognized by the Hellenistic kingdoms as something better than barbarian, and every advance on the side of Hellenism had been received with great pride and self-conscious sensitiveness. Though they had conquered all the Greeks in Italy, and now in Sicily, and defeated the greatest Hellenistic captain of the day—Pyrrhus—in fair fight, still they felt themselves quite outside the real home of civilization, and longed to be recognized as worthy of friendly relations with Eastern courts. Their efforts to obtain this were positively amusing. When Ptolemy Philadelphus sent to ask their friendship the year after Pyrrhus left, they accorded him every honour, and what was more, the solid advantage of a free port at Puteoli. When the Punic War was over, they were sent to Ptolemy Euergetes, hearing he was at war with Syria, to offer help, but the war was over. Strangely enough, we are told that Ptolemy's opponent, Seleucus II., asked them for an alliance, which they promised in a reply *written in Greek*, on the condition that he should free from all burdens the people of Ilion (Troy), the ancestral relations of the Romans. What profound amusement must this letter have created in the East! And how publicly it must have been discussed when we find that the Acarnanians appended to their appeal this memorandum, that they alone of all the Greeks had not joined in the expedition against Troy. How the stupid snobbery of the Romans must have delighted these people who believed in no claim beyond Alexander!

When the Ætolians, in spite of Rome's warning to desist, invaded Acarnania again, Demetrius let loose upon them the wild Illyrians, who plundered Epirus, defeated the Achæans and Ætolians, and spread terror all through Western Greece. We cannot say why these terrible pirates had kept quiet so long, or how it was that now they suddenly appear in such power on the scene. Unfortunately for themselves, they carried their depredations as far as the opposite shore, and robbed Italian coasts and ships. Then Rome interfered in force, humbled Queen Teuta, made subject allies of Dyrrachium, Apollonia, and Corcyra, and sent polite embassies to Achæans and Ætolians to explain their action, and deprecate any sinister construction of their interference in Hellenistic affairs.

So far all was well; the terrible scourge which had threatened Greece was stopped, and the Greek Leagues treated the Roman envoys with all distinction; but the cloud in the west was still there, and any good prophet might have foretold the coming danger. Meanwhile, Demetrius had been so busy with his northern wars, that Aratus was able to enlarge greatly the League in Southern Greece. Sparta was paralyzed by the reaction after Agis's death. Presently (B.C. 229) Demetrius II. was killed; his son, Philip V., was an infant, and the usual struggle for the existence of the Macedonian throne began. All seemed smooth and prosperous for both Achæan and Ætolian Leagues. Let us turn at this moment, and see what was doing in the Eastern Levant, where, as in Greece, secondrate powers were striving to hold in check the dangerous power of Egypt, the claims of Syria, and the depredations of their own barbarians the Galatians.

XX.

COMMERCE AND CULTURE AT PERGAMUM AND RHODES.

WE left the eastern part of the empire in considerable confusion. Ptolemy Euergetes, after his victorious campaign in Asia, had occupied Syria up to the port of Antioch, had seized possessions in the Levant up to Thrace, and, in order to distract permanently the attention of his rival Seleucus II., had set up and encouraged the younger brother, Antiochus Hierax

COINS OF RHODES AND PERGAMUM.

to contest the succession. After long and various struggles, this latter was conceded the crown of Asia Minor, limited by Mount Taurus; but his ambitious and wild nature, ever finding support in the policy of Egypt, could not keep at rest. He attacked the Galatians, and was thoroughly defeated, and his expeditions so disturbed Asia Minor, that these marauders broke loose from their appointed region, and began again to plunder and levy black-mail all over the Greek cities within their reach.

It was then (perhaps B.C. 235) that Attalus I., who had succeeded to the possession of Pergamum in 241, met and vanquished the Galatians in a great battle, which gave him such popularity that he was able to assume the title of king, and extend his influence far beyond his inherited dominion. He next defeated the turbulent Antiochus Hierax, who was killed in his flight in Thrace, perhaps on his way to Macedonia. When this pretender was gone, it was evidently Euergetes' policy to raise the power of Attalus against Syria, and so the court of Pergamum continued to

COIN OF PHILETÆRUS.

flourish till it controlled the larger part of Asia Minor. In his long reign this king represented almost as much as the King of Egypt, the art and culture of Hellenism. His great victory over the Galatians was celebrated by the dedication of so many splendid offerings to various shrines, that the Pergamene school made a distinct impression upon the world's taste. Critics have enumerated seventeen remaining types, which appear to have come from statues of that time — the best known is the so-called *Dying Gladiator*, who is really a dying Galatian. But quite recently the discoveries of Humann at Pergamum have brought to light the great frieze round the altar of Eumenes II., dedicated to celebrate this and subsequent victories, and now the history of Greek art must include a new chapter on the style and character of the Pergamene school.

Perhaps the literature of the Court was even more remarkable. Starting on the model of Alexandria, with a great library, Attalus was far more fortunate than the Ptolemies in making his university the home of Stoic philosophy. Criticism, too, was not behindhand; and in the next reign, Crates was an expounder and recensor of the text of Homer hardly inferior to the great Alexandrians, of whom we shall presently speak. The amiable character of the royal house, whose successions, though generally indirect,[1] were marked by no murders and jealousies, seems to have given a tone to the society of its capital, and few Hellenistic cities bear a more enviable character, not

---

[1] Here is this very curious genealogy, curious because none of its rulers succeeded by murders or banishment of their relatives, as was the fashion elsewhere even in direct successions.

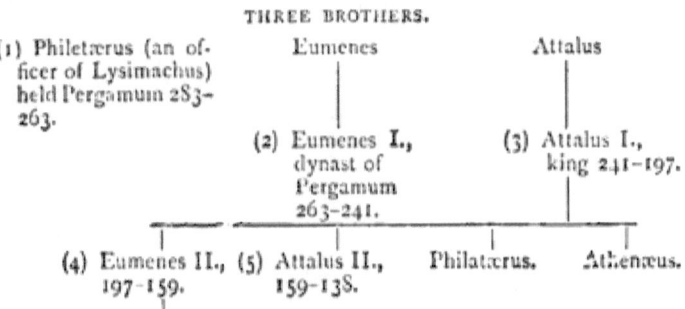

only for art and letters, but for that obscurity as regards private life which implies orderly peacefulness in comfortable homes.

Indeed its only rival in this respect was Rhodes, the great city representing its island since B.C. 408, when it was founded by voluntary amalgamation of lesser towns. After long and varied conflicts between its people, a democracy backed by Athens, and its aristocracy, backed in turn by Sparta and Persia, we find it already in Alexander's day a republic of importance, famed for its honour and good conduct. It appears to have taken some such place in the marine of those days as Hydra did in the Levant of the last century—a small rocky island with a safe harbour, a vigorous population of adventurous mariners, and so high a code of commercial morality that every one trusted them with investments, and they acquired such wealth as not only to decorate their town with handsome buildings and comfortable dwellings, but to own considerable property on the adjoining coast. Such was the case with Rhodes. The siege by Demetrius showed not only the power but the virtues of this merchant aristocracy (see p. 61). They rebuilt their shattered city with great magnificence. They used the metal of Demetrius's abandoned engines for the famous Colossus, a bronze figure of the sun about one hundred feet high, which, however, was thrown down and broken by the earthquake of B.C. 227, and lay for centuries near the quays, the wonder of all visitors.[1] It was doubtless during the same period

[1] It is said that the Saracens sold the remnants of this statue for old metal when they captured Rhodes. See "The Story of the Saracens," chapter xxx.

THE LAOCOON.
(Rhodian work of this period.)

that Rhodes perfected that system of marine mercantile law, which was accepted not only by all Hellenistic states, but acknowledged by the Romans down to the days of the empire. It is hardly possible that the polite interchange of good wishes, which Polybius implies as having taken place (B.C. 304) with Rome just after the great siege, could have established any marine treaty.[1] We do not know what the detail of their mercantile system was, except that it was worked by means of an active police squadron, which put down piracy, or confined it to shipping outside their confederacy, and also that their persistent neutrality was only abandoned when their commercial interests were directly attacked. In every war they appear as mediators and peace-makers. There is an allusion in the *Mercator* of Plautus, to young men being sent to learn business there, as they are now sent to Hamburg or Genoa. The wealth and culture of the people, together with the stately plan of their city, gave much incitement and scope to artists in bronze and marble, as well as to painters, and the names of a large number of Rhodian artists have survived on the pedestals of statues long since destroyed. But two famous works —whether originals or copies seems uncertain—still attest the genius of the school, the *Laocoon*, now in the Vatican, and the *Toro Farnese*. In literature, they rather encouraged and cultivated eloquence and poetry, than produced it themselves. Apollonius takes his name Rhodius from his long residence there. Æsthines, the rival of Demosthenes, had long before

---

[1] This passage (xxx. 5, ed. Hultsch), which historians assume as evidence for an embassy, does not seem to justify any such inference.

settled there as a teacher of rhetoric, and down to Roman times it was regarded as one of the best places to send young men for their education.[1]

At the present juncture Rhodes was determined not to allow Euergetes to monopolize the trade and dominion of the Eastern Ægean, and therefore they violated their old traditional friendship with Egypt, by resisting his further encroachments. All details of this war are lost, but the Rhodians evidently got what they wanted. It was perfectly well known they would only fight as long as their commerce was in jeopardy, and would make the easiest and most generous terms to preserve peace. So in the following period we find them in their glory, and second to none of the smaller powers in importance. Indeed their navy made them in many respects a first-class power. For though it was never very large—seventy-two ships is the largest fleet we ever hear of—the efficiency of their sailors was such, that they could always contend successfully against heavy odds. They had inherited completely the naval prestige of Athens in its best days. Like the English of the last century, they were afraid of nothing on the sea, they delighted in bold adventures both of war and of wandering, and so they devoted themselves to preserving the balance of power among the surrounding kings which would insure their liberty and respect.

Nothing proves Rhodian greatness, or the solidarity of the Hellenistic world, more curiously than what happened in 227 B.C., when the earthquake almost

---

[1] Julius Cæsar studied elocution here for two years. See "The Story of Rome," p. 217.

THE TORO FARNESE.
(Rhodian School.)

destroyed their city. They sent around an embassy to tell of this calamity, and to solicit subscriptions, or rather to demand them in the name of commercial credit. It was plain that unless they were set up again, the whole trade of the Mediterranean would be bankrupt. They may have been bankers for half of the trading cities of the Levant. Polybius gives us a list of the chief kings and cities who sent them contributions, which is quite astonishing. It made no difference whether they were at war with one another, or had been so with Rhodians. Even wars could not be carried on without credit, and so all united to set Rhodes up again. Seventy-five talents were sent

COIN OF RHODES.

from Gelon and Hieron, tyrants in Sicily, to supply oil, and ten talents to increase the number of their citizens, probably by paying fees of admission for the poor, ten talents for sacrifices, fifty catapults—altogether one hundred talents; Syracuse was made a free port to them, and moreover they set up at Rhodes a monument representing the Commonwealth of Rhodes crowned by that of Syracuse. Ptolemy announced to them a present of three hundred talents of silver, an enormous quantity of wheat, materials for twenty ships, viz., hewn beams of deal, masts, tow, tar, &c., three thousand talents of copper to restore the Colossus, four hundred and fifty artizans and their pay for a year. The king of Macedonia (it was now a new Antigonus) sent one hundred talents of silver, and a vast supply of pitch, tar, iron, lead, timber, and wheat. The king of Syria sent five five-banked ships ready, wood, resin, ropes, and wheat, but instead of money granted a freedom of all his ports. The gifts of many lesser kings, and of free cities, Polybius says, it would be hard to enumerate.

So, then, the Hellenistic world, besides its unity of language, had an unity of Commerce, of which the centre was then apparently Rhodes, and the Rhodian system must have been fair and generous, or it would not have commanded such support. It is remarkable that the Rhodians were nevertheless hard masters to their subjects on land, especially to the tract of Southern Asia Minor (Caria and Lycia), which they called the *Perœa*, where they levied very severe taxes. A few years later, the king of Pergamum argued at Rome that for a free city of Asia Minor to be under his direction is far happier than to be left independent, and so at the mercy of the Rhodian merchants, who could make any terms they liked by stopping its trade.

We may now leave the East for a while, where Seleucus II., killed by a fall from his horse in 226 B.C., was succeeded by his son Seleucus III. (Soter), who carries on with doubtful success the same struggle, in the East against revolted satraps, in the West against the power of Pergamum. Ptolemy Euergetes is growing old, and disposed for peace, and so there is for the moment no advance of world-problems there, while in Macedonia and Greece arise new leaders, and a conflict of the most momentous import.

XXI.

THE RISE OF ANTIGONUS DOSON AND CLEOMENES
(B.C. 229-223).

WE left the throne of Macedonia vacant, the Illyrian pirates crushed by the power of Rome, which had set foot on the coast of Epirus, the royalty at Sparta in the hands of a stupid and selfish Conservatism, the free, or would-be free, cities with no policy possible save that of joining either the Achæan or the Ætolian Leagues, the one offering a fair and attractive Constitution, the other more active and effective military support, with corresponding dangers to those that spurned it. If the Achæans had then possessed an able military leader, they might have embraced all Greece; as it was, the struggle with the Ætolians would have been more than doubtful; but the issues were altered and widened by the rise of two men, one in Macedonia, and one in Sparta, who possessed these qualities, and compelled the Leagues to fall back into the second place. Let us sketch their advent and power in turn.

When Demetrius was killed, he left everything in confusion. The northern barbarians were victorious, Thessaly fell away to the Ætolians: Corcyra was in the hands of the mighty Romans, who had overthrown

Carthage in Sicily, and mastered all the Greeks of
the West save the nominal kingdom of Hiero at
Syracuse: they had even seized Sardinia and Corsica,
and when the Carthaginians essayed to create an
empire in Spain, had ordered them (B.C. 228) to halt
at the Ebro. Though they had offered apologies to
the Greeks, it must have been clear to any politician
that here was a new element of danger, only to be
met by all the strength of Hellenism put together.

We know very little of the first years of Antigonus
Doson; what we do know shows that he fully understood, and strove to solve the problem as a matter of
duty to his country. He was now in the prime of
life; son of Demetrius the Fair, who had been slain
in Cyrene (p. 119), and therefore first cousin to the late
king. Assuming at once the regency, he was so
scrupulous in guarding the interests of the boy prince,
Philip, the son of Demetrius II., that he married
Philip's widowed mother, and postponed his own children deliberately and honestly to Philip's claims. Even
in his will he had left careful directions for his protection. All this shows how far personal ambition
was from his mind. As well as we can make out, his
first care was to attack and defeat the Ætolians; and
yet he made with them so favourable a treaty, as to
keep them with sufficient power to rival the Achæans,
nor did he fail to set them on to make further conquests in Peloponnesus. Elis was always their ally;
they now advanced further, and presently Mantinea,
a new member of the League, revolted from the
Achæans. Leaving, then, these rival interests at war,
and perceiving that the Romans intended for the

present no further advance, he was bold enough to seize possessions in Caria, probably with the connivance or advice of the Rhodians and free cities of Asia Minor, who still dreaded the supremacy of Egypt. Thus he passed by the outlying Egyptian posts in Thrace, and effected a hold upon the coast from whence he could directly threaten Egypt. This he did evidently for the purpose of paralyzing this resource of help, when he advanced against Athens and the Peloponnesus. Egypt had always assisted them against him, and it was at Cos, off this coast, that his great namesake Gonatas had decided the last war with Athens in his favour (p. 118). We do not know what means Euergetes took to oppose him, but there seems a curious decay in the activity of this once mighty conqueror in his later years. With all his power he seems going asleep, and does nothing in the way of diplomacy beyond paying subsidies now to one, now to another, of the warring powers.

The firm and wise action of Antigonus Doson soon re-established the power of Macedonia, and so he was able to begin the campaign he had nearest his heart, the reduction of all Greece under his power, especially the Achæan League. We may be sure that he would have subdued the Ætolians last, and then have been prepared to offer a firm front to the Romans; but just at this time, when he had been two years king, arose the most dangerous complication that any man could have to face, a young man of genius in the very position where that genius could have full scope.

After the death of Agis, his brother had been exiled, and the other king Leonidas, the chief of the Conservative reaction, led affairs back into their old condition, poverty, debts, discontent, despair, and the subjects were kept down by the strict surveillance of the ephors. Yet their watch was not well kept, they allowed a certain Stoic philosopher, Sphæres, to teach his doctrine and write books on sovrantry and the antiquities of Spartan policy, which evidently attracted and stimulated the better and sounder youth. Leonidas had insisted on the widow of Agis marrying his own son, the youthful Cleomenes, that she and her infant son might be under control, yet it was probably she, more than Sphærus, who converted the king's son to the theories of Agis, to great reverence for his purity and self-sacrifice, and profound pity for his tragic end. No quality was, however, stronger in Cleomenes than patience. While maturing his plans he kept on terms of filial respect with his father, of obedience to the ephors.

Succeeding to the throne in 227 B.C., he at first gave all his attention to military matters, and to rendering the army thoroughly efficient. He soon showed himself a thorough general, and more than able for any opponent in the Peloponnesus. His difficulty was not only to urge the ephors to war with the Achæan League, but to be permitted to carry it on till he had endeared himself to the soldiers, created a body of mercenaries faithful to him, and shown the cities of Argos and Arcadia that he was a better friend than Aratus or the Ætolians. The ephors, on the other hand, were exceedingly jealous of his successes, and more than once recalled him when he was on the point of making important conquests. During this early period, or first two years of his reign, his stepson, the child of Agis, died suspiciously, and the brother of Agis, who was living in exile, when invited home by him, was forthwith murdered, thus leaving him the sole heir of both the royal houses of Sparta. We are unable to discover whether, with all his high qualities, Cleomenes did not promote their deaths, as necessary to the policy he afterwards disclosed ; or whether his enemies the oligarchy did not compass them, for some hope of weakening his power by the odium they produced ; or whether they did not happen, the one from natural causes, the other from some private quarrel. The ancients were divided into enthusiastic admirers of Cleomenes, or of his rival Aratus, and decided according to this bias. We are disposed to side with those who acquit the king of all such charges, seeing that his life was one not only of noble self-devotion, but of extraordinary patience in waiting for the right moment to launch his schemes.

The action of Aratus, on the other hand, was distinctly that of a weak and jealous man, who felt unable, and therefore was afraid, to meet Cleomenes in battle, who not only sacrificed noble colleagues like Lydiades, by leaving them unsupported in action, but betrayed the interests of the League over and over again to maintain himself in power. What astonishes us most is the forbearance, or rather the obstinate weakness, of the Achæans for Aratus, whom they not only re-elected every second year as Commander (continuous re-election being forbidden), but allowed him to hamper and thwart the Commander of the alternate years. It is plain that there was a great fear among the propertied classes of radical changes in the constitution of the League. The schemes of Agis show that abolition of debts and redistribution of lands were in the air; pauperism was showing its hideous face beside the accumulated wealth of the day, and there were eager crowds in every city anxious to invade the privileges of the favoured few. It is one of the clearest proofs of the aristocratic character of the League, that the party of Aratus were for so many years able to thwart this feeling, though their external policy was in consequence of it wretchedly weak and disgraceful. They were evidently protecting their home interests at the cost of everything else, and we are disposed to guess that the actual men who managed this miserable diplomacy were old men, who believed that in wiliness and scheming lay the virtues, which are really the outcome of broad and straightforward views. Aratus was indeed not old in years, but an old statesman, and his way of managing affairs would recommend itself to old men. He always avoided pitched battles, but managed surprises by stealth and corruption. He avoided public discussion, and came to the assemblies with everything settled beforehand by cliques and caucuses.

At last Cleomenes was ready for his *coup d'état*. In the year 226 B.C., possibly having learned that the oligarchy were preparing to get rid of him, he managed to leave all his Spartan troops, whom he had wearied with long marches in garrison, about Orchomenos and Mantinea, and marched with his mercenaries straight for Sparta. He had been taught by the fall of Agis that constitutional proposals would not only be thwarted by the aristocracy, but would result in his own ruin, so he chose a bolder course. Marching in towards night, to give an account to the ephors of his campaigns, he ordered his advanced guard to set upon and slay them forthwith. One only, left for dead, escaped to a temple. The few who rushed to their aid were slain also, and the city occupied. Next morning when the people were summoned to the assembly, they found all the ephors' official chairs overthrown, save one, which Cleomenes intended to occupy. He declared to the people that he had abolished the usurpers of the Spartan throne, and would now proclaim a new constitution for the citizens, with abolition of debts and distribution of lands. Thus the sole king of Sparta became a military despot, in fact a tyrant except for this, that he was the lawful heir to the ancient throne. His reforms were actually carried out, but the details are lost. He obtained by them not only a body of four thousand citizen infantry, whom he armed as a Macedonian phalanx, abandoning the old Spartan tactics, but he brought upon his side all the radical party in the Peloponnesus. His monarchy had a democratic basis; it proclaimed the abolition of a rich aristocracy, and the generous treatment of the poor. Thus, in many ages and various societies, has a king become powerful by advocating the cause of the people against the aristocracy. He had by him as his constant adviser Sphærus, the Borysthenite, whose teaching of Stoical doctrines we have already noticed; and Plutarch, in his parallel between the two revolutionary kings of Sparta and the Gracchi, does not fail to bring out this among many curious analogies. Blossius of Cumæ played the part of Sphærus in Rome.

The picture we have of Cleomenes as king is peculiarly charming. Far removed by his Spartan traditions from the ostentation of a Demetrius, the splendour of a Ptolemy, in fact from the semi-oriental luxury of all the Hellenistic courts, he was perfectly simple in his habits, affable to all that sought him, full of grace and high breeding in his manners, and exceedingly stirring and practical in the control of affairs. He had that ineffable charm about him which is the apanage of a splendid ancestry, and which is very rarely attained by any upstart monarch. He even relaxed, for hospitality's sake, the strictness of his fare, which was Spartan on principle, saying that he must not *laconize* too strictly with strangers. He even countenanced dramatic representations. He was the idol of the people and the army. No wonder, then, that he soon began to make such way against Aratus, as to make it plain who would presently be lord of all the Peloponnesus.

XXII.

THE CLEOMENIC WAR (B.C. 224-221) TO THE BATTLE OF SELLASIA.—THE POLICY OF ARATUS.

ARATUS saw clearly that by himself he was lost; the League was evidently threatening to go to pieces, if he did not find some means of counteracting Cleomenes. He still drew his pension from Egypt, but, as we have noticed, the policy of that kingdom was gone to sleep, and he could expect from that quarter no help sufficient or effectual to save him. The Ætolians seemed to be on some terms of understanding with Cleomenes; they ceded to him quietly three towns in Arcadia which had joined their League. Polybius even suggests that there was a secret alliance; but in the whole struggle they never once interfered actively, a very strange fact for so thoroughgoing and active a body. The real solution seems to be that they were kept quiet by Antigonus, who was awaiting the chance of interference by allowing a crisis to come on in Southern Greece. This was not long in maturing.

The town of Megalopolis, nearest to Sparta of the League, was in most danger, and had frequently been exposed to loss of territory and siege from Cleomenes. Aratus got this town to propose an embassy to Antigonus for protection, in case the League was unable to afford it. Such a several action in foreign policy was totally at variance with the first principles of the Federation, or indeed of any Federation, and we shall see that it was through this violation of principle that the Romans ultimately destroyed the League. Aratus, who was probably unable to persuade the assembly to approach their old foe directly, succeeded in getting this separate mission allowed. Shortly after, when another man, Hyperbatos, was Commander (B.C. 224), Cleomenes won another decided victory over the Achæans at Hecatombæon, who lost severely in booty and prisoners. It is quite possible that Aratus may have been secretly content at the slaughter of his fellow-citizens, for it decidedly hastened the completion of his policy. However, the demands of Antigonus, which were now repeated, were very difficult to satisfy; for he would not interfere without the possession of Corinth, the key of the Peloponnesus, and how could the Corinthians, free members of the League, who had been saved by Aratus himself, tolerate such a proposal.

Meanwhile Cleomenes sent very different offers to the League. He only wanted *hegemony*, a military leadership, which had long since been voted to Ptolemy in return for his subsidy. He sent back many of his prisoners. The League was summoned to Lerna to meet him, and would certainly have nominated him, when a sudden illness, a violent hæmorrhage, laid him postrate. Never was there a more splendid chance for a great man more clearly lost by an accident, for when he had slowly recovered, and sent to renew the discussion at Argos, Aratus had found time to pull the strings and neutralize his opponent's influence. He offered him such insulting conditions of conference (forbidding the king's troops to approach Argos, and offering hostages for his security), that Cleomenes, in bitter impatience, broke off the parley with an angry public letter accusing Aratus of treachery and treason, and again declared war against the League. We may nevertheless wonder that this great man, who had shown such patience in earlier years, did not submit to disagreeable conditions to gain his point. Probably he mistrusted his own safety, or had ascertained that Aratus had secured the vote against him. At such a special meeting, called soon after another special meeting, the bulk of the poorer voters would not attend, and the decision would lie in the hands of Aratus's rich friends.

In the war that ensued the whole League went to pieces. Cleomenes captured cities on the Achæan coast, others revolted to him, even Argos and Corinth; Ægion, Sicyon, and the Acropolis of Corinth, were the only strongholds which remained to Aratus. He applied, or professed to apply, to Athens and Ætolia for help. Cleomenes was besieging Sicyon, he was cut off from the citadel. Although he had assumed dictatorial power, and behaved with considerable cruelty, it availed him nothing. At last he brought the rest of the League (Megalopolis and the original Achæan towns except Pallene) to such a pitch that, at a formal meeting at Ægion, they besought him to call in Antigonus. With this plea he excused himself in his memoirs. He could not even be an honest traitor. We may well imagine the rage of the Corinthians. They summoned Aratus to a conference to explain his conduct. He came with fair words, and besought the assembly to keep quiet; then seeing his personal danger, escaped on horseback before they could seize him. His large possessions at Corinth, granted to him as the successful deliverer of the city, were forthwith confiscated and handed over to Cleomenes. Antigonus was only waiting to advance and seize his prey—the Acro-Corinthus; but Cleomenes barred the isthmus with his army, so that the advance by land was impossible. The sea, however, was open to the Macedonian, though he seems to have been very slow to take advantage of it, and Ptolemy, who was supplying Cleomenes with money, sent no fleet to support him. It is very likely, though our authorities are silent about it, that the whole of Antigonus's available fleet was off the Carian coast, watching Egypt, and ready to fight any relieving squadron sent out. Thus Antigonus may have been really unable to transport his large army across even a narrow bay. Had he done so, the issue would probably have been different. Meanwhile, the citadel of Corinth was being held against the town and the army of Cleomenes by Aratus's garrison. Antigonus, who had advanced in great haste, was already in perplexity for want of provisions, when the decisive move was played by Aratus, inducing his partizans in Argos, whom the generous Spartan had neither executed or banished, to revolt from the Spartan alliance, and besiege the Spartan garrison in their citadel. Argos, as will be seen in the map, lay behind Cleomenes, and with Sicyon to aid it could cut off his retreat.[1] He at once sent a detachment to support his garrison, but it was defeated, and its leader slain, and he had no course left but to abandon the isthmus and retire, saving his troops at Argos, and marching in perfect order to the south.

Antigonus was thus master of the situation, and acted accordingly. Aratus and his friends, though treated with external courtesy, were obliged to see the statues of tyrants which they had overthrown set up again, and those of patriots which they had set up overthrown. They had to tolerate garrisons where Antigonus chose to put them, and to undertake the support of his large, and no doubt insolent, army. Such was the master whom the wretched traitor Aratus had substituted for the generous Cleomenes; who was like a Free Trader dealing with Protectionists —all his acts of generosity and candour were utilized without thanks, and turned against him without any scruples whatever.

We should have expected that Antigonus would advance at once, and finish the war by an active campaign against Sparta itself, but we find that he did no such thing. This and the next summer (B.C. 222) he spent in ordering the Northern Peloponnesus,

[1] In this complicated campaign the contending parties were at this moment sandwiched as follows: Antigonus at the isthmus facing the army of Cleomenes, with whom were the Corinthians. Behind Cleomenes the citadel of Corinth was held by the Achæans in Antigonus's interest. Further south Argos had just gone over to Antigonus's side, besieging in its turn Cleomenes' garrison in the citadel of Argos.

keeping there a sufficient army only to guard his fortresses, and allowing Cleomenes to make many brilliant and successful raids. In one of these he actually captured Megalopolis, and generously summoned the population which had fled to Messene to return and accept his alliance. In this policy he was opposed by Philopœmen, a young citizen then heard of for the first time, who rose to be leader of the Achæan League. Cleomenes was obliged to plunder the city, and make it as harmless as he could without being able to hold it. Antigonus and Aratus tolerated this possibly because Megalopolis was full of ardour and loyalty to the democratic interests of the League, and maintained a strong philosophic spirit keenly opposed to the temporizing craft of Aratus. If the facts be indeed so, how infamous the character of Aratus! On the other hand, Mantinea, which had twice revolted from the League, was captured by Antigonus, and treated with a savage cruelty quite beyond the ordinary laws of war—here, too, with the sanction of Aratus, who refounded it under the name of *Antigoneia*. If there be no excuse for Aratus, it is evident as regards Antigonus that he was playing his game elsewhere. He reduced, during his two years of inaction in the Peloponnese, his forces to the minimum which would keep the Spartan army on foot, and urged against them the Achæan League, who on their side expected that he would fight their battles; but he knew that by protracting the war he must wear out Cleomenes' resources, and that for want of funds the Spartan must in the end give up the contest. For this purpose he seems to have set in motion every device possible to weaken Egypt, and so force Ptolemy to abandon the subsidizing of Sparta.

The East had again been thrown into confusion by the murder of the young king Seleucus Soter (III.), who was warring in Asia Minor to recover his possessions from the usurpation of Attalus. He left an infant son, who was proclaimed king for a moment; but the troops called upon Antiochus, younger brother of the dead king, to assume the throne, when it was refused by his uncle Achæus, who had accompanied the troops against Attalus, and now took up the campaign with great vigour, recognizing his second nephew as king. Indeed Achæus very soon recovered all the territory won by Attalus, took the great fortress of Sardis, and even besieged Pergamum. The new Antiochus (III.), who was living as regent in Babylon, left the eastern provinces of Media and Persia under the control of two trusted officers, Molon and Alexander, delegated to Achæus the rule in Asia Minor, and established himself in Antioch with the open determination of at once attacking the Egyptian possessions in Cœle, Syria. In his first campaign Antiochus was checked by Egyptian garrisons in the strong passes, and returned to Antioch. Polybius speaks of his being under the influence of a sort of vizier, the Carian Hermeias, who jealously excluded other advisers, and urged him incessantly to war against Egypt. Very likely this Carian was acting in Antigonus's interest. His schemes were thwarted by the revolt of the two officers Molon and Alexander, in the eastern provinces, who defeated the first expedition sent against them, so that Antiochus himself was obliged to turn eastward, much against the will of Hermeias, who felt forced to go with the king to keep himself in power, and to exclude all rivals at the court. The conquests of Achæus more than counterbalanced this check— Attalus, Egypt's ally in Asia Minor, was almost crushed, Antigonus held part of Caria.

We may be sure that active negotiations were going on between Macedonia and Egypt, and that one of Antigonus's chief objects was to force Ptolemy to give up his ally Cleomenes. Perhaps, indeed, it was part of the arrangement to postpone a decisive battle in Greece. At all events, with these rising dangers from Syria, and apparently with the concession of Caria by Macedonia, Ptolemy was at last persuaded to send word to Cleomenes that he had better settle with Antigonus, for that he need no longer expect support from Egypt. It is said that Cleomenes, who was quite prepared for this result, and had ships prepared at Gythium, the nearest port to Sparta, to carry him and his friends away, determined to fight one great battle before he abandoned his kingdom. If all this account be true, we may rather wonder that the prudent and practical Antigonus should have attacked him, and risked a great defeat, when he had the game so completely in his hands. Yet this is what happened. In July, B.C. 221, Antigonus, marching with a large army which even included Illyrians, whom he obtained by alliance with Demetrius of Pharos, of notoriety in Roman history, found Cleomenes in a strong position defending the defile, which leads down one of the river courses running to the Eurotas, near Sellasia. The Spartan army occupied the heights on both sides of the narrow valley, and the right bank was held by the king's brother Eucleidas, on so steep a height that attack seemed hopeless. Yet it was here that the Illyrians, actively supported by Philopœmen and the Achæans, who charged the centre in the valley of the river, defeated the enemy and carried the heights. If we are rightly informed, Eucleidas, on his steep hill, made the same mistake as that of Sir G. Colley on Majuba hill against the Boers. He stood so strictly on the defensive that he allowed the enemy to scale the height without disconcerting them by an active offensive movement. As it was, our Achæan authority, Polybius, pretends that but for Philopœmen's entreaties to be allowed to charge the centre, the battle had been lost. When Cleomenes saw his left wing gone, nothing remained for him but to throw himself on the enemy, whose principal strength was massed against him. His attack failed, and he escaped with a few friends from the bloody field. Coming to Sparta, he advised submission to Antigonus, rested himself but a few moments leaning against a pillar, and took ship with his friends for Egypt.

The reader will not fail, it is hoped, to consult the closing chapters of Plutarch's *Life* of the hero, touching beyond description, showing how he was received in Egypt, first with indifference, then with gradually growing admiration, by Ptolemy, who saw in him the means for future victories; but the old king died just now, and his son, a young fool, left all public affairs to narrow and jealous ministers, who feared and disliked Cleomenes, and finally persuaded the king to put him under arrest as dangerous. Then he broke loose with his twelve companions, and called the Alexandrians to liberty. The people stared at him, and perhaps laughed—they hardly knew the meaning of the word; so having failed to force the prison, where he doubtless had more friends, these noble visionaries committed suicide together, a resource their master Sphærus had probably often recommended to those whose life was a failure. The mother and children were murdered by way of vengeance by the Egyptians; and so disappears the best and worthiest member of one of the oldest and most splendid royalties on record. He was practically the last king of Sparta.

The victory of Antigonus at Sellasia was disturbed by the news that Illyrian tribes had broken into Macedonia, and he hurried away—not, however, without setting the Peloponnesus in order by establishing a League of which he was the head, and to which all subscribed at once except the Eleans. Sparta, under its old oligarchy, had, moreover, a Bœotian officer appointed as its superintendent. Antigonus found the marauders in his kingdom; he immediately gave battle, and defeated them completely; but the exertions and shouting of commands caused him to burst a blood-vessel, and he died immediately after his victory. Thus this great man was carried off in the early years of his maturity,[1] and just when he had apparently succeeded in all his designs. He had done what no one had ever accomplished before; he had

---

[1] Our authorities speak of his failing health, and how he had foreseen and provided for his death by a careful will.

kept the Ætolians quiet or powerless for nine years; he had got rid of his only dangerous enemy in Cleomenes; all the Peloponnesus would soon be under his absolute control; Athens and Ætolia must follow; already he had relations with the Illyrians. Thus he could have made a bulwark which might have resisted what all the East saw coming with dread—an invasion of the Romans.

XXIII.

THE CONDITION OF THE HELLENISTIC WORLD IN 221 B.C.

POLYBIUS chose the year 221 B.C. for the opening of his great history of the civilized world, because, in his opinion, it marked a curious turning-point in the affairs of men. Several of the greatest monarchs of the world died at that time—Antigonus Doson, Ptolemy Euergetes, Cleomenes; Antiochus III. of Syria was only just come to the throne, a mere youth; and other inexperienced youths, Ptolemy Philopator and Philip V., ascended the vacant thrones. To those who expected a Roman invasion it must now have seemed inevitable, and at this time they could have conquered the Empire of Alexander with no difficulty. But suddenly there arose for them too the cloud in the west; Hannibal was before Saguntum, and crossed the Ebro, and for the next twenty years they were struggling for bare existence against the mighty Carthaginian. So then the interference of Rome was stayed, and Hellenistic life was allowed another generation of development.

Yet it seems as if its natural period were drawing to a close. Egypt, so brilliant in her first three kings, produces nothing more upon her throne than fools and debauchees, at best pedants. Macedonia, with her splendid line of Antigonid kings, all sacrificing every energy to the largest patriotism, descends to a selfish tyrant and a penurious fool. Syria produces, indeed, her Antiochus the Great, with his far-reaching campaigns and early activity ; but in middle life his power seems gone, and he falls before the Romans in a single sham battle. The chief glory of Hellenism falls to the secondary powers, not only Rhodes and Pergamum, but to the many free Greek cities like Byzantium and Cos, and even to the kings or dynasts who occupied kingdoms reaching from real Greece to the pure East. The kings of Bithynia, Cappadocia, and Pontus built Hellenistic capitals, set up Hellenistic art, and cultivated Hellenistic letters. Even the savage Galatians, like the rude and barbarous Ætolians in Greece, spent their plunder in adorning and beautifying their capital, and acquired some knowledge of the current idiom of the world.

We do not meet any deep reassertion of Oriental nationality till we reach the kingdom of Atropatene, in Northern Media, now seized by the Arsacids, who dated their advent with the year 250 B.C., when they successfully revolted from Antiochus Theos, and, as the Parthian monarchy, were long the mainstay of Orientalism against the inroads of the West. Yet even to them Greek artists wandered, and were understood, and far beyond them were still in Bactria dynasts with Greek coinage and Hellenistic traditions. We have seen how the Roman senate zealously affected to belong to the same great unity—an unity so like the " European culture " of to-day ; and we can imagine with what anxious care the Greek letter to Seleucus II., with its absurd reference to Ilium, was read and re-read by those who posed as Greek scholars at Rome, lest a solecism might betray the vulgar upstart. If the eastern limit of Hellenism was therefore the rising Parthia, in the West it reached as far as Carthage, whose Semitic origin had stamped upon it an indelible contrast to the Greeks, deepened by centuries of commercial jealousies. Possibly even in Carthage there may have been more Hellenism than we imagine. The innumerable spoils in art and slaves which they carried off from Sicily cannot but

COIN OF ANTIOCHUS III.

have affected the Punic merchant-princes. Yet we hear of Hannibal conferring with Scipio (before the battle of Zama) through an interpreter—nowhere in his campaigns do we hear of his speaking Greek.

This common language, then, was the largest bond of all the civilized world; next to it the wide extension of commerce whose objects ranged from the silk of China to the silver of Spain, from the polar bear of Siberia to the tropical rhinoceros. Trade routes from Ceylon and the Ganges to the Mediterranean were the constant preoccupation of Syrian and Egyptian kings, and more than one war was waged for the sake of these communications which were the source of enormous wealth. Unfortunately, with the increase in the quantity of precious metals, and the opportunities of gaining great fortunes, came the contrast of pauperism, and we know that Antioch and Alexandria had their hungry, desperate mobs, just like Paris and London. In Greece we saw that the Land question, so familiar to us in the Rome of the Gracchi and in modern Europe, was in full agitation. We may be sure that the leaders of the poor did not fail to make use of the arguments of the Stoics, aristocratic though these philosophers were, to show that all men were equal before God, and therefore entitled to the same rights and privileges ; but they were not represented by literature, which was all in the pay of princes, and so we only hear indirectly of such an agitation when a king like Agis takes the side of the people.

It is remarkable, but not surprising, that in none of the new centres of culture, except perhaps Alexandria, did there spring up any really original and vigorous literature. Such a growth must come fresh from the bosom of the people itself, and can only come in the language which expresses all the history of that people's growth. This had been eminently the case with older Greek literature ; but in the new Hellenistic centres Greek was after all an artificial plant, universally cultivated for purposes of trade and intercourse, but for that purpose only. As well might we have expected original French literature from the courts and courtiers of Germany, Poland, and Russia, because for a century back they spoke that language constantly and familiarly. There was no want, indeed, of new books in such seats of learning as Pergamum or Alexandria, Rhodes or Tarsus. So at Athens the heads of the schools poured out floods of tracts upon the world; but these books were not literature in its high and pure sense. The Alexandrian literati affected to compose in all styles and metres. Every learned man ought to be able, they thought, to write tragedies, lyric poems, hexameters, epigrams, and in various dialects. This is the case even with Theocritus, who has a true vein of poetry. They spent their time, too, in angry literary disputes, in satires and lampoons, in minute and trivial criticisms. The coteries of the museum at Alexandria were probably quite as narrow as those of the Oxford and Cambridge Dons now-a-days. There was the same weighing of syllables, the same mania for emendations, the same glory to be obtained by this barren ingenuity which lays exclusive claim to the grand title of scholarship; but then the field was new, and a great harvest to be reaped. The studies of Aristarchus were indeed an epoch in human letters, and his perfecting of the method of his predecessors in ascertaining the true words of an ancient author has probably saved for us the great body of the older Greek poets. For by the school of Aristarchus, though they naturally began with Homer—the Bible of the Greeks, all the other old masters, Hesiod, Pindar, Aristophanes, Sophocles, were not only amended and purified, but explained; and it is to these commentaries, composed while there was yet a living tradition of the sense, that we owe our understanding of innumerable riddles of vocabulary and allusion, otherwise insoluble. Any reader who desires to prove this may do so by examining the *scholia* on Aristophanes the comic poet, derived at second or third hand from the Alexandrians.

With the taste for the novel and for the story of personal adventures which has been noted above (p. 146) came in also the habit of personal memoirs, such as those of Aratus and of sundry Ptolemies, from which the historians drew the piquant details which we so enjoy in Plutarch, who has drawn freely from these writers. Hence it is that this historian has had an influence on the world so much greater than Thucydides. He is biographical, personal, modern, and does not disdain those details which earlier historians thought beneath the dignity of their subject. There was at this epoch a great delight, too, in antiquities as such, in the research of old traditions and origins—a study never popular till a nation has grown tired, and looks back upon its youth to distract its disgust and weariness with the present.

These researches, together with the larger familiarity men attained with various religions or cults, led to an interest in the philosophy of religion, and so naturally to advanced scepticism, which was backed up by the philosophical scepticism of the schools. These were so indifferent about what religion they believed; kings were so tolerant of all faiths; that people soon began to think them a mere fashion, and this advanced scepticism found its most famous expression in the work of Evemerus of Messene (*circ.* B.C. 300), who boldly asserted that all the gods were but deified men, and all faith but the effect of the knave working upon the fool. How fashionable this book must have been is proved by its translation into Latin by Ennius, while Rome was yet far from such an attitude. Had a Roman composed such a work, he would certainly at that date (B.C. 200) have been driven from the state with execration; but the Romans would tolerate anything Greek, as authorized by all civilized peoples.

Perhaps the developments of positive science were the most striking feature of all in this complex world. Medicine, surgery, botany, as well as pure mathematics and mechanics, made great strides. We read with astonishment in Athenæus the account of the gigantic ships which were built at Syracuse and at Alexandria to hold kings and their courts, and convey all the delights and luxuries of a palace and a park over the water. Presently we come upon Archimedes, and his wonderful defence of Syracuse (B.C. 212), which shows us that in all its applications, mechanics had attained a condition not despicable even for our modern science.

XXIV.

THE LAST INDEPENDENT SOVEREIGNS OF THE EMPIRE.— THE FATE OF ANTIOCHUS III. AND PTOLEMY IV. (PHILOPATOR).

THE reader may now study to advantage the following table of chronology for the generation before us:

PERGAMUM AND RHODES.	MACEDONIA AND GREECE.
Attalus reigning since 241 B.C.	
	Philip V. ... ... acc. 220 B.C.
War of Rhodes and Byzantium 219 B.C.	War of the Leagues begins. Demetrius of Pharos conquered by Romans... ... 219 B.C.
	Peace between the Leagues 217 B.C.
	Treaty of Philip with Hannibal 215 B.C.
Attalus joins Ætolians and Romans against Philip 211 B.C.	War with Ætolians and Romans 211 B.C.
	Peace with Ætolians and Attalus 206 B.C.

SYRIA.	EGYPT.
Antiochus III. ... acc. 222 B.C.	Ptolemy IV. (Philopator) acc. 221 B.C.
Insurrection of Media and Persia	
Battle of Raphia ... 217 B.C.	Battle of Raphia ... 217 B.C.
Capture of Achæus at Sardis 213 B.C.	Death of Ptolemy ... 204 B.C.
Eastern campaigns... 212-7 B.C.	
Conquest of Arabia ... 206 B.C.	

ROME.

Conquest of Demetrius of Illyria by Æmilius—Capture of Saguntum by Hannibal 219 B.C.

Hannibal crosses the Alps 218 B.C.

Thrasimene... ... ... 217 B.C.

Cannæ... ... ... 216 B.C.

Treaty with Ætolians... 211 B.C.

Scipio crosses to Africa 204 B.C.

We may take up Antiochus "the Great" first, as he was the first of the new generation of kings to succeed, and was actively engaged in putting down the Eastern revolt of Molon and Alexander, and in threatening war against Egypt for the possession of Cœle-Syria, when the others came to the throne. We have mentioned (p. 213) his first failure against Ptolemy, and the anxiety of his vizier Hermeias to hurl him against Egypt, probably at the instigation of Antigonus; but the revolt of the "Upper provinces" became so serious that the king himself was obliged to turn eastward. Here we find how deeply the Seleucid house had impressed the legitimacy of its power upon the eastern populations. Molon had easily defeated Antiochus's generals; he seemed on the point of establishing a new independent kingdom like Atropatene and Bactria, but on the appearance of Antiochus his soldiers deserted him, and went over to their lawful sovereign. The crime of treason by pretending to the crown was regarded as the most heinous of offences, and these insurgents had only their choice between suicide and death by torture, which was regarded as lawful in this case, as it was in the Middle Ages. In fact, the divine right of kings was even more ostentatiously put forward in Hellenistic days, for as it was usual to pay divine honours to the king himself, revolt seemed a direct act of sacrilege. Thus the body of Molon was gibbeted by order of the king in a conspicuous place.

It is quite the same feeling which dominates at another corner of his empire; while the king was arranging his eastern affairs, and had invaded the territory of Artabarzanes in Northern Media, his uncle Achæus, who had so loyally ceded the throne to him in the first instance, set up by his own great successes, and by promises from Ptolemy, assumed the royal tiara and the title of king, and advanced upon Syria, hoping to reach and occupy it before Antiochus could return from the East. As soon as his soldiers learned his object, however, they refused absolutely to be led against their lawful king, and Achæus was obliged to content himself with ravaging Pisidia, and appeasing his troops with plenty of plunder. When Antiochus returned to Antioch, he sent a royal protest to Achæus, charging him with high treason, and with being the ally of Ptolemy, but postponed a campaign into Asia Minor till he had assayed the recovery of Cœle-Syria. No doubt he encouraged Attalus to keep up his war with Achæus, and so divert him from further interference in the Syrian war.

He then began by carrying Seleucia on the Orontes by assault, his seaport town which the Egyptians had held ever since Euergetes' invasion; and through the treason of the Ætolian officer holding the passes into Palestine for Ptolemy, he was able to advance as far as Gaza, but not before much time had been spent in diplomatic negotiation, of which Polybius has left us an interesting abstract. The point at issue was whether after the original division of the Diadochi, when Syria fell to Antigonus, its subsequent conquest by the first Ptolemy had been for himself, or for the purpose of establishing Seleucus there; also, waiving this point, whether Seleucus's occupation of Syria after Ipsus (B.C. 300) should not count as lawful conquest, though not in strict accordance with the previous arrangements of the three kings. These negotiations were diligently kept up by the Egyptians, because the young king Philopator had neglected his army, and nothing was in readiness. So a great number of Greek mercenaries were hired, principally Ætolians, and great drilling went on at Alexandria, while the Syrian envoys were going to and fro to Memphis by the eastern (Pelusiac) mouth of the Nile, and saw nothing of it. At last, when they had had enough of parley, Antiochus being peremptory about holding Cœle-Syria, and about excluding all consideration of the rebel Achæus, the hostile armies met at the great battle of Raphia, near Gaza (B.C. 217). At this engagement, though the African elephants of Ptolemy would not for a moment face the Indian elephants of Antiochus, and though Antiochus gained considerable advantage with his cavalry, the shock of the phalanxes decided the matter, and he was defeated with a loss of twelve thousand men. Finding further conquests were hopeless, he returned to Antioch, and offered terms which were far too readily accepted by Ptolemy who recovered Palestine and Phœnicia, but was content apparently to forego the possession of Seleucia.

Antiochus was, however, hurrying at any cost to turn against Achæus, who now ruled over all Asia Minor, with the exception of some Greek towns, and of the fortress of Pergamum, in which he had besieged Attalus. In a campaign of two years Antiochus recovered all his dominions, and shut up Achæus in Sardis. Then, with the aid of clever Greeks, he stormed the city, but still Achæus held out in the impregnable citadel. Meanwhile, the Egyptian vizier Sosibius was doing all he could to save Achæus, by negotiating through private agents at Rhodes and Ephesus to manage his escape through the enemy's lines, and it seems that in these wars, conducted chiefly through Cretan and Ætolian mercenaries, there was always a good understanding among the hostile armies, since many now opposed to each other had before served together under the same banner; but the Cretans, who took the matter in hand, negotiated with Antiochus also for the treacherous surrender of Achæus, and having taken bribes from both sides, thought it their interest to cheat the Egyptian who was far away. In a thrilling narrative, Polybius tells us of this night adventure, in which they arranged for Achæus to leave his fortress secretly, and make his way through the enemy's lines. There had been much mutual suspicion, and the night was pitch dark, so that the conspirators could not be sure that Achæus was among the fugitives, and it was not till they saw one of the party being carefully and respectfully helped down the precipice, by those who could not forget their court manners, that they made sure of their man, and carried him bound to the tent of Antiochus, who was sitting up alone, after his state dinner, in intense excitement. When he saw his great enemy thrown bound upon the floor, he burst into tears, but not of compassion, for next day when his council of " Macedonians " met, amid the wildest excitement, it was decreed that Achæus should be mutilated first, then beheaded, then have his body sown up in an ass's skin and gibbeted.

These details contrast strongly with the conduct of Antiochus in the great Eastern campaign which he presently undertook. No sooner was he master of Asia Minor (B.C. 213) than he turned to the reconquest of those further provinces, which had long asserted themselves as independent kingdoms. He attacked the rising Parthian kingdom, he forced the so-called Parthian passes, and penetrated into Bactria, where he found Euthydemus established as king. We have in Polybius fragments concerning his wars in Parthia, Hyrcania, and Bactria, in all of which he was ready to establish the reigning sovran, if he promised obedience and loyalty. His principle was to admit the claims of the descendants of rebels to some consideration, seeing that they had not revolted against himself, while he punished upstart or personal opponents, like Molon and Achæus, with the most cruel vengeance. Euthydemus explained to him that by destroying the new dynasty in Bactria, it would be laid open to devastation and rebarbarization at the hands of the Turanian hordes, the nomads of the steppes.

So after making peace and alliance, the king turned eastward on the track of Alexander, and made his power felt by the sovrans on this side of the Indus. He obtained from them elephants and treasure. He even returned by the southern route which Alexander had found so difficult, wintering in Caramania or Gedrosia, and not content with these achievements, made conquests in Arabia, still probably imitating not only the campaigns, but the plans of Alexander. Then after several years of glorious wars, in which he had incurred much personal danger and shown great personal bravery, he returned (B.C. 204) to Antioch, loaded with the treasures of the East, and justly hailed with the title of "the Great." Ordinary readers only meet this king late in his life, when he appears so dilatory and feeble in his campaign with the Romans, but Polybius notes specially the great contrast of his earlier and later years. The fatigues of war and pleasure seem to have exhausted his energy, and from his return, which we have just noted, he seems to have done nothing to sustain his well-earned title

During all this time his rival Ptolemy had been leading a slothful and luxurious life at Alexandria. Content, after his victory at Raphia, with any fair terms, so as to secure peace and return to his pleasures, he is only known through the number of his mistresses, and their statues throughout his city, and for the enormous state ship which he built to carry his whole court and all his luxuries up and down the Nile. His affairs were managed by Sosibius, afterwards by a Greek lady and her brother, whom we shall meet again; and though Polybius mentions that he was involved in some other war or insurrection late in his reign, it was of no import, nor distinguished by any brilliant action. The epitomator of Polybius has not even mentioned where it was waged. The murders of his early years— including his mother, brother, wife and sister, and uncle, as well as that of Cleomenes and his family —are attributed by Polybius to his minister, and we know that literature and science continued to flourish at the Museum during his reign ; but if Egypt did not visibly decline, it was owing to the greatness and energy of his predecessors, not to any merit of his own. We know that he so increased taxation as to alienate permanently the Jewish nation, which had hitherto preferred Egyptian to Syrian rule ; and, nevertheless, so low were his finances that he issued a copper token money, which had the names, and affected the value, of silver coins. It was the nearest approach the ancients made to our paper currency. The revolts and internal troubles of the succeeding reign are chiefly attributable to this king's injustices. He died in 204 B.C., when Antiochus had just completed his Eastern campaigns. The heir to his throne was a child of four, known as Ptolemy (V.) Epiphanes.

COIN OF PTOLEMY V.

XXV.

THE CONDITION OF PERGAMUM AND RHODES.

BEFORE we return to the third monarchy, Macedonia, and consider the king who was to fall before the Romans, let us take a brief view of the action of the now important secondary powers, during the activity of Antiochus III. and the sloth of Ptolemy IV. Polybius gives a very interesting glimpse into the conditions of Greek trade at this moment in his elaborate preface to the war of the Rhodians and Byzantines (B.C. 219). Laying aside his speculations as to the ultimate filling up of the Black Sea by the deposit of the great rivers which flow into it, he is most instructive on the course of the current which carries vessels naturally into the harbour of Byzantium, while those who try to reach the opposite Chalcedon only do so with great difficulty. This natural advantage secured for Byzantium the command of the vast trade of the Euxine in the necessaries of life (says Polybius), cattle, and slaves; in its luxuries, honey, wax, salt fish, hides; and sometimes in corn. The Greeks would be deprived of all this benefit were there not a strong city established there—for the Galatians on the one side, and Thracians on the other, would stop and plunder everything. Hence Byzantium was absolutely necessary to the Hellenistic world, as holding the key to all this commerce, and to all the cities settled on the coasts of the Euxine; but their difficulties were also colossal—nothing could pacify or settle the barbarous Thracians, their neighbours, whom they could neither buy off nor conquer, but who always came down upon their suburbs, and carried off all that they had in the fields, so that they were really like an outpost in an hostile country, holding the strait for the Greek world with great loss and discomfort to themselves.

This state of things had long been suffered when the Galatians supervened, and established a kingdom (that of Tylis) in Thrace, close to Byzantium. These marauders were so much worse than the Thracians, that the tax they levied on Byzantium by way of blackmail was gradually raised to eighty talents a year (£20,000). Upon this the people of the city sent embassies to their neighbours throughout the Ægean, and asked for a subsidy to help them in their trouble, as they held a post of importance to all civilization. We may fancy that the late successful petition of the Rhodians (p. 195) encouraged them to hope for some success; but when they failed, they determined to levy customs on the passage of the straits. Whereupon there was a great outcry in the trading world, and a general appeal to the Rhodians, as the leaders in mercantile affairs, to interfere. It was as if the present powers of Europe were to appeal to England to interfere in keeping the Suez Canal open to European traffic. The Rhodians therefore protested, and getting worsted in argument went to war—as usual, with money and allies rather than with their own forces. They secured the active help of Prusias, king of Bithynia. The Byzantines applied to Attalus and Achæus, who were then at war, Achæus being master of almost all Asia Minor, and both promised to help them—a curious evidence of the interest this war excited. But the Rhodians bought off Achæus by persuading Ptolemy to give them up Andromachus, Achæus's father, who was kept a hostage in Egypt. So the war of Byzantium and Prusias continued, till in the end the Rhodians gained their point and forced the straits to be kept an open highway for ships.

Of course Attalus was not able at the time to help, nor do we know of his taking an active part in the history of Asia Minor for the next few years. He kept warring with Achæus in the interest of Antiochus, who accordingly made a favourable treaty with him; and as his position was now secured by the capture and death of Achæus, he was able to turn to Western politics, and he joined the coalition made by Romans and the Ætolians against Philip of Macedon in 211 B.C. This brings us back to Europe, to Macedonia and the Greeks, whose history was very agitated and serious during the period before us.

XXVI.

THE REIGN OF PHILIP V. OF MACEDON, UP TO HIS INTERFERENCE IN EASTERN AFFAIRS.—HIS WARS IN GREECE.

THANKS to the able policy of Antigonus Doson, Philip V. was the first king of Macedonia, we may say for centuries, who succeeded peacefully, and without a struggle, to the throne. He was an agreeable youth of courtly manners, trained in Hellenic politics by the wily and experienced Aratus, with whom the late king had desired him to be intimate. The northern barbarians were quiet, and the Illyrians were cowed by a new and stronger interference of the Romans (B.C. 219), who ousted Demetrius of Pharos, their former ally, from all his possessions, and sent him, a mischievous fugitive, to haunt the court of Macedon.

Troubles soon arose from the Ætolians, whom Antigonus had so marvellously coerced and controlled, without having the time to subdue them into his alliance. Their jealousy of the spread of the Achæan League led them to attack it, nominally to protect the eastern towns of the Peloponnesus, which had long been allied with them. In the complicated wars which ensue during this generation, the usual combination is this: Ætolia, Elis, Messenia, and Sparta, against the Achæan League, who call in the help of their ally, the Macedonian king. The Ætolians were his natural enemies, and they always claimed, and generally held, towns in Thessaly, thus threatening his land communications with Southern Greece.

The details of the struggle which follow are not of large interest, and may be disposed of in brief summary; the world-feature is the ambition of Philip to join in the great Punic War against Rome, and the momentous consequences of this folly. The Ætolians succeeded in detaching Sparta from the League, where two kings were again set up for a moment, one legitimate, the other for a large bribe; but they soon made way for the tyrant Machanidas, so that Sparta too has her epoch of tyrants from this time on. The Ætolians also got aid from Attalus, who from the first opposed the young king of Macedon; but the latter was so quick and brilliant in his movements, as to show plainly he was no contemptible foe. He even succeeded in a raid on the Ætolian capital Thermus, which he took and sacked. So a peace came about in 217 B.C., as the Ætolians were worsted and tired of unprofitable fighting, and Philip had his eye upon the West.

Indeed, all Greece saw the storm coming, and even the sensible men among the Ætolians advised peace and union in the face of the tremendous conflict now commenced in Italy. It was plain that as all ancient nations thought conquest legitimate, the victor in this struggle would next attack the Hellenic peninsula.

It seemed clear, too, that the Romans were the nearest and most dangerous neighbours. They had just reasserted themselves and triumphed (B.C. 219) over Illyria. The only question was the alternative between strong, combined neutrality, or active interference on the side of Carthage. When, therefore, the news of the defeat of the Romans at Thrasymene, came to Philip, as he was sitting with Demetrius of Pharos beside him, at the Nemean games (B.C. 217), it was easy to persuade him to join Hannibal. Hence he, too, was glad of peace at home.

Demetrius was a fugitive from the Romans, who even demanded, but could not then enforce, his extradition; he was an adventurous Illyrian pirate, who loved war for its profit, and had, at the time, nothing more to lose. Yet his general advice was perhaps right, if Philip had only possessed other responsible advisers who could carry out practically this large and difficult policy. Though chosen by Antigonus, they seem all to have been as worthless as Aratus, and wholly unable to grasp the situation. Hence fatal delays, occupied in fighting with Illyrian chiefs, and not spent in building a fleet fit to protect his transport ships to Italy. It was only the news of Cannæ (B.C. 216) that stimulated him to action; but as Hannibal commanded no port, the ambassadors Philip sent by way of Croton were taken by the Romans on their way inwards, and though they lied themselves free, were again captured with the treaty in their possession, so that the Romans, not Philip, got news of the threatening prospects on the east side of Italy, and forthwith kept a fleet of observation cruising in the Adriatic.

In spite of these precautions, Philip did manage to reach Hannibal with another embassy, and made a treaty with him in 215 B.C., after much precious time had elapsed ; but so far as we know its terms, he did not even get a promise of possessions in Italy, which were the dream of his ambition; he stipulated only the aid of the Carthaginians to recover all the Roman conquests on his own coast (except the property of Demetrius of Pharos) and to subdue all Greece ; but even now he did nothing but attack, and fail to take, Corcyra and Apollonia. No doubt he was afraid to face the Adriatic fleet of the prætor Lævinus—perhaps the refusal to give him Greek Italy had cooled his ambition—and he remained warring with Illyrian chiefs ; moreover, he had no friendly port for the reception of his invading troops. This point was not secured till Hannibal captured Tarentum in 212 B.C., the only year of great Carthaginian successes in Spain, and the Romans were now so alarmed at the prospect of a Macedonian invasion, that they prepared to occupy Philip by raising up enemies against him in Greece.

In this they easily succeeded. For the momentary anxiety for peace and union under Philip was gone. During the year since 217 B.C., he had estranged cities and people by his caprice, cruelty, and injustice. He got rid of the remonstrances of the veteran Aratus by poisoning him in 213 B.C. ; he sacked Greek cities, and sold free citizens into slavery ; in fact, he behaved as an Oriental tyrant, and not as the president of Free States.

So then the Romans, who had just conquered Syracuse (B.C. 212) and Capua (B.C. 211), sent their Admiral Lævinus to the synod of the Ætolians, to incite them to war with Philip. Of the conquests made, the Romans were to have the movable property, as they intended no extension of empire; the Ætolians the land. Neither were to conclude a separate peace with Philip. Thus the Romans, who had before appeared in Greece as the promoters of order and the chastisers of piracy and freebooting, now appear as the deliberate promoters of it; but we must consider their desperate circumstances. They were still fighting for existence, and must have thought all means lawful to occupy Philip in his own country.

So we have a new war of Macedonians, Illyrians, Ætolians, Eleans, Messenians, Spartans (under Machanidas, the new tyrant), and also Attalus, against the Achæans and Philip—the Achæans strengthened by the return of Philopœmen, a competent general. This man, together with Philip, who displayed in the difficult and various movements of the war very great ability—it is his best period—actually resisted the coalition successfully, especially when Attalus was attacked by Prusias of Bithynia, and the Romans, now threatened with the new invasion of Hasdrubal, sent no more help; but they had done enough to show that a new power of the first class, ruthless in politics and very cruel in war, was now to take part in Hellenistic affairs, and it was not difficult to predict the end. For the present, however, the Greeks and Macedonians were allowed to fight it out among themselves, and when Philopœmen slew Machanidas the Spartan in a great battle at Mantinea (B.C. 207), and Philip sacked Thermus, the Ætolian capital, both sides were prepared to listen to the neutral powers, Egypt, Rhodes, Athens, &c., who had repeatedly offered mediation (in 209, 208, and again in 206) on the basis of the *status quo*. The Romans were much put out at this peace, for Philip came out of the war so powerful, that even now an invasion of Italy seemed quite possible, and was generally expected; and though the Romans were evidently going to conquer Carthage in the great struggle, they were so completely exhausted that they dare not undertake a new war. So they forthwith sent a consul with an army to Epirus, who strove hard to make the Ætolians join him. They refused, but he was able to intimidate Philip into a peace with Rome. This sealed his fate, and the fate of the East. It was the last moment when the power of Macedonia might have turned the scale in the world's history. A descent with the new fleet he had built upon South Italy would proably have kept Scipio there, and might have given Hannibal help enough for another and a decisive victory.

We have now reached a new turning-point in the history of Alexander's Empire. Antiochus had just come back victorious from the East, and ready for new conquests. Ptolemy Philopator had just died, and was to be succeeded by an infant, in hands of the viziers and favourites of the late king. Rhodes, at the head of all the Greek coast cities, was prospering, and perpetually striving to mediate between warring neighbours, and keep the world at peace.

Attalus was beginning to interfere with his fleet in external politics, as far as Greece, especially against Macedonia, which threatened him on the north-west of his dominion. Philip and the Greeks had worn out their force by two civil wars, if we may so call them, and the Hellenic peninsula was still divided among free cities, tyrants, leagues, and Macedonian subjects. In spite of Philip's ability when hard pressed, and the solid worth of Philopœmen at the head of the Achæan League, it was now plain that very shortly there would be a conflict with the Romans, who had been provoked in their great distress, and shown that their eastern shore was not protected by the Adriatic from the risk of Hellenistic raids. Pyrrhus had once made such an invasion, and Philip had threatened it; this danger, then, must be removed at the earliest opportunity.

COIN OF PHILIP V. OF MACEDON.

XXVII.

STATE OF THE HELLENISTIC WORLD FROM 204 TO 197 B.C.—THE FIRST ASSERTION OF ROME'S SUPREMACY.

As we approach the close of our period, the relations of the various parts of the empire become so close, that it is no longer possible, or indeed needful, to consider them in separate sections. It was now clearly Philip's policy to conciliate all his neighbours by every fair concession, and strive to unite all Hellenism to meet the coming attack from the victorious Romans. With the most inconceivable stupidity and selfishness he did the very reverse. He annoyed the Romans by sending underhand assistance to Carthage; he not only treated the free Greek cities with insult, but even tried to get rid of Philopœmen, who was daily attaining more influence in Peloponnesus in military matters, by assassins, whose attempt was foiled and discovered. He then set the new tyrant of Sparta, Nabis, an infamous robber chief, the friend of pirates and outlaws, to harass the Achæan League. It seems that the military greatness of Philopœmen has been exaggerated by his panegyrists, Polybius and Plutarch, for though he fought

THE VENUS FROM MILO.
(Our best specimen of Greek art about 200 B.C. which reverted to the ideal types of Phidias for its models.)

some successful battles with Nabis, he was wholly unable to subdue him. Had he been the brilliant general they assert, such could hardly have been the case.

While this conflict was going on in Greece, and Philip was losing favour and influence there, he had taken in hand a new conflict, which showed how degraded he had become. Without the smallest ground of quarrel, he entered (B.C. 203) into a treaty with Antiochus III., who was longing for some new conquest, to attack and dismember the kingdom of Egypt, now in the hands of a child of six and his tutors. Antiochus advanced against Cœle-Syria and Phœnicia, which he twice before in his early years failed to conquer, while Philip demanded for his share the numerous coast and island cities in the Ægean Sea, from Thrace to Caria, which were allies or subjects of Egypt. The war, as it was begun on shameful principles, so it was carried out by the mercenaries of Philip with shameful excesses. He began himself by the capture of the northern towns Lysimacheia, Perinthus, Chalcedon, Kios, Thasos, all close about the Propontis, and in alliance, not only with Egypt, but with the Ætolian League, or Byzantium, or the king of Bithynia.

He thus challenged the enmity of all these powers, and if the Ætolians did not move, the rest did, and speedily brought with them Attalus and the Rhodians, who had in vain interposed by embassies to save these towns, seeing clearly that Philip would attack them next. So when his fleet came as far south as Samos, the new allies, especially the Rhodians and

Attalus, fought him a great sea-battle, in which he was defeated. The death of the Rhodian admiral Theophiliscus, however, and the heavy losses to Attalus's ships in the battle, so paralyzed the allies, that he was able to land and devastate cruelly the land of of Pergamum. When this fleet was refitted and strengthened, so as to be again mistress of the sea, he escaped home with difficulty, through their ships, to Macedonia (B.C. 200). It shows us, however, how completely Rome was already regarded as the arbiter of Eastern affairs, at least as far as Egypt, that all the allies injured by Philip sent ambassadors to complain at Rome. From this time onward for half a century there was hardly a moment when crowds of ambassadors were not besieging the senate-house, and trying to bribe or persuade influential people at Rome to get them a hearing.

Let us turn back for a moment to the accession of the child Ptolemy Epiphanes. He was in the hands of the late king's mistress Agathoclea, her brother Agathocles, who was in fact vizier, and much hated and feared by the people, and Sosibius, the son of the former minister. The will of the late king making the arrangement was at once suspected as forged, and popular discontent arose. To meet this these persons followed the usual course of policy in such cases. They gave largesses to the mob, and Agathocles sent away all the important rivals he had on public missions, to announce the accession to Philip, to Antiochus, &c. Scopas the Ætolian was sent to collect troops from his home; but they were not able to get rid of Tlepolemus, the Greek general who

FIGURINE FROM TANAGRA.

(Showing real life, as opposed to the ideal figure in the last cut. This terra cotta figure represents an ordinary Greek lady of the third century B.C.)

superintended the grain supply of Alexandria, and was stationed at Pelusium. Their attempts to implicate this officer in treason failed with the "Macedonians," as the Household Troops of Alexandria were still called. Attempts at repressing popular feeling were worse than futile. All the walls were found written over in the morning with incitements against the Ministers. Gradually the tumult spread, the royal child was supposed to be in danger, and Polybius gives us a most graphic account of the wild excitement in Alexandria, children joining in the noise, torches and troops hurrying through the streets, the minister's mother a suppliant in the temple of Demeter, and driving from her with horrible curses the women who wished to console her. To save their lives, the cabal gave up the child, who was carried in triumph, crying and terrified, to the theatre. The opposition coaxed from him an order for the punishment of the "enemies of the people," and sending him home to the house of Sosibius, they proceeded literally to tear in pieces in the streets the wretched impostors who had thought to hold Egypt in their hands.

The new regents, for the moment Tlepolemus and Sosibius, were men of very different character, the one a reckless and generous soldier, the other a prudent diplomatist. The former could not refuse any demand for money, and squandered the king's treasure; the objections of Sosibius only caused the transference of the great seal and charge of the king to his rival.

Meanwhile the attack of Philip and Antiochus on Egypt's allies had begun. The Rhodians seem to have been left to manage the naval war. The Ætolian Scopas was sent against Antiochus who had invaded Palestine. After some brilliant successes gained by Scopas, he was defeated by Antiochus, at Panion, in Cœle-Syria; and the Jews, who were generally staunch to Egypt in these quarrels, sided this time with Antiochus, owing to the ill-treatment they had lately received from Philopator. It seemed now as if Antiochus would really invade Egypt, but meanwhile the Romans, who had finished the Punic War, and were preparing to attack Philip, sent an embassy of three of their most distinguished nobles to announce their victory to Egypt, to thank the nation for its support of Rome in great trial, and also to request an alliance against Philip. It seems that the Regency not only accepted this message with cordiality, but begged for interference against the aggression of Antiochus. Moreover, they actually asked the Romans to undertake the protection of the young king, and we have extant a coin of M. Æmil. Lepidus, one of the ambassadors, which has stamped upon it the Roman putting a diadem on the boy's head, with the words, *tutor regis* (see p. 298).

The first message of the Romans to Antiochus seems to have been unheeded; a second induced him to propose a marriage of his daughter with the young Ptolemy, when he was of sufficient age, and a promise to make the territory he had conquered her dowry. This vague offer, which was not seriously intended, was at the time accepted by the Senate, as Rome was now entering upon her second war with Philip.

The Senate had only two difficulties to deal with, in opening this war. It seemed to them essential, diplomatically, to put Philip in the wrong by making him appear the aggressor; that was not a serious obstacle, as his recent acts showed him to be quite a tyro in diplomacy. They had, however, further to persuade the Roman assembly that Philip was actually threatening Italy, for the late exhausting war had made the very name hateful, and the people longed for peace. The ostensible cause was an attack which he made on Athens, to avenge for the Acarnanians the murder at Athens of two young men who had violated (it was said ignorantly) the Eleusinian mysteries. His devastation of Attic territory, and of its art-treasures, naturally caused great commotion in the Greek world, and more embassies were sent to complain at Rome. The Senate, which now began to pose as the admirer of Hellenedom and protector of Grecian liberty, took up the matter, and on sending M. Æ. Lepidus on a mission to the king, found him in the midst of a bloody and successful campaign about the Hellespont. This was evidently to cover his rear when the Roman war began. He was just besieging Abydos with circumstances of great horror, the whole body of the inhabitants during three days after the capture, committing suicide *en masse* rather than become his subjects. Such was already the result of Stoical teaching on the world! The Rhodians and Attalus were unable to check him, and when the Roman envoy used bold language to him, demanding restitution of cities taken from the allies, cessation of hostilities, and indemnity for damage to be fixed by arbitration, Philip answered haughtily,[1] and when he had finished his bloody work at Abydos, hurried back to find a Roman army landed at Apollonia, and a Roman fleet at Corcyra.

There were only two legions sent, on account of the unpopularity of the new war, and because the Senate intended to carry it on by diplomacy, and the help of Greek allies rather than with Roman blood. So then the Senate set to work to isolate Philip, and to secure as many allies as possible. They were sure of the Rhodians and Attalus, but in Greece only of Athens, for their old allies the Ætolians had been on distant terms with them, ever since they had concluded peace without Rome's leave, and the rest were waiting to see the turn of fortune. Each side was anxious to secure the Achæans, but at the crisis Philopœmen was defeated in trying to secure (against the law), a re-election as President, and a second time he sulkily left his country in the lurch, and went off to Crete. He was the only man able to keep Nabis in check, and now the Achæans were in this great difficulty, either to quarrel with Philip, and expose themselves to him and Nabis, or to offend the Romans, who were distinctly the greater power. After long and anxious discussion they determined to remain neutral. So did the Ætolians, till they saw the first Roman successes, then they joined the stronger side.

Still Philip showed, as usual, great military ability in the actual campaign. He kept the Romans out of

[1] He told Æmilius that he would excuse his impertinence because he was a young man, a handsome man, and a Roman.

Macedonia at the difficult passes through Mount Pindus, which separate Epirus from Macedonia, and it was only after nearly two years' efforts that Flamininus was able to manœuvre a passage for the Roman army into Thessaly. Why they did not operate with a fleet on the east side of his dominions does not appear; but some of the delay was caused by incompetence of consuls, and mutiny of troops in the Roman camp—a new and strange feature. When Flamininus had secured his military position in Thessaly, he spent the winter in further isolating Philip, and in persuading the still neutral states to join Rome. After a most exciting debate at their congress, the Achæans at last consented, with the greatest hesitation and fear, to join Rome. Philip attempted negotiations, and even obtained a truce of two months, to discuss terms with the Senate; but the determination was fixed to confine him to mere Macedonia, to clear all his garrisons from Greece and Thessaly—in fact, to reduce him to the original limits of Macedonia, in the days of Demosthenes.

Thus it was that the issue came to be fought on the hills not far from Tempe, called Cynoscephalæ, or *Dogs' Heads* (B.C. 197), where, for the first time since Pyrrhus, the open order of the Romans met the phalanx of the Hellenistic kingdoms. Roman officers afterwards told Polybius they had never seen anything so terrible. On level ground the phalanx was invincible, unless attacked in the rear, but it was quite unfit for rapid advance or for rough terrain. In this particular instance the battle came on unexpectedly, the

Roman cavalry stumbling in a fog upon the Macedonian which was on the hills. First successful, then defeated, then reinforced, the Macedonians urged and persuaded their king to bring up his infantry in two phalanxes, to decide the day. The right phalanx, charging down hill, was victorious, but the left did not reach the summit either in time or in order, and was easily broken, especially by the elephants on the Roman side. The victorious Romans then found themselves almost on the rear of the winning phalanx, and surrounded it. As the sign of surrender, the raising of the sarissa, or long pike, was not understood by the victors, thirteen thousand of the Macedonians were slaughtered on the field. The king escaped, burnt all his secret papers, and offered negotiations.

Of course the lesser and smaller allies, who had only joined at the eleventh hour, and who, except the Ætolians, had given little help in the war, loudly demanded the extinction of Macedon. But the Roman general was calmer and wiser. He knew how long and difficult had been the effort to penetrate through the passes into this kingdom; he knew that the king had still resources; with the aid of Thracians and Dardanians he might have begun again a tedious and dangerous struggle. He rather desired, while making the king impotent to subdue or dominate Greeks, still to keep him strong enough to act as a bulwark against the barbarians, who were the real danger to Greece. Moreover, not only had a great revolt broken out in Spain, but Philip's Eastern ally, Antiochus, who had behaved with curious and culpable sloth in not making a diversion or in coming to his aid, was now in conflict with the Rhodians, and there thus appeared new complications on the Eastern horizon. Philip was merely ordered to reduce his army and fleet, to give up all his Greek possessions, and to abstain from any attacks on the allies of Rome.

Here, then, we may pause, for the first blow has been struck from the West at the Empire of Alexander. It may of course be said that an earlier limitation came from Sandracottus (Chandragupta, p. 65 when he occupied the provinces reaching to the Indus, and made Seleucus cede to him the Indian portion of the great conqueror's acquisitions; but these remote provinces can hardly be called any portion of the Hellenistic world. More serious and real was the rise of Arsaces in 250 B.C., for not only did he establish in the province of Atropatene, hardly touched by Alexander, a lasting Oriental monarchy, but he cut off from real Hellenism the kingdom of Bactria, which had clearly made no inconsiderable effort towards that unity of culture which marked the empire.

Yet all these outlying losses were as nothing compared to the humiliation of Macedonia, the real core and backbone of the whole system of kingdoms sprung out of the empire. The highest military class in Egypt and Syria were still called Macedonians, yet we hear of the Egyptian regent Sosibius (the younger), at this very time, when he had come back from a visit to Pella, looking upon all the Alexandrian Macedonians with that supreme contempt that an Englishman of the better classes feels for the non-sporting, over-polite, city-lounging nobility of most foreign countries. In the mountains and glens of that rugged home there was a fine and hardy population who had conquered the world, and had not forgotten it, yet they were now defeated, shackled, confined, and shorn of all glory, save their imperishable traditions. So then we need not wonder that they prepared for another struggle, hopeless as it was, and that it required another great and difficult war, and another great battle, to complete their subjection. If they fell now, they fell through the isolation into which they had been brought by the vices of their king, the jealous and shortsighted meanness of their Greek neighbours, the helplessness of Egypt, and the criminal folly and delay of the king of Syria. To all these retribution was at hand.

XXVIII.

THE HELLENISTIC WORLD FROM B.C. 197–190—THE SECOND ASSERTION OF ROME'S SUPREMACY.—MAGNESIA.

THE further proceedings of Flamininus in Greece after the battle of Cynoscephalæ are recorded in every Roman history, and perhaps best in Mommsen's, if we allow for his contempt of the claims of small states, and his open assertion that the strongest have a right to rule. Flamininus was at that time no mere Roman proconsul, but an individual possessing great influence in the state, because he was supposed to know all about the Greek world, and was a proper representative of the Senate in the East on account of his culture. The majority of the nobles at Rome were still mere outsiders as regards Hellenistic culture; they spoke Greek not at all, or badly, and they were not only very sensitive to ridicule for being barbarians, but anxious to maintain the dignity of Rome in the East. Flamininus, on the contrary, posed as a man of the new culture, and fit to talk with kings and at synods in Greek; he was very vain of this, and desired to be handed down to posterity as the benefactor and liberator of Greece. Hence, in the first place, his declaration of the freedom of all the

Greeks who had been direct subjects of Philip, at the Isthmian games (B.C. 196).[1] The rest were assumed to be free. Hence, too, his extreme forbearance to the insolence and turbulence of the Ætolians, who had given him active help in the campaign, notably at the critical commencement of his great battle with Philip, and had obtained from him neither the plunder of Macedonia, nor an extension of their League into Thessaly. Hence, again, his forbearance to the Bœotians, who took to murdering single Roman soldiers; and even to Nabis, whom he subdued in a campaign at the head of the combined Greeks, but whom he did not, as he ought to have done, execute or depose. So he left Greece free indeed, but free to her own internecine quarrels, as the history of the next fifty years shows with lamentable iteration.

Still more imprudent was his persistence with the Senate—to which they at last gave way against their better judgment—on withdrawing all Roman troops from the three fortresses formerly held by Philip, Demetrias, Chalchis, and Corinth. For Philip's old ally, Antiochus the Great, was clearly preparing to dispute with the Romans part of their profits; he was at Ephesus, making his plans to succeed to the power of Philip in the Ægean; he had just received with every distinction the mighty Hannibal, whom the Romans, still fearing, had driven from Carthage, where he had introduced dangerous popular reforms. In the face of this manifest and serious danger, the sentimental Roman assembled all the Greeks at Corinth in B.C. 194, and announced to them the immediate

---

[1] See "The Story of Rome," p. 161.

evacuation of the "three fetters" which had so long galled their patriotism, and checked their liberty in going to war.

These declarations of independence, made not by the people themselves, but by their masters, had been ridiculous enough in the days of Polysperchon, of the first Demetrius and the first Ptolemy. It was now only the promise of the Cyclops, that the smaller states should be devoured last, after they had helped with treasure and with blood to subdue the greater kingdoms of the Hellenistic world.

When Flamininus was declaring Greece free and ungarrisoned, Antiochus was already making conquests and establishing his advanced posts in Thrace.

There is said to be honour amongst thieves ; it was not the case with the royal thieves of that day. Philip and Antiochus had agreed to conquer and divide Egypt, and Philip had carried out his part of the bargain by active naval hostilities, while Antiochus was conquering Cœle-Syria and Palestine ; but no sooner did he see Philip engaged with the Romans, than instead of coming to his aid, and helping the cause of Hellenism, he stood aloof, disregarded his appeal, and clearly adopted the policy of seizing not only Ptolemy's, but Philip's outlying possessions. He attempted the conquest of the Ægean islands, and of those parts of the Propontis and Thrace which had at times been claimed by Egypt, but were really the proper apanage of the Macedonian kingdom. So the old allies became bitter enemies, and Philip for once dealt honestly with the Romans when he sent them aid in their war with his own ally. This

Antiochus, justly surnamed the Great in the history of Oriental Hellenism, is quite a different person when we meet him in Roman history. The reader will remember the remark of Polybius quoted above (p. 231) on this point.

Of course the mainstay of the Romans, so long as the war remained on the coasts of Asia, was the power of Rhodes and Pergamum, but they had to do with Antiochus in Europe first. The offers by Egypt of aid in troops and money were politely declined by the Romans, we may fancy because the main body of Egyptian mercenaries at that time were Ætolians, and the Ætolians were the people urging Antiochus to come to Europe; just as Eumenes, the successor of Attalus at Pergamum, was perpetually urging the Romans to undertake a war which must turn out to the profit of his smaller kingdom. The Ætolians persuaded those Thessalians and Peloponnesians who usually stood with them to join the king of Syria, and so he came to Greece in title the Generalissimo of the Ætolian League. The king came, however, with a small army, instead of a great host; he did no more than seize Eubœa and Chalcis, and secure Thermopylæ; but the Romans held Thessaly. Then Antiochus retired to Chalcis, to celebrate a new marriage with a beautiful Greek girl, instead of working his campaign diplomatically. It was clear what the end would be.

In the spring of B.C. 191, the Roman army arrived under Acilius Glabrio, with the elder Cato as one of his tribunes, other men of consular rank also serving under him. He brought Numidian cavalry and elephants, and by dint of foreign auxiliaries raised his force to forty thousand. Antiochus sought to hold Thermopylæ against this superior army, till his absurdly delayed reinforcements should arrive from Asia. As usual, this position was turned, by sending Cato round the mountain pass inland, where the Ætolians kept slack watch and were surprised; so the Syrian was defeated, and had to fly to Asia, abandoning all the strong positions he had gained. Among the Greeks the Ætolians only resisted, and defended themselves, so that with difficulty a truce was arranged between them and the consul by the friendly and forgiving Flamininus. There followed a long and arduous struggle on the coast and among the islands of Asia Minor between the fleets of the Romans, Rhodians, and of Eumenes on the one side, and that of Antiochus on the other, in which Hannibal was absurdly given a command, and fought his only sea battle, without success, off the coast of Lycia. Meanwhile Seleucus, the king's son, was besieging Pergamum, which was only saved from capture by the constant diversions produced by Achæan troops thrown into the town. At last, after many conflicts, the supremacy of the sea was settled by the great battle of Myonnesus (B.C. 190), fought in presence of Antiochus's land army, and thus the passage of the Roman army to Asia was secured. Had Antiochus garrisoned Lysimacheia on the Propontis, the difficulty would not have been so easily settled.

The campaign was under the nominal command of the great Scipio's incompetent brother Lucius, but the victor of Zama was there and inspired confidence.

On the other side was a great army, drawn from all the far provinces of the kingdom, and arrayed in all their various splendour, as we may read in the description by Livy. They met on the plain near Magnesia (B.C. 190). Hannibal was with the king, but it is strange that we do not hear of his being entrusted with a division, not to say with the command. We hear, indeed, that he was regarded with jealousy by the Syrian generals and courtiers, and that his advice was systematically disregarded. With the troops as they stood at Magnesia, it is likely that not even he could have won a victory. They were discomfited and scattered, with a Roman loss of three hundred foot and twenty-four horsemen. Had Antiochus given him full play when he first arrived; had he been allowed to organize and drill the Greeks and Syrians, and act on his own judgment, we may be sure he would quickly have altered the whole face of the war.

Now all was over with a single battle. Antiochus the Great made peace on the Roman terms; he abandoned all Asia Minor, and had to support the Roman army at a cost of thirty thousand talents during its stay in Asia. Thus the second of the Hellenistic kingdoms fell, at a single blow, from the position of a great power, never to rise again; nor is there an example in history of a more disgraceful fall. The Macedonians, as we shall see, were as yet far from subdued; the Egyptians, though now under Roman tutelage, kept their individuality, and long after made national revolts, which showed their tough resistance to the foreigner. Syria gave up with a single half-hearted campaign. The battle of Magnesia was more a great pageant than a real fight; and yet the description of this pageant seems to indicate to us that under Antiochus the kingdom was being orientalized, and was losing its Hellenistic side. It went to pieces like an Oriental army, and the king acquiesces like an Oriental despot, when he is beaten. He was killed next year at the head of the Persian Gulf by the people whose temple he was plundering to fill his failing treasury. We leave him without regret—a brilliant youth disgraced by a sensual and silly old age.

If the king of Syria had surrendered Asia Minor without a blow, the Romans were determined not to accept it without establishing there a thorough terror of their name. They made their boundary-line from the Taurus Mount to the Halys, and in the year following, the new consul, C. Manlius Vulso, led his army through the interior of the country, making it his special object to attack and subjugate the Galatians, who were now permanently settled, and had avoided all offence or cause of war. If this military parade through the new subject-provinces was indeed required, we cannot but agree with the historians who see in the expedition of Manlius a new and terrible feature. The Romans who had appeared in the East as liberators were rapidly to become plunderers. The first armies which were levied to subdue Macedonia came unwillingly to the enrolment. The plunder of Cynoscephalæ and Magnesia opened out a new discovery—that war in the East for the Romans was what war in the East had been for the Greeks and Macedonians, a splendidly lucrative pursuit. It has also been justly remarked by historians, that if it took a couple of centuries to degrade the Greek into the Greekling of Roman days, it only took a generation or two to degrade the old dignified Roman of the Punic wars into the shameless and brutal spoiler of the Gracchan days. Nor is it hard to account for this remarkable difference. It had been observed long before in Greek history, how the rude and honourable Spartans turned tyrannical and venal as soon as they had conquered all opposition and had become a dominant nation. In both cases an uneducated people came suddenly to dominate around them, and the uneducated are never able to resist prosperity like those who have been trained by high culture to know the true value of the world's gifts.

XXIX.

THE HELLENISTIC WORLD FROM THE BATTLE OF MAGNESIA TO THE ACCESSION OF PERSEUS (B.C. 190-179).

DURING the great struggles which we have been relating, we have been almost silent as regards Egypt, where the child Ptolemy Epiphanes was growing apace under various tutors and governors. What happened at his accession was told above (p. 251). In the fragmentary records of his reign, we find a whole series of military and civil officers, almost all threatening revolt, and all disposed of successfully by their rivals. What became of Tlepolemus we know not, but we know that a succeeding commander of the forces, the Ætolian Scopas, notorious for his rapacity and injustice in the management of the League's affairs, played the same part in Egypt. He had commanded in the campaign against Antiochus, not without success, in spite of his great defeat at Panion, but in times of peace he assumed great state at Alexandria, demanded and squandered enormous pay, and even refused to appear before the ministers of the king when summoned to their council. He was arrested and put to death by Aristomenes, a new minister who was very faithful to his trust, and who seems to have managed affairs wisely.

The accidents of history have preserved to us not only the curious scene of riot at Alexandria on the occasion of Epiphanes' accession, but also the decree of the priests and ministers at his formal coronation, or *Anacleteria* (proclamation as king). The coronation took place in the ninth year of his reign (B.C. 196), when he was by no means of age, and at Memphis, the ancient capital of Egypt. The ceremony, which is described, shows very clearly how the Ptolemies had taken care to succeed to the indigenous dynasties. Coming to Memphis by state barge, he was met by the assembled priests; crowned in the temple of Ptah with the double crown (Pschent) of Upper and Lower Egypt. Then was passed the decree in honour of the king, which is the text preserved on the famous Rosetta stone, now in the British Museum. This stone has a celebrity quite apart from its historical value, in affording us the key to the deciphering of the hieroglyphic and demotic characters, in which the old language of Egypt was written. We have now another stone, the inscription found by Mariette and Lepsius in 1865 at Tunis, recording the decree of the priests assembled at Canopus in the ninth year of Euergetes (see p. 157). But nothing will ever displace or obscure the celebrity of the Rosetta stone.[1] Found by the French in Napoleon's expedition in 1799, and packed up for France, it fell, upon the capitulation of Alexandria after the battle of the Nile, into British

[1] Casts of this stone are preserved in America.

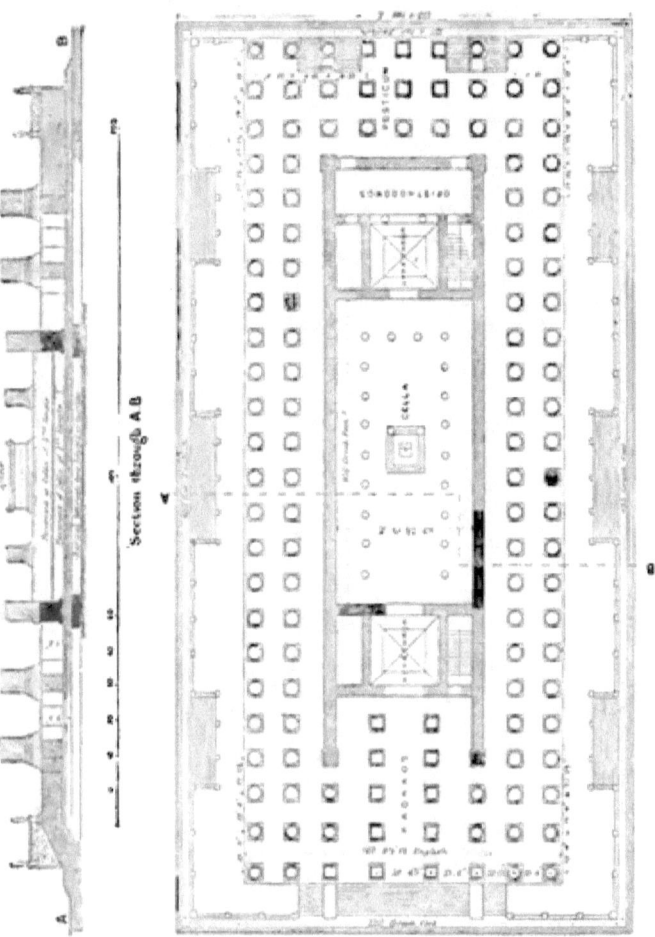

PLAN OF TEMPLE OF DIANA AT EPHESUS.
(Rebuilt on this plan in the third century B.C.)

hands, and was sent to London; but it was many years before the key was found by Champollion. The Greek text was of course easy enough—the other two were the secret. Luckily the names of the king and queen, Ptolemy and Cleopatra, appeared in such a place in the Greek text as to correspond to two oval rings in the hieroglyphic characters, which were filled with signs. These then seemed to represent the letters of the names. Starting from this clue, Champollion made out the alphabet, if such it may be called, helping himself by a thorough knowledge of the Coptic language, the daughter of the old Egyptian, which gave him the names of many objects represented in the tomb-paintings with their names written over them.[1]

The text of the inscription is in substance this: After a long enumeration of the titles of the king—to whom Ra has given victory, beloved of Ptah, &c.—the date is fixed by the names of the various priests serving that year as the priests of the older Ptolemies and their queens now deified. Then a preamble describes the good acts of the king, how the taxes were lessened, crown debtors forgiven, prisoners released, crown allowances to the temples increased, the duties and taxes of the priests diminished, the pressgang for the navy abolished, and so forth—all this in accordance with the wishes of his grandfather, thus carefully slighting his father Philopator. In

---

[1] Champollion's own account is in his *Précis du système hiéroglyphique*. I have given the history of the discovery and its development down to our own days in my "Prolegomena to Ancient History," Longmans, 1871

consequence of all this, the decree orders that the king shall be worshipped in every temple of Egypt, his statue carried with the gods in all processions, and this decree carved at the foot of every statue of the king in sacred (hieroglyphic), common (demotic), and in Greek writing.

We now know that this famous declaration had more than a mere formal meaning. The cruelties of Philopator as to taxing, and the systematic employment of Greeks, not only in the army, but in all good civil offices, excited a national opposition to their rule. We hear of the Egyptian troops rebelling and being conquered with difficulty, then later on of a rising in Upper Egypt, and even of a Madhi who was to be a deliverer of the people from the foreign yoke. The decree of Memphis, then, was a declaration obtained from the priests, who represented the national party, that the young king was indeed divine and the lawful and legitimate possessor of the crown of Egypt; and this declaration was not obtained without large concessions in the way of taxes remitted, and of privileges conferred upon the temples. National reactions such as this were the second weapon which the age developed, to undermine and destroy the conquests of Heilenism. As the Parthian monarchy was based upon national principles, so the Egyptian revolts, which continued at intervals down to the final conquest of the Romans, partook of this character; and the third outlying kingdom, which stood independent longer than all its great neighbours, the kingdom of Pontus, represented in its turn not Hellenism, but Orientalism.

These considerations will justify this brief delay on

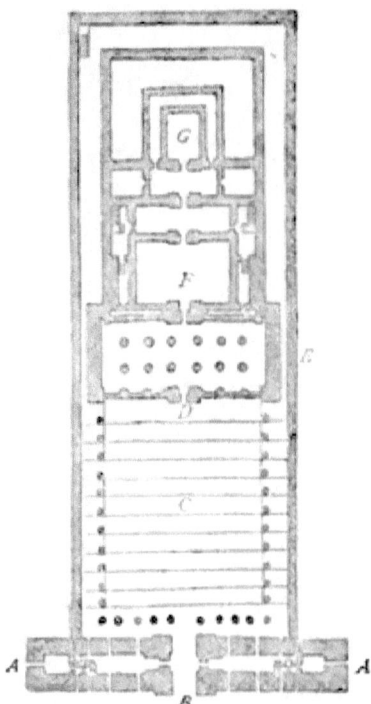

PLAN OF EGYPTIAN TEMPLE.

(We come first to a great Pylon (*A*), or pair of lofty buttresses on either side of the main gate (*B*), then a great open court (*C*), surrounded by a huge colonnade; then a second gate (*D*), leading to an ante-chamber supported by still huger pillars (*E*), then the gate (*F*) into the temple proper with various chambers, of which the inmost (*G*) held the shrine of the god.)

a curious moment of Egyptian history. As regards its external politics during the reign of Epiphanes, we have already mentioned that the struggle in Syria ended by the young queen obtaining Palestine, nominally at least, for a dowry. The possessions through the Ægean had fallen away, consisting as they did of the protectorate of free cities which now appealed to the Romans; Cyprus and Cyrene were perhaps the only outlying possessions now remaining to Egypt.

The condition of Pergamum, on the other hand, underwent a mighty change, for, with the exception of those Greek towns which were independent of him at the date of the battle of Magnesia, and a small portion of Caria granted to the Rhodians, Eumenes obtained the whole of Asia Minor, and the European shore of the Hellespont. This, in addition to immense sums in compensation for damage, which Antiochus was compelled to pay him, made Eumenes quite the greatest sovran of the East, at least in appearance; but there was this weak point, that the League of free cities along the coast, with the Rhodians at their head, were opposed to him in interests; and as the sentimental fashion of the day went for "freedom of all Greeks," the cities left under his rule were sure to be discontent, and struggled to escape into the League of Rhodes. The commercial power of Rhodes amounted on that coast to almost a monopoly of profits in seafaring. It was afterwards asserted before the Senate by Eumenes, during one of his quarrels with the Rhodians, that freedom under them was a subjection far stricter than to be a member of his kingdom; and this was very probably true.

The large fact, and that which dominated the world, now was this : that all these powers were only kingdoms, or leagues, or free cities, in a secondary sense—that they really depended on the nod and beck of Rome. As yet the Romans showed no desire to make any direct conquests beyond the seas. As yet they did not require any contributions to support the myriad paupers of Rome ; but with the notions of the ancients, and especially of the Romans, about the rights of conquest, it was quite clear to any observer that the moment policy or convenience at Rome required it, all these kingdoms and free states would pass into the condition of absolute and heavily taxed subjects.

Thus we may say that the day of Magnesia marks definitely the fall of the Empire of Alexander under the power of the Romans. Henceforth the chief part is played by those second-rate powers, to whom, in return for their services, the Romans had given largesses and privileges. These, the Achæan League, Pergamum, Rhodes, were set up to watch and control the remaining fragments of the great kingdoms ; but it very soon appeared that these smaller states would carry on a perpetual conflict for balance of power or for supremacy, like the greater kingdoms of Hellenism, but on a smaller scale. The Achæan League, Pergamum and Rhodes, are like a little Macedonia, Syria, and Egypt in their relations, and their complicated wars and diplomacies can hardly be called world-history, and may therefore be left to the special historians of that period.

The larger events, on the other hand, which make

this generation of deep interest to humanity, are
essentially a part of Roman history, and are therefore
narrated in every good book—and how many there
are!—on that subject. Here we may be very brief,
for the empire we have been considering is gone to
pieces. The great kingdoms are now isolated, and,
with the exception of one attempt of Syria on Egypt,
and one more struggle for independence in Macedonia,
these kingdoms either continue a bare existence,
tolerated by the Romans, or are actually broken up
by the conquerors.

All the world, says Polybius, sent embassies of con-
gratulation to Rome upon the battle of Magnesia, and
thus that great thoroughfare which had grown up
under the empire all through Egypt, Asia Minor,
and Greece, began to extend to Italy. The Mediterranean from Rome to Antioch, from Alexandria to
Pella, was the high road of civilized men, all speaking
the language, and possessing or affecting the culture,
of Hellenism. And this was the lasting result of the
conquest of Alexander, which the Romans neither
could nor would destroy. But at the moment before
us, all the Eastern world went to Rome to see what
they could get, and of course many of them were not
satisfied. The Achæans, who overrated their part in
the campaign, wanted to extend their league over all
Greece, and were restricted, with much grumbling and
discontent, to the Peloponnesus. Philip's share in the
campaign was really serious, for he had secured all
the Roman communications with Asia; but then he
was dangerous, and must be left in weakness and dependence. So he was deprived of Thracian coast

towns, which were given to Eumenes to keep watch over him, and was not allowed to hold the islands of Thasos and Lemnos. Indeed, all the rest of his days he was exposed to insult at the hands of the Romans; he was compelled to answer accusations and explain his acts at the demand of former subjects. The Ætolians showed their stubborn fighting qualities even after the great victory, and it required a special campaign of the Romans, and some long and desperate sieges, to reduce them to subjection.

The state of the world for about ten years after Magnesia was not indeed such as to alarm the Romans, who were occupied, as we see from their annals, with a peculiarly obstinate Ligurian war, combined some years with outbreaks in Istria and the Pyrenees. Every year we hear of consuls and armies being sent to Liguria, and it is a wonder that this exercise did not keep up the old military spirit which we find so curiously decayed in the next Macedonian war.

Antiochus the Great was succeeded by his younger son, Seleucus Philopator, who reigned obscurely and ingloriously for twelve years (B.C. 186-174), but still kept up the tradition of the Hellenistic kings by marrying his daughter to Perseus, the prince of Macedonia.

The wretched king of Egypt lived on in sloth and luxury, undoing what had been done by his able ministers, and reversing his early reputation, till he was poisoned in 181 B.C. when about to make another campaign into Palestine against the king of Syria.

Meanwhile Philip, now in the decline of life, had

been in vain trying to recover himself by annexing a few towns, and still more by re-colonizing deserted tracts in the inner and northern parts of his dominion; but his watchful neighbours cited him before a Roman Commission, sent out to inquire into his doings, and he was compelled (B.C. 184-183) to give up not only the towns in Thessaly which had been formerly granted to him, but his remaining coast towns in Thrace. The deeply offended king gloomily determined to spend the rest of his life in preparing for another contest; but he was delayed by a sad tragedy in his own family, which reminds us strongly of the history of Lysimachus of Thrace (see p. 72). There arose violent jealousies between his elder son Perseus, and his younger and more brilliant Demetrius, whom the Romans had often received at Rome, and favoured (with a policy now becoming systematic) as a rival and spy resident in the kingdom of a doubtful ally. The suspicions raised by Perseus were increased by the charge that Demetrius was a "friend of the Romans," and desirous of removing his father. He was poisoned, but before long the old king found out the deceit and false charges of Perseus, and died an embittered and broken-hearted man (B.C. 179).

The long reign of Philip—over forty years—had seen the decadence of the Empire of Hellenism. When he succeeded, Macedonia was still a strong empire, stronger indeed than it had been for nearly a century, through the genius of Antigonus Doson. Succeeding with the fairest prospects, he was a character only kept within the bounds of good sense and justice by the sternest adversity. As soon as he found himself idle or safe, his lusts and tempers broke out. It was possibly a misfortune to the world, certainly to himself, that he was not obliged, like almost all his predecessors, to recover by arms the kingdom to which he had succeeded by right.

We are very fully informed by Polybius and Livy of the political relations which developed themselves during these years between Rome and the various states of Greece. While elsewhere there were large kingdoms and single persons to be considered, here there were a great number of varying polities— Leagues, free cities, some tyrants, all in strained relations, and all appealing perpetually for Roman decisions, and protesting against those decisions when they were given. It is not our duty here to give more than a general sketch of these constant and wearying quarrels, which ended, of course, in the pacification of Greece by a bloody armed intervention; but the method of Roman absorption is so explicitly shown, and so well recorded in the case of Greece, that it will reward the reader to follow a short summary of it.

It is clear that the Roman policy was shifty and uncertain because opposite views were held by strong parties in the state. The older school, such as Cato, understood nothing but military conquest and occupation; they were therefore cautious about advancing far from Italy, but if they did so it was for the permanent enlargement of the state. On the other hand, there was a school of younger statesmen, like Flamininus, who were ready to interfere diplomatically everywhere, but without any intention of conquest, who thought to control a great empire by playing off a number of allied or subject powers one against the other. This was the view which at first became popular in the case of Greece, especially on account of the sentimental favour with which the free Greek cities were regarded at Rome. Up to the war with Antiochus, these smaller states were eminently useful in isolating the three kingdoms, Macedonia, Syria, and Egypt. This importance, however, and the generous language used as regards the liberty of the Greeks, were understood by them in a far different sense from what was, or could have been, intended at Rome. Flamininus might indeed think that gratitude would prevent this liberated people from taking side against the Romans; but if they did, their liberties must be forthwith cancelled. It was found presently that even before such an event happened it might be necessary to interfere, for it was single free cities or small states, all impotent and insignificant, which the Romans intended to have in the East, not Leagues which took the liberty of enlarging themselves and growing into important powers. Such Leagues, even if wholly unable to oppose Rome, were inconvenient from the weight which they had with their neighbours, and the independent way in which they could remonstrate and protest.

The first conflict of the kind arose, as we have observed, with the Ætolians, who were the earliest to see the real character of the Roman interference, and who were urgent in calling in Antiochus to aid them. They also incited Nabis of Sparta to attack the Achæans, the friends of Rome, and recover the territory adjudged to them by Flamininus. Consequently a new war had broken out (B.C. 192) between Sparta and the Achæans under Philopœmen, now returned from Crete, and appointed General of the League. Nabis had been worsted, but when the Romans were informed of it, they would not allow the Achæans to finish their victory, and compelled a peace. This again was Flamininus's doing. It was even alleged by the Greeks that he was jealous of the military successes of Philopœmen; but this is on a par with the constant allegations of the Ætolians that he was bribed during his previous settlement of affairs after his victory. These latter, however, though they murdered Nabis in their attempt to seize Sparta, together with Chalcis and Demetrias, by their vigorous action induced Antiochus to come over into Greece.

The result has already been narrated. After the battle of Magnesia the Ætolians still held out obstinately, and were at last conquered and crushed for ever; but the very year that marks their downfall marks the greatest geographical extension of the rival League. All Peloponnesus had now joined, or been forced to join the Achæans, and they aspired to unite all Greece. This it was which the Romans would not tolerate any more than the resurrection of Philip's power. They forced the Achæans to give up Zakynthos (Zante), an island which had been taken and joined to the League, and warned them not to go to war without consulting Rome. They no doubt treated with distinction certain rich men, and made agents of them, while we find patriotic statesmen becoming more and more democratic, and leading a party which gradually conceived suspicion, then aversion, then hatred towards Rome.

Moreover, the blunders of the League gave Rome constant ground for interference. The pretended union of all Peloponnesus under the League was a mere sham. Even when Nabis was gone, the town of Sparta again revolted, and expelled the Achæan party. Then Philopœmen led them back, demanded the leaders of the revolt, who were all massacred, some with, some without the form of a trial, and proceeded to the most sweeping and high-handed executions and confiscations, making, in fact, a clean sweep of everything distinctively Spartan, even so far as the formal abolishing of the Lycurgean laws. Of course the defeated party ran to Rome. The Romans ordered a commission to inquire into the case; they received separate missions from the Spartans; what was worse, they gave a half-hearted decision, ordering peace and the return and pardon of exiles, and taking from the Achæans the power of condemning the Spartans in their congress, though they left Sparta a member of the League. This capture of Sparta happened in 188 B.C. and these negotiations were protracted four years.

Then came a similar difficulty with Messene. Philopœmen hurried to put down this revolt, and advancing too precipitately, was captured and killed (B.C. 184). There resulted wars with Messene and with Sparta, which took its opportunity of revenge; the Romans declined to interfere; and it was only with the greatest energy and caution that Lycortas (Polybius's father), the new leader of the League, managed to produce a kind of peace, or rather pause in these miserable quarrels, in 181 B.C. Thus we have the condition of things matured, which led to the last Macedonian war, and then to the subjugation of Greece.

COIN OF PERSEUS, KING OF MACEDON.

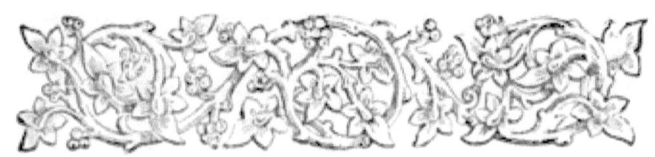

XXX.

THE STRUGGLE OF PERSEUS WITH THE ROMANS.—THE THIRD ASSERTION OF ROME'S SUPREMACY.—PYDNA (B.C. 168).

PERSEUS succeeded his father in 179 B.C., and soon showed that he did not possess the private vices which ruined Philip's influence. He was, like him, a thoroughly trained soldier, but strict in his morals, and courteous in his manners. He had of course inherited a deep hatred for the Romans, and had also been trained for many years in the only policy which could lead him to any reasonable success. It was his clear determination to foster the Hellenistic feeling against the Romans, to enter into friendly relations with all Greek states, and so to prepare for himself a general alliance when he struck his blow; for two things were certain. He would be watched and accused at Rome by the king of Pergamum, as soon as there was a suspicion of war preparations. He would not be joined by the Greeks till some decided success had excited them, for the fear of Rome was great, and the cautious would always keep a fair face to the Western barbarians till they saw a chance of throwing off their hated sway. For these reasons, Perseus prepared as quietly as possible, and five years passed before he made any public demonstration of his power.

Meanwhile, things had been gradually growing worse in Greece and Asia Minor. The Romans had everywhere created or excited a philo-Roman party in the states, which acted in their interests, and believed, or professed to believe, that there was no peace or security for property without close and actual dependence upon Rome. On the other hand, there was a large nationalist party everywhere, violently opposed to the unionists, branding them as traitors, and constantly asserting the right of every Greek state to legislate for itself. The halting and uncertain tone of the Roman Senate fed the hopes and the animosities of both parties. On the one hand, the Senate had often admitted, and publicly admitted, the principle that each Greek state ought to have liberty and home-rule. On the other hand, every practical politician whom they sent to the East as Deputy or Commissioner, found that active interference with this liberty was necessary, if the life and property of the richer classes were to be safe, and if the Romans were not prepared for a proximate declaration of independence on the part of the Greeks. Let us add that the Roman temper and tone of mind—proud, narrow, ill-educated, nay, even stupid as compared with the quick-witted Greeks, was profoundly unsympathetic, and that therefore Rome came to be disliked on account of the haughty and imperious manners of even worthy and respectable men. Above all, they constantly interfered in what we may call state property, in an unjust or inexpedient way.

They first sanctioned the Achæan League, and granted territory on the mainland to the Rhodians. Then, when members of the League, or the cities of the Rhodian *Peræa*, as it is called, complained of harsh treatment, and appealed to Rome for liberty, they were protected against their masters, who were not allowed to enforce the acknowledged law or existing contracts against them.

There are curious analogies to all this in the actual state of Ireland (1886); and as here the opposed parties are so hostile and embittered that neither will acknowledge any virtue or honesty in the other, so we find that by the patriot party in Greece, every Romanizer is set down as a traitor and a villain. During the pause in actual war which we have now reached, Callicrates was the head of the Roman party in Achæa. He is accused by Polybius of going to Rome (B.C. 180) as one of the three commissioners, and there making a secret arrangement with the Senate, by convincing them that no peace or obedience could be secured in Greece without everywhere protecting the aristocrats, and demanding their restoration to their properties, whenever they had been exiled. At the same time Polybius pretends that the Achæans, or his brother-envoys at Rome, had no inkling of all this, for he was elected President in 179 B.C.

It is plain that here, too, a land-question was at the root of things. The decay of Greece had increased pauperism; the power of Rome had already stopped the lucrative mercenary wars between the sovereigns of the Hellenistic world, and the poor—

we saw it as early as Agis and Cleomenes—turned their attention to despoiling their richer neighbours. In democratic constitutions the only possibility of safety for the rich minority was the support of Rome, a foreign power bound to the world to permit no violent disorders among its subject states.

This sketch of the state of feeling among the Greeks shows what good cards were in Perseus's hands, had he known how to play them. Everywhere the popular party found that the control of Macedonia would be infinitely preferable to that of Rome. Even the Rhodians foresaw that in the end Rome would ruin their trade.

In 174 B.C. Perseus made his first demonstration; punishing the Dolopians for the murder of a Macedonian official, and making a solemn display of his army at Delphi. Of course Eumenes ran to Rome with complaints and warnings, and each side began to foresee the coming struggle; but when Perseus sought allies among the Greeks, though he found the poorer classes everywhere in his favour, and in many places bloody insurrections against the better classes showed how they understood his interference, the Roman party were able to get his proposal for a formal alliance with Achæa rejected. On the Asiatic coast, where Eumenes was feared and hated, both the great towns on the Hellespont and the Rhodians were disposed to take his side; but all were very much afraid to declare themselves.

Envoys from Rome went to Macedonia in 172 B.C., to complain that the king had not observed the terms of the treaty with Philip. He answered as if he were prepared for war, and rejected all liability for his father's acts. So the war opened in the end of the year, by the arrival of troops from Italy at Apollonia. Then it appeared that Perseus, who had spent years in preparation for this struggle, had not the decision to act. Instead of at once mobilizing his army, invading Greece, and getting his numerous partizans in every state to join him, he sat quiet while Roman envoys went all through Greece and the Ægean to intimidate the Hellenistic world, and demand support and sympathy. The king even allowed himself to be deluded by his Roman guest friend, Quintus Marcius, into sending a deputation to Rome, to discuss terms of peace when war was already determined. This Q. Marcius plays an ugly part in the history of the time; his diplomacy consisted in nothing but shameful falsehoods, and excited indignation among the older nobles at Rome.

Both the diplomacy and the strategy shown in this war show a curious and rapid degeneration in Roman character. Though the Romans had secured at least material support from all the Greeks, and had an ample army and fleet, the first campaign was so incompetently managed by the consul P. Licinius Crassus, that Perseus gained one considerable victory, and with any energy on his part could have destroyed the Roman army. Along with this incompetence, the Romans also developed great cruelty and barbarity, even in the treatment of friendly states. These causes naturally excited the sentiments and fed the hopes of the national, now the Macedonian, party in every state, and so the war assumed a very serious appearance. The consul and admiral of the next year (B.C. 170) succeeded no better, and were guilty of similar acts of monstrous oppression and cruelty. All this time Perseus hesitated in his strategy, and still worse in opening his treasure and paying the northern barbarians, who were his only efficient allies. The next consul, our lying friend Q. Marcius, was more active, and actually took his army over the shoulder of Mt. Olympus down desperate precipices into Macedonia; but when there his communications were interrupted, and his advance stopped by Perseus, who occupied a strong position, and for want of commissariat he could do nothing.

It was not till the famous L. Æmil. Paullus, the brother-in-law of the great Scipio, and father of the Scipio who destroyed Carthage, was appointed, that the war was brought to a close by first manœuvring Perseus out of his strong position, and then defeating him at Pydna.[1] (June 168 B.C.) In this battle the phalanx again attacked and defeated the Roman infantry, and Paullus confessed that he had trembled for his army; but Perseus, commanding his cavalry, according to Alexander's fashion, would not charge when the legions were in confusion, and the rapid advance of the victorious phalanx threw it out of order. Then the Romans rallied and destroyed it. These facts show the profound knowledge possessed by Alexander of the possible uses of the phalanx, which he never used for attack. Had an officer like Philopœmen commanded the Macedonian cavalry at Pydna, and charged when the legions were in dis-

[1] See "The Story of Rome," p. 163.

order, the Macedonians must have won; but now the king fled to Samothrace, where he was taken prisoner by the Roman admiral.

Even Æm. Paullus, though he was able to recover the discipline of the Roman troops in action, and make them an efficient army in the field, was unable to stem the tide of rapacity and injustice which seemed to have invaded the conquering people in a generation. He indeed, a Roman of antique virtue, had also a respect for the art and culture of Greece, and would gladly have shown sympathy for his vanquished enemy; but the decree of the commission upon Macedonia, to which he was obliged to agree, was perhaps the most cruel ever made by Rome. The kingdom was first stripped of all its better classes (including every official), who were all transported to Italy — to live, we suppose, in seclusion and wretchedness, if not in positive captivity, in country towns, among their conquerors. The king himself, after being exhibited in the triumphal procession of Paullus, disappears in hopeless misery, we know not whether to be put to death, or to suffer death in life, in captivity in some Etrurian town. His son afterwards earned a poor living as an auctioneer's clerk; nor was this last scion of great royal houses treated with any respect by the Roman aristocracy. Macedonia was cut into four divisions, and so isolated that no inhabitants of one were allowed to acquire property or marry in the next. Of course Roman traders— and here the policy of protecting them by tyranny and oppression first appears—who could cross these frontiers, soon got all the remaining wealth into their hands; and so great was the wretchedness of the land, that bloody raids and insurrections compelled the Romans twenty-one years after to reduce it to a direct Roman province. It was all very well to demand only half the tax paid to the former kings. The mines were closed, the export of timber prohibited—in fact, everything was done, and done but too successfully, to reduce this noble and free people to starvation and ruin.

Also, by special order of the Senate, the wretched Epirotes, who had shown active sympathies with Perseus, were invaded by Paullus, their cities sacked, most of them massacred, and 150,000 people sold as slaves.

Even their trusty agent and friend Eumenes was charged with being half-hearted—we know not how truly—insulted by being deprived of Thracian cities, and shown clearly that now, when he was no longer of use to the Romans as a policeman, or a spy, they had no regard whatever for his past services. They set the king of Bithynia and the Galatæ to encroach upon him, so that it was only with the greatest forbearance and diplomacy that the kingdom was kept alive, and bequeathed to his faithful brother Attalus II., who had been often set on by the Senate, but in vain, to dispossess his brother. As is well known, the next king, Attalus III., thirty years later (B.C. 133) bequeathed his kingdom directly to the Roman people as their property. There were not wanting people to assert that the will was forged, and from the general character of Roman diplomacy, such a charge is far from incredible.

The treatment of Rhodes was not less scandalous, and affords another example of the brutal way in which the Romans determined to monopolize the trade of the world. They had just discovered what riches could be acquired by foreign mercantile speculations, and they determined to keep this source of wealth to themselves by ruining every other trading power. The Rhodians, however, gave the Romans a sentimental grievance by offering to mediate between them and Perseus. They had come to the camp of Q. Marcius to promote peace, as they had done in every Hellenistic war for a century, seeing that their trade interests were strictly the interests of peace. The lying consul, for the purpose of getting them into a scrape, insinuated that they had better go to Rome, where they would be well received. This embassy was of course regarded at Rome as the grossest impertinence. The news of Pydna which arrived at the time made it even ridiculous. Thus the war party, and the mercantile party, who urged them on without appearing on the scene, caught at the opportunity of ruining these ancient and respectable allies. They were very near being destroyed like Macedonia. It was thought a great concession that they were only deprived of all the territory on the mainland, granted them by Rome after the battle of Magnesia, and ruined in commerce by the declaration of Delos to be a free port. It is evident that one of the regulations of the Rhodian League was to require fixed harbour-dues in every port, by which vessels were naturally brought to the largest and best mart in the League. The income of Rhodes from this source fell at once from £40,000 a year to £6,000.

Thus the Romans, having crushed their enemies in the East, proceeded to crush their allies. They knew full well that Rome had done only too much to earn Hellenistic hatred, and that while these smaller states kept carefully within all the bounds of the treaties, public opinion was more and more setting against themselves. The most signal instance of this was the famous case of Achæa. The League had honourably supported them in the war with Perseus, and had carried out all the wishes of the Romans, nevertheless their friends and agents could tell them that the national feeling was intensely bitter against them. Q. Marcius tried all his lying to get them into trouble; but the honorable conduct of their leaders made it difficult. At last the Romans held a formal inquisition into private opinion (B.C. 167), and when the honest Xenon declared that the national party were ready to stand any fair trial, even in a Roman court, he was taken at his word, and a thousand leading men were deported to Italy, where they were kept without trial for seventeen years, in spite of constant embassies and remonstrances, till at last the surviving three hundred came home (B.C. 150), savage and furious enemies of Rome, and lost to all feelings but revenge. Thus came on the desperate outbreak of 146 B.C., the invasion of Mummius, the capture and sack of Corinth. This and the sack of Carthage in the same year completed the policy of the mercantile party. Rome had now no commercial rival on the Mediterranean.

If Achæa was ruined and driven to desperation by this foul injustice, the world has gained by it the invaluable history of Polybius. He was one of the thousand captives; he had lived a life of great activity and of official prominence in the League, of which his father, Lycortas, had been frequently president. He had carried, as a youth, the ashes of Philopœmen to the tomb. He had been on embassies to Egypt and Pergamum. After Pydna, he had hunted with Paullus's sons in the rich preserves of Perseus, forgotten during the war and full of game. He had studied not only politics, but military affairs. Now he was carried to Italy, and by the influence of Paullus settled in his mansion at Rome, and in the society of the noblest and best citizens. They it was who informed him about the doings of the great Scipio in the second Punic War, about the management of war and peace by the Romans, and who prompted him to write the great history of the world from the outbreak of the second Punic War (B.C. 221) to the fall of Corinth (B.C. 146). This book gives us the key to the history of Hellenism. It is written, of course, in the Roman interest; it doubtless exaggerates the merits of Scipio to suit the tastes of his descendants, to whom Polybius read these chapters. It is also a special pleading for the Achæan League, and for the national party in that League; but nevertheless it is a great and wise book, and teaches us even in its fragments more history than all the other Greek historians put together.

XXXI.

THE LAST SYRIAN WAR, AND FOURTH ASSERTION OF ROMAN SUPREMACY. THE CIRCLE OF POPILIUS LÆNAS (168 B.C.).

THE obscure Seleucus (IV.) Philopator, king of Syria, had died in 175 B.C., and was succeeded by a man who made some stir in the world, his elder brother, Antiochus Epiphanes, who reigned B.C. 175–166. We have two pictures of this king, who had lived several

COIN OF ANTIOCHUS IV.

years a hostage at Rome. Born in 221 B.C., at the opening of his father's reign, he had seen the rise and fall of the kingdom under Antiochus the Great, and was thirty-one years old when the terms of the peace in 191 B.C. sent him to Rome. Thus he was forty-five years old when he succeeded, of an age and experience from which we might have expected a steady reign; but Polybius, who has described the extraordinary feasts and pageants he gave, apparently in imitation both of Alexandrian and Roman processions, gives us plainly to understand that along with high and brilliant qualities there was a vein of madness in the king. He rode up and down his state processions as his own master of the ceremonies, a thing unheard of in those stately courts, and sat down at table with the lower classes at his great feasts. In Josephus and in the book of Maccabees, he is painted as a brutal tyrant, profaning the temple of the Jews, and causing wanton and ruthless bloodshed. Both pictures are doubtless true, and are interesting, as they give us some knowledge of the last real king of Syria, as Perseus was the last real king of Macedonia.

He maintained the policy of his house by taking advantage of the war in Macedonia, and the occupation of all the Western world, to attack Egypt. His sister Cleopatra (Queen of Egypt) was just dead, and her infant son Ptolemy (VI.) Philometor had succeeded. Cœle-Syria, or its revenues, had been Cleopatra's dowry, and now Antiochus refused to pay, and reclaimed it. He was more successful than any Syrian king had yet been. Winning a great battle on the borders of Egypt, he actually penetrated the country, reached Memphis, and had the boy-king completely in his hands; but the Egyptians deposed and expelled their king, who had come to terms too easily, and set up his brother, Euergetes II., known as Physcon, in his stead. Antiochus returned to restore Philometor, and besieged the new king in Alexandria, when his brother took the occasion of Antiochus's brief absence to join the Egyptian party, and both made war on

Antiochus. Meanwhile they sent urgent messages to Rome, praying for interference and succour. The Roman ambassadors, the same who had been sent to Rhodes just after the battle of Pydna, met the king within four miles of Alexandria, apparently about to become permanent master of Egypt, and they handed him the Senate's missive forbidding his war. He asked time to consider, when Popilius Lænas drew his famous circle round him in the sand with his stick, and told him to decide before he stepped out of it. This was a very different kind of embassy from that of the Rhodians, who had come on the same errand a short time before, to whom he answered that

COIN OF LEPIDUS TUTOR REGIS.

he was only restoring the Egyptian people their lawful king. He knew the Romans well; no doubt he knew Popilius personally, and he saw that his day was come. He gave up his war, and returned through Jerusalem to his capital.

Here, then, was the climax of Roman interference. The threat of an envoy was sufficient to close the last Syrian war, and stay the conqueror when on the eve of completing his conquest. Thus the Empire of Alexander passed under Roman sway. We have, indeed, lists of Syrian and Egyptian kings, reaching down to the time when Pompey and Cæsar respectively made the final settlement of these kingdoms (B.C. 49 to 47), and abolished the existing sovereigns; but this long list is merely a succession of names. They have neither influence upon the world, nor power in their own country. They either keep beyond the limits of Roman politics, or submit tamely to what the Senate orders. Whatever spirit still subsists in the nations was no longer a Hellenistic spirit, but that of the original nations. The bitter revolts and war against Julius Cæsar at Alexandria were essentially Egyptian revolts. The wars of the eastern provinces of Syria againt Rome were essentially Parthian. With the year of Pydna (168 B.C.) the whole matter was decided. The struggles of the Achæan patriots and the sack of Corinth were only small items in this settlement. The Empire of Alexander, founded by a single genius, broken up by ambitious generals, held together in spirit and in culture by unity of language, of interests, of commerce, sank into dependence upon Rome, and ceases to have any other than a spiritual history.

It only remains for us now to sketch briefly the present effect of this Hellenism upon Rome, and to show that even when the empire and its component kingdoms were gone, the ideas of Alexander long continued to dominate the civilized world.

XXXII.

THE INFLUENCE OF HELLENISM ON ROME.

WHEN the Romans suddenly found themselves a great and conquering power, when circumstances, as it were, thrust upon them sovran authority, they were as inferior to the East in culture as they were superior in force of arms, and they knew it. For a long time back, as far as the Decemvirs, who drew up codes of law, and the censors, established to look after the population and its taxing, they had been in the habit of sending occasional embassies to learn from the Greeks—generally, indeed, from the Athenians; but their closer intercourse with Greeks only dates from the time when they had conquered the Samnites, and came in direct contact with the Greek cities of Italy, with the result that Pyrrhus came over from Epirus, and they made trial of Greek arms as well as Greek courtesy. The legends told about this war show the anxiety of the Romans to appear equal in manners to the polite Hellenistic princes. Thus, then, there grew up a desire to enter into the circle of these civilized nations, retarded, it is true, by the Punic wars, but still always increasing as the world became one by commerce and language. It is possible that the Rhodians had communicated with Rome before

300 B.C. It is certain that the second Ptolemy sent them an embassy before the first Punic War (B.C. 273). Thus they became recognized by the Hellenistic world, and they learned to know the Greeks, but not the Greeks of the old days; not the Greeks, like Pericles, and Epaminondas and Demosthenes, but their degenerate descendants who have occupied us so much in the great struggles of surrounding kingdoms.

At this time the Romans were just struggling into a Literature of their own; what it would have been we know not. For whatever points of weakness the Greeks—the nearest and best known to them of the Hellenistic world—possessed, their books were vastly superior to anything attempted at Rome. Thus it was inevitable that the Romans should imitate what they found, and that their literature must be moulded upon Greek models. I shall not lay stress on the old translation of the Odyssey into the rude Latin verse by Andronicus, who flourished as early as 240 B.C., but rather urge that he was the first to exhibit plays, tragedies, and comedies, and so introduce that kind of Greek amusement in Rome. Though, of course, there were but few who could follow Greek, even the Senate adopted the language about that time in sending replies to the Eastern powers. We have also noticed above their ludicrous attempt to pose as members of the Hellenistic world through their descent from the Trojans.

Presently come the times when Roman influence extended itself to the eastern side of the Adriatic, and Romans began to go as soldiers and diplomatists to Greek cities. We still feel, in our scanty evidence, the strong contrast observed among all men, between the calm, self-possessed, unlearned Romans, and the over-acute, mercurial, unstable, brilliant Greeks. It was a time, nevertheless, when the greater nation was deeply impressed with, and anxious to emulate, the less. To learn Greek must have become an important part of a Roman noble's education, especially if he meant to pursue diplomacy; but far beyond that, all felt obliged to pick up some of the current Greek ideas, in order to show that they too had attained Hellenistic culture. It is very curious and significant that Ennius, the Roman poet who introduced Greek hexameters into Latin, and gave the whole succeeding literature its Greek tone—translated for his people the most fashionable piece of Greek scepticism, the "Sacred History" of Euemerus of Messene, written at the court of Casander of Macedonia. The book was not new in Greece, and was noted for a blasphemy of scepticism even exceeding the license of these freethinking days. Euemerus held that except the nature gods, such as the sun and moon, all these personages were but deified mortals, who had lived long ago, and were dead—nay, their very tombs could still be found. It is hard to picture what would be the feelings of a quiet country Greek at hearing such a doctrine about Zeus, and Apollo, and Demeter, all of whom were entwined with his holiest associations. Possibly Euemerus meant to justify the deification of the Hellenistic sovrans, such as the Ptolemies and Seleucids, a practice which did not invade Italy till the days of Augustus. Such, however, was the Greek book chosen by Ennius to introduce to Roman society, and many who were learning Greek must have studied it.

In a previous chapter I pointed out how the same kind of thing took place as regards the stage. The plays translated and arranged by Plautus, and afterwards by Terence for the stage at Rome, were of a kind deeply antagonistic to the sound and healthy morals of the simple Romans of the third century B.C. The misfortunes of young girls, the profligate life not only of fashionable young men, but even of old men and married men, the prominence of parasites, and panders, and prostitutes—all this condoned and pictured as the life of refined and gentlemanly Athenians, as the highest outcome of good breeding—what could it produce at Rome except a very great moral earthquake, a feast upon the fruits of the tree of the knowledge of good and evil, a breakdown of all the old traditional education, and an epidemic of crude and disgusting scepticism?

People of high intellect and culture can resist such influences. The sceptics whom we find nowadays among the upper and thoughtful classes are not coarse and brutal. They do not violate decency and traditional morals, nor do they offend the sentiments of their believing neighbours; but the vulgar, the uneducated, or the half-educated who run into scepticism are very different indeed. If they adopt agnosticism or egotism as their creed, they parade it to the offence or the damage of their neighbour, and even vindicate with cynical frankness what those around them regard as gross crime.

One cannot but feel this kind of difference between the Romans and the Hellenistic states in the second century B.C.

In diplomacy, for example, there was as much playing with the truth among Syrian and Egyptian statesmen as there is now among Russians in their management of foreign affairs, or among Englishmen in party politics; but if we except the pirate Ætolian admirals of Philip V., who set up shrines to Impiety and Perjury, and who were regarded as outlaws and assassins by all the civilized states, we meet no such systematic and barefaced lying as was practised by Q. Marcius in his transactions with Philip, the Achæans, and the Rhodians. So also the manner in which the Senate first pampered and rewarded a power, like that of Eumenes, and enriched it at the expense of its neighbours, then jealously pulled it down the very instant their purpose had been attained, shows not only a total absence of justice, but a want of shame in parading this policy which astonishes us. Even worse, their usual method of accomplishing this end was to set up the son or brother of their ally as a pretender, and let him see that they encouraged his treachery, thus sowing the seed of crime in families, and violating the purest and best feelings of our nature. It is natural for the weak to have recourse to treachery and falsehood, but when the strong do so, it is from deliberate immorality, and from a feeling that it is more astute or more convenient to win by fraud than to employ force.

It seems, then, that sudden contact with this luxurious, rich, often depraved but highly cultivated East, had at first the most serious effects upon the Roman world. It encouraged not only lies, but brutality and cruelty, for we find that they behaved in their campaigns as hardly any Hellenistic power had, and we know that they were ready to massacre the inhabitants of any city for the mere benefit of their trade.

All these things rapidly bore their natural fruit. When diplomatists work only by lies, and generals go out to fight for booty, the better qualities soon die out, and selfishness soon breeds incapacity. The conduct of the war against Perseus shows the most extraordinary decadence in Roman warfare. Generals and troops were equally bent on plundering their helpless friends, and avoiding an encounter with their enemies. We have a lively picture (in Plutarch's *Life*) of the difficulties which the austere and the honourable Paullus Æmilius found, in making a serviceable army out of his materials; and we are told that if Perseus with his cavalry had supported the phalanx, before which the legions quailed, even Paullus would have been defeated.

So, then, the first spiritual result of Alexander's Empire on Rome was decidedly a failure. It was the shallower and somewhat debased Greek culture which we call Hellenism, which, in its superficial aspects, attracted and conquered the Romans. The old conservative people, like Cato, kept aloof from it. Some few really superior men, such as those whom Mommsen calls the Scipionic circle, felt their way through the mists of error and decay around it, and found the great truths which lay within; but the majority of fashionable young Romans took their notions from the plays, and their experiences at the court of Alexandria or at Athens, where all the sycophants and panders showed them vices by way of education.

Polybius gives us some curious details of how this Græcomania affected the Romans. He tells us of a certain Aulus Postumius, a young noble who affected Hellenism to such an extent as to disgust all his friends at Rome, nay even so as to disgust them with this kind of culture generally. At last he produced a Greek poem, and a history, in the preface of which he asked for pardon if, Greek not being his native tongue, he were guilty of solecisms. On this Cato remarked, that had he been ordered to write in Greek by some literary body, such excuses might find their place; but that now he was like a man putting down his name for an athletic contest, and then asking pardon of the spectators when he showed neither strength nor endurance. The rest of his life was, says Polybius, on a par. He copied the bad points in the Greeks, their love of pleasure and their idleness. He feigned sickness during a campaign in Greece, but was the first to write to the Senate about the battles, and describe his share in them.

Polybius further gives an account of the games produced by the prætor L. Anicius, who, in concert with Paullus, had subdued the Illyrians and Genthius their king, brought captive to Rome with Pesceus. He sent for all the best artists from Greece and setting up a great stage in the Circus, brought in all the flute-players. They were ordered all to blow together, and their chorus to dance. When they began their stately and orderly performance, it was voted slow by the audience, and the prætor sent them word he wanted something more lively in the way of a contest. Probably he thought the Greek word for a contest meant strictly a fight. When the artists were puzzled at this, one of the lictors explained what was meant, by turning them round at one another and gesticulating to show a fight. Then they saw their duty, and forming their chorus into two parts all blew at random, and advanced against one another, and retired. But when one of the chorus squared up in a boxing attitude at one of the great flute players, there burst out shouts of applause. Then solo dancers and boxers together with trumpet blowers ascended the stage, and there ensued a free fight, to the enthusiasm of the Romans. Polybius adds that what he has to say about the tragedies and their performance will seem ribald talk. Unfortunately his remarks are not preserved. Such was the culture of the Roman public after nearly half a century of contact with Hellenism.

The reaction upon the East was not less unfortunate. As the Roman snob wanted to pose as an Athenian, so the princes of the East, especially those who had been hostages or envoys at Rome, learned all the faults and insolences of the Roman character; and if they could not pose as Romans, at least professed to admire everything that was done in Rome, and to flatter and corrupt the Italians who came in contact with them. The pictures drawn by Polybius of the Philo-Roman party are those of a very hostile witness, and perhaps not more trustworthy than the characters now given by Irish politicians to their opponents ; yet we cannot but admit some truth in Polybius's case. He exaggerates their guilt when he omits giving the one strong motive of these anti-national politicians. They had property, and they felt that if a home democracy prevailed they would be despoiled. This was a strong and natural motive, and palliates their want of patriotism ; it is hard for men to admit that a policy of plunder is to be endured, even when it assumes a more respectable name. Still, when the anti-national party triumphed, they got small profit by their victory. Roman selfishness and greed very soon made terrible inroads upon the prosperity of the Hellenistic world. We know from the increasing depopulation of Greece, how wretchedly that country and Macedonia must have fared. The great marts of the Greek world, Corinth and Rhodes, were ruined, and the main industries of Macedonia forbidden by law. Still worse, the Rhodian control of the seas fell away with their decadence, and Cilicia and Crete began to swarm with those pirates who justified their cruelties as fair reprisals upon Roman injustice, and increasing their power as the carelessness or home policy of Rome prevented interference, became at last a disgrace which was used by party men to overthrow the constitution of the Republic.

While all these public mischiefs were developed there was secretly and almost silently a great gain to the civilized world being secured. The purest and best of the Romans were in real earnest learning from the best of the Greeks that knowledge of philosophy, of history, of poetry, of the plastic arts, which was ultimately spread over the world in Roman form. While Plautus and Terence were rendering Greek comedy into Latin, and tragedy was similarly handled, men like Polybius lived in great Roman houses, and by long and intimate intercourse produced that effect which the brilliant lectures of philosophers on stray visits could not attain.

Polybius speaks as if he were the only one of the Achæan exiles who had this good fortune, but we may be full sure that many others of the Scipios' friends chose educated men among the thousand captives who were kept so many years in Italy, and thus the fashion came in of having a learned Greek in the household, like a domestic chaplain. Presently the Romans imported from Alexandria grammar and criticism; then the Alexandrian poetry, and a school of Latin elegiac and lyric poets arose, based upon the fashionable Hellenistic poets, Philetas, Callimachus, and their fellows. It was to these, and not to the older and purer models, that the first Latin poets turned.

Then came the transference of the other art. In architecture especially (in which the Romans were great practical men), they added the Greek architrave in its newest or Corinthian form to the Roman arch, and in this mongrel style built vast temples over the world—Roman, indeed, in vastness and real meaning, but Hellenistic in beauty and expression. When the splendours of Palmyra and Baalbec rose in the old homes of the Seleucid Macedonians, they represent the spirit of the Empire of Alexander which had never died; which, after centuries of foreign life in the heart of Rome, came back to adorn the distant regions, where it had made its earliest and perhaps its greatest conquests.

THE END.

LIST OF NAMES EASILY CONFOUNDED.

In order to save the reader from confusion in reading a history where the same names are so constantly repeated, a catalogue is appended of the principal namesakes, with such details as will enable any intelligent person to distinguish them easily.

Agathocles, eldest son of Lysimachus (married to Lysandra), an able general, and heir to the throne of Thrace; murdered by Ptolemy Keraunos and Arsinoe.
———— of Syracuse, famous adventurer and tyrant of Syracuse, whose daughter Lanassa first married Pyrrhus and then king Demetrius.
Agis III., king of Sparta during Alexander's campaigns; defeated and slain by Antipater.
—— IV., king of Sparta about 244 B.C., social and political reformer; put to death by the ephors.
Alexander the Great, strictly Alexander III. of Macedon.
———— IV., his son by Roxane, murdered by Casander while yet a boy.
———— the Molossian, brother of Olympias, and hence brother-in-law to Alexander the Great, who made campaigns in South Italy, and was there killed.
———— son of Pyrrhus, his successor on the throne of Epirus, and last king.
———— son of Casander, put to death by king Demetrius.
———— satrap of Persia who revolted under Antiochus III.[1]
Antigonus, called Monophthalmos, the one-eyed, satrap of Phrygia under Alexander, then the foremost among the Diadochi, father of king Demetrius; killed at Ipsus (B.C. 301).
———— Gonatas, his grandson, king of Macedonia for thirty-four years.
———— Doson, nephew to Gonatas, son of Demetrius the Fair, king of Macedonia.

[1] There are fourteen other Alexanders known in the history of the period.

Antiochus I., called Soter, son of Seleucus I. Soter, king of Syria and the Eastern provinces.
———— II., called Theos, his son and successor.
———— Hierax, younger son of Antiochus II., ruling Asia Minor and warring against his brother, Seleucus II.
———— III., the Great, younger son of Seleucus II., king of Syria for thirty-five years; defeated at Magnesia (B.C. 190).
———— IV., Epiphanes, eldest son of Antiochus III., King of Syria, was master of Egypt till stopped by the Romans.[1]
Arsinoe, daughter of Ptolemy Soter and Berenice, married to king Lysimachus; then betrothed to Ptolemy Keraunos, who murdered her children; then finally married to her brother Philadelphus.
———— daughter of Lysimachus by Nikæa, first wife of Ptolemy Philadelphus, but divorced, when he married his sister, the other Arsinoe just named.[2]
Attalus, a Macedonian prince, uncle to Philip of Macedon's second wife Cleopatra, and general of Philip.
———— brother of Philetærus, the first dynast of Pergamum.
———— I., king of Pergamum, son of the last.
———— II., king of Pergamum, son of the last; succeeded his elder brother Eumenes.
———— III., king of Pergamum, son of Eumenes II., the last king of Pergamum.
Berenice (Bernice), daughter of Lagus, married to Ptolemy I., her half-brother, and mother of Ptolemy II. and his wife Arsinoe.
———— daughter of Magas, betrothed to Demetrius the Fair, then married to Ptolemy III.
———— daughter of Ptolemy II., and married to Antiochus II.; murdered by his first wife.[3]
Demetrius I., king of Macedonia, son of Antigonus, and known as Poliorcetes, the Besieger.
———— of Phalerum, philosopher, and viceroy of Athens under Casander B.C. 317-307, till expelled by the former Demetrius, when he went to Egypt to Ptolemy I.
———— the Fair, younger son of Demetrius I., sent to Cyrene by his brother Antigonus Gonatas.
———— II., king of Macedonia, son of Antigonus Gonatas, killed in battle B.C. 229.
———— of Pharos, an Illyrian prince defeated by the Romans; adviser to Philip V.[4]

[1] See under "Seleucus" the alternation of the two names in the Seleucid dynasty.
[2] Arsinoe was, moreover, the name of at least fifteen towns founded by the Ptolemies.
[3] We know of ten cities called by this name.
[4] Eight other Demetrii are known in the period.

NAMES EASILY CONFOUNDED.

Eumenes of Cardia, private secretary, afterwards general to Alexander the Great, supported his family against Antigonus, and after great wars was taken and put to death in Gabiene.

———— I., brother of Philetærus of Pergamum, afterwards dynast there.

———— II., cousin to the former, son of Attalus I., king of Pergamum.

Philip of Macedon, Alexander the Great's father, known as Philip II.

———— Arridæus, half-brother of Alexander the Great, known as Philip III. (Alexander's successor).

———— IV., son of Casander, titular king of Macedon just before Demetrius I.

———— V., the antagonist of the Romans, father of Perseus; son of Demetrius the Fair.[1]

Ptolemies occur in regular succession as kings of Egypt, denoted by numbers and distinct epithets, viz.: I., Soter; II., Philadelphus; III., Euergetes; IV., Philopator; V., Epiphanes; VI., Philometor; VII., Euergetes II.

Ptolemy Keraunos was the eldest son of Ptolemy I., Soter, exiled; for a year king of Macedon.[2]

Seleucus I. (Nicator), general of Alexander, then king of the Eastern provinces, father of Antiochus I., grandfather of Antiochus II.

———— II. (Callinicus), son of Antiochus II., fourth king of Syria and Eastern provinces.

———— III. (Soter), son of the last, also king of Syria.

———— IV. (Philopator), younger son of Antiochus III., king of Syria; succeeded by his elder brother, Antiochus IV. (Epiphanes).[3]

---

[1] Seventeen other Philips occur in the history of the time.

[2] Fifteen other Ptolemies occur besides these kings.

[3] The cities Seleucia on the Orontes and Seleucia on the Tigris should also be carefully distinguished. There were eleven other cities, of less note, called by the name.

INDEX.

A

Abydos, siege of, 253
Academy, the, founded by Plato, 97; importance of its teachers, 107; furnishes model for Alexandrian Library, 143
Academy, the New, embraces the conclusions of Scepticism, 103
Acarnanians apply to Rome, 184
Achæan League, 62; its opposition to Antigonus Gonatas, 118; its spread, 168-169; its character, 178; its officers, 179; defeated by Cleomenes, 208; remains neutral in war between Philip and Rome, 254; joins Rome, 255; treatments of by Rome, 277; attains its greatest magnitude, 282; supports Rome against Perseus, 294; leading members of, transported to Rome, id.
Achæus, expedition of, against Attalus, 213; revolts against Antiochus III., 227; besieged in Sardis, 229; his death, 230
Açoka embraces Buddhism, 140
"Acontius and Cydippe," 152
Adule, inscription of, 160
Ægion meeting-place of League, 179
Ætolian League, opposition of, to Antigonus Gonatas, 118; its spread, 162; its character, 181; its effects on Greece, 182; its attitude in Cleomenic War, 207; enmity of against Macedonia, 238; makes treaty with Rome, 241; joins Rome against Philip, 254; supports Antiochus, 262; its opposition to Rome, 281; crushed, 282
Ætolians offer to mediate in Siege of Rhodes, 62; importance of 79, 91
Agathocles, minister of Ptolemy Epiphanes, 248
Agis, schemes of, 172; death of, 173; dealings of, with Aratus, 174
Alexander the Great, begins new epoch, 2; parentage and youth of, 4-7; accused of being implicated in his father's assassination, 8; present at Chæronea, 9; his improvements on Philip's military system, 10; Illyrian campaign, id.; destroys Thebes, 11; starts for Asia, 15; defeats Persians at Granicus, id.; at Issus, 20; his military tactics, 23; takes Tyre, id.; wins battle of Arbela, 24; marries daughter of Darius, 28; and Roxana, 33; marches into India, 36; wounded by the Malli, 37; his mode of life, 40; his death, 41; his children, 42; influence of his example in producing monarchical form of government, 56; contrast between him and the philosophers, 99; modifies Greek idea of monarchy, id.; the one lasting results of his conquests, 277
Alexander's Empire passes finally under Roman sway, 298; injurious effects of on Rome, 305
"Alexandra" of Lycophron, 151

Alexandria (Egypt) founded, 24;
description of, 120-122; scholarship of 222; Library of. (*See Library.*)
American Federation compared to Achæan, 182
Anacleteria explained, 268
Ancyra, monument of, 83
Andronicus translates Odyssey, and writes plays, &c., 301
Antigoneia founded, 212
Antigonus Monophthalmos, general under Alexander, 8; Satrap of Phrygia, 46; assists Eumenes in Paphlagonia, *id.*; conquers Eumenes, 50; drives Seleucus from Babylon, *id.*; murders Cleopatra, 54; wars with Ptolemy, 58; coalition against, 65; his defeat and death, 67
Antigonus Gonatas, claimant for throne of Macedonia 73, 75; defeats Celts, 80; wars with Pyrrhus, 87; parentage and youth of, 115; reign of, 117; his efforts to counteract Ætolian and Æchæan Leagues, 118; joins Ætolian League, 169
Antigonus Doson, history of, 200; campaign of against Egypt, 201; called by Aratus to aid Achæan League, 209; becomes master of it, 211; takes Mantinea, 212; defeats Cleomenes, 215; death of 216
Antioch, description of, 136
Antiochus I. Soter defeats Celts, 80; difficulties of his reign, 136; his literary patronage, *id.*; his war with Eumenes and death, 137
Antiochus II., Theos, origin of surname of, 137; his successes and death, 138
Antiochus Hierax, 158; obtains Asia Minor, 187; attacks Galatians, *id.*; defeated by Attalus, 188
Antiochus III., the Great, accession of, 213; campaigns of, *id.*; his successes against Molon, 227; his campaign against Egypt, 228; captures Achæus, 230; attacks Parthians, *id.*; hailed as "the Great," 231; makes treaty with Philip, 247; campaign against Egypt, *id.*; defeats Scopas, 252; attacks Macedonian possessions, 261; takes Eubœa, 262; defeated at Thermopylæ, 263; and at Magnesia, 264; death, 265
Antiochus IV., Epiphanes, accession of, 296; his character, 297; his Egyptian campaigns, *id.*; restrained by Rome, 298
Antipater, General under Alexander, 8; his arbitrary conduct complained of by Olympias, 40; receives government of Macedonia, 45; disinherits Casander, *id.*; wages Lamian War, 48; procures death of Demosthenes and Hypereides, 49; his settlement of Greece, *id.*; becomes guardian of Royal House, 51; death of, 51; leaves Polysperchon regent, *id.*
Apollodorus, subject of tragedy by Lycophron, 84; subdued by Antigonus Gonatas, 116
Apollonius Rhodius, Librarian at Alexandria, 144; his poems, 151
Arabia circumnavigated, 160
Aratus, makes peace with Antigonus Gonatas, 119; early life of, 164; frees Argos, 167; takes Corinth, 168; dealings of, with Agis, 174; his policy, 180, 203; his death, 240
Aratus the Astronomer, 136; poem of, 151
Arbela, battle of, 24
"Arcadia" of Sannazaro, 146
Architecture of Rome indebted to Greece, 309
Areus, Spartan commander in Chremonidean War, 117
Argos, battle at, 87; freed by Aratus, 167
Aristarchus of Samos, 144, 222
Aristomenes, Minister in Egypt, 267
Aristophanes, of Byzantium, 144
Aristotle, teacher of Alexander, 9; theoretical nature of his philosophy, 97
Armenia, kingdom of, 90

INDEX.   317

Arridæus, see Philip Arridæus
Arsacids seize Atropatene, 219, 257
Arsinoe, married to Lysimachus, 71;
  to Ptolemy Keraunos, 74; to
  Ptolemy Philadelphus, *id.*; her
  complaisance, 132
Athens, governed by Demetrius of
  Phaleron, 51; hails Demetrius
  Poliorcetes king, 56; heads Greek
  coalition in Chremonidean War,
  117
Atropatene, kingdom of, 90; its revolt,
  139; seized by Arsacids, 219
Attalids, princes in Pergamum succeed to Asiatic part of Lysimachus'
  dominion, 46
Attalus I. defeats Galatæ, 83, 188;
  and Hierax, 188; joins Rome
  against Philip, 236; defeats Philip,
  248
Attalus II. succeeds Eumenes, 292
Attalus III. bequeaths his kingdom
  to Rome, 292
Attica, devastated by Philip, 253
Autonomy, communal, 57; instinct
  of a Greek mind, 176

B

Babylon, History of, translated by
  Berosus, 137
Bactria, conquered by Alexandria, 35;
  kingdom of, 90; its revolt, 139;
  cut off from Hellenism, 257
Berenice, married to Ptolemy Euergetes, 119
Berosus, the Chaldæan, 137
Bessus murders Darius, 28; executed
  by Alexander, *id.*
Buddhism, spread of, 140
Byzantium attempts to levy customs,
  235

C

Callicrates makes secret arrangement
  with Rome, 287
Callimachus, librarian at Alexandria,
  144; poems of, 151; his "Acontius and Cydippe," 152
Cardahar, etymology of name, 92
Canopus, decree of, 268

Cappadocia, kingdom of, 90
Carthage, interference of, in struggle
  between West and East, 88; Hellenism in, 220
Casander, disinherited by Antipater,
  45; opposes Polysperchon, 51;
  re-introduces order into Athens, *id.*;
  secured in possession of Macedonia,
  52; murders Roxana and her son
  Alexander, 53; his policy, 58; his
  death, 70
"Cassandra," see "Alexandra"
Cato, Tribune at battle of Thermopylæ, 263; his policy, 280
Catullus, poem of, 160
Celts, invasion of, 16; cross into
  Asia Minor, 80; settle in Galatia,
  80; defeated by Romans, 83, 265;
  effects of their invasion on Hellenism,
  84; attacked by Hierax, 187;
  defeated by Attalus, 188
Champollion discovered alphabet of
  hieroglyphics, 271
Chandragupta, alliance of, with Seleucus, 65
Chremonidean War, 117
Cilician Pirates, 308
Cleanthes, teacher of Stoicism, 105
Cleomenes, successes of, 202; his
  reforms at Sparta, 205; defeats
  Achæans, 208; his campaigns
  against Achæan League, 209; besieges Corinth, 210; takes Megalopolis, 212; defeated by Antigonus,
  215; flies to Egypt, *id.*; death of,
  216
Cleopatra, sister of Alexander, 43;
  her intended marriage, 46; murdered, 54
Colossus of Rhodes, 190
Coma Berenices, poem of Catullus,
  160
Comedy, the New, life depicted in,
  109, 110; influence of, on Roman
  morality, 303
Corinth, battle at, 117; taken by
  Aratus, 178; besieged by Cleomenes,
  210; decadence of, 308
Coron, battle at, 73
Cos, battle at, 118
Cosmas Indicopleustes, 160

Crannon, battle of, 49
Crassus, Licinius, Roman general against Perseus defeated, 289
Craterus, death of, 46, 50
Crates, 189
Criticism, origin of, 145
Cynoscephalæ, battle of, 255
Cyrene, expedition of Demetrius the Fair to, 119

D.

"Daphnis and Chloe" of Longus, 151
Darius present at Issus, 20; his flight from Arbela, 27; his murder, 28; his character, id.
Delos declared a free port, 293
Demetrius Poliorcetes, hailed as king by Athenians, 56; his successes against Casander, 59; besieges Rhodes, 60; his victories in Greece, 65; recalled by Antigonus, 66; present at Ipsus, 67; his adventures and final capture by Seleucus, id.
Demetrius Phalereus rules Athens, 51; originates Alexandrian Library, 143
Demetrius the Fair, brother of Antigonus Gonatas, 117; his death, 119
Demetrius II., history of, 162; wars with Ætolia, 185; death of, 186
Demetrius of Pharos expelled by Rome, 237; adviser of Philip V., 239
Demetrius, son of Philip V., death of, 279
Demosthenes, opinion of, concerning Alexander, 10; banished from Athens, 40; death of, 49
Diadochi, division of empire among, 49; assume titles of kings, 56
Dolopians punished by Perseus, 288

E

Egypt, conquered by Alexander, 24; ruled by Ptolemy son of Lagus, 45; attacked by Perdiccas, 47; its natural security against invasion, 48; its traffic, 89; its supremacy in the East, 158; attacked by Antiochus III., 247; national opposition of, to rule of Ptolemies, 272; its gains and losses in territory, 275; attacked by Antiochus IV., 297; finally settled, 299; early intercourse of, with Rome, 301
Elegy, origin of, 146
Ennius translates Euemerus, 302
Epicureanism, rise of, 101; its teaching, 103, 104; its cosmopolitanism, 105; its points of dissimilarity to Stoicism, 105, 106; teaches Quietism, 106
Epicurus, teaching of, 103
Epigoni, 76
Epiphanes, see Ptolemy
Epirus, rise of kingdom of, 92; abolishes royalty, 170; treatment of by Rome, 292
Eratosthenes, works of, 144; his discoveries, 164
Esne, temple of, 160
Eucleidas present at Sellasia, 215
Euemerus of Messene, 223, 302
Euergetes, 194; and see Ptolemy
Eumenes of Cardia assisted in Paphlagonia by Antigonus, 46; supports Perdiccas, 47; declared public enemy by Macedonians, 50; his wars with Antigonus, id.; his death, id.
Eumenes I., repels Antiochus Soter, 137
Eumenes II., friendly to Rome, 263; his increase of dominion, 275; loses favour of Rome, 292
Eurydike, wife of Philip Arridæus, murdered, 52
Euthydemus, sovereign of Bactria, 230

F

Federations among Greek cities, 57; their increase in wealth and reputation, 62; necessity for, 177
Flamininus, Roman general against Philip, 255; defeats him, 256; Policy of, in Greece, id.; and 280; character of, 259; forbearance of, 260.

Freeman, Professor, on Federation, 176, 182.

G
Galatæ, see Celts
Gaugamela, battle of, 24
Glabrio, Roman commander against Antiochus, 262
Granicus, battle of, 15
Greek Literature, see Literature
Greek language used by Rome in correspondence with foreign powers, 301
Greek, translations into, made by order of Antiochus Soter, 137
Greeks, freedom of, declared, 260

H
Halicarnassus taken by Alexander, 19
Harpalus, flight of, from Babylon to Athens, 40
Hecatombaeon, battle of, 208
Hellenedom, politics and intellect of, fused with Eastern manners, 34
Hellenism, general epoch of, 55; effects of Celtic invasion on, 84; golden age of, 111; two special epochs of, 113; last independent act of, 114; wide-embracing character of, 137; extended to the boundaries of the Tartars, 139; unity of language in, 154, 220; commerce of, 198, 221; power of falls to secondary states, 219; boundaries of, 220; literature and scholarship of, 221, 222; religious feeling of, 223; science of, 224; losses of, 257; efforts of Rome to get a place in, 300; unfavourable influences of, on Rome, 305; reaction of Rome on, 307; arts of, spread over the world in Roman form, 309
Hellenistic cities, objects of the foundation of, 92; composition of their population, 94; their uniform construction, 95
Herakles illegitimate son of Alexander, 43; his elevation and death, 54

Hermeias of Caria, 213
Homer, text of, emended, 144
Horace, models of, 153
Hyperbatos, Commander of Achæan League, 208
Hypereides, death of, 49

I
Idyll, the pastoral, origin of, 146
Indicopleustes, 160
Ipsus, battle of, 67
Illyria cowed by Rome, 237
Issus, battle of, 20

J
Jews alienated from Ptolemies' side with Antiochus, 252

K
Keraunos, see Ptolemy Keraunos

L
Lævinus sent to synod of Ætolians, 241
Lamian War, 48
Land Question at Sparta, 172
Laodike, wife of Antiochus Theos, 138
Leonidas, King of Sparta, 173
Leonnatus, death of, 46, 49
Leosthenes, Greek commander in Lamian War, 48; killed, 49
Lepidus, Roman Ambassador to Egypt, 252; and to Philip, 253
Library and Museum of Alexandria, foundation and character of, 143, 144
Literature, character of, at Alexandria, 145; at Pergamum, 189
Literature, poorness of, in Hellenistic centres, 221; effect of on Roman Poetry, 309
Literature of Greece, influence of on Roman Literature, 301
Longus, "Daphnis and Chloe" of, 151
Lucretius, exponent of Epicureanism, 104
Lycia, League of, 183
Lycophron, tragedy of Apollodorus by, 84; his "Cassandra," 151

Lycortas, General of Achæan League, 283
Lysimacheia, founded, 58; battle at, 80
Lysimachus, satrap in Thrace, 26; his expedition against Antigonus, 66; his power, 69, 70; slain, 73

M

Macedonia, description of, 89; Roman decree against, 291; division of, id.; trade of, paralysed, 292
Macedonian Army, change in habits of, 34; discontent of, 36; mutiny and submission of, 38
Macedonian governors, corruption of, 39
"Macedonians," Household Troops of Alexander, 251, 257
Machanidas, tyrant of Sparta, 238; death of, 241
Magnesia, battle of, 264
Malli, taken by Alexander, 37
Manetho, translates History of Egypt, 137
Mantinea, taken by Antigonus, 212; battle at, 241
Marcius, Quintus, diplomacy of, 289; enters Macedonia, 290
Margos of Keryneia, 178
Marine Law established, 58, 193
Megalopolis joins Achæan League, 171; proposes embassy to Antigonus, 207; taken by Cleomenes, 212
Meleager declares Philip Arridæus king, 44
Memnon, commands for Darius, 16; his death, 19
Mentor, General of Darius, 16
Messene, Wars of, with Achæans, 283
Molon, revolt of, 213; his death, 227
Monarchy becomes accepted form of Government, 55; its nature, id.; recommended by Greek philosophers, 56
Museum, origin of the title, 143; of Alexandria, see Library
Myonnesus, battle at, 263

N

Nabis, tyrant of Sparta, 244; attacks Achæans, 281; his death, 282
Neoptolemus, death of, 50

O

Olympias married to Philip of Macedon, 7; accused of being implicated in the assassination of her husband, 8; complains of Antipater, 40; murders Arridæus, 52; her death, id.

P

Panion, battle of, 252
Paphlagonia obtained by Eumenes, 46
Parmenio, General under Alexander, 8
Parthia, foundation of monarchy of, 219; attacked by Antiochus, 230
Pater, Mr. Walter, exponent of Epicurism, 104
Paullus Æmilius defeats Perseus at Pydna, 290
Peræa, 198, 287
Perdiccas appointed regent, 44; attacks Egypt, 47; killed, 48
Pergamum, kingdom of, founded, 91; neutrality of, 114; becomes leader of Hellenism, 159; its school of sculpture, 188; and of literature, 189; its strength and its weakness, 275
Peripatetic school of philosophy, 107
Persæus, Stoic philosopher, 100
Perseus, son of Philip V., 279; his preparations against Rome, 285; punishes Dolopians, 288; begins war with Rome, 289; defeats Licinius Crassus, id.; defeated at Pydna, 290; his death, 291
Persian Empire, character and topography of, 31, 33
Phila, sister of Casander and wife of Demetrius Poliorcetes, 68
Philadelphus, meaning of, 132
Philetærus, first of Attalids, 91

Philip II. of Macedon compared to Peter the Great, 4; to Victor Emanuel, 7; his marriages, *id.*; his assassination, *id.*

Philip Arridæus, son of Philip II., 43; proclaimed king, 44; murdered by order of Olympias, 52

Philip V., accession of, 237; wishes to join Punic War, 238; campaign of, against Ætolian League, *id.*; makes treaty with Hannibal, 239, 240; inaction of, 240; tyranny of, *id.*; makes peace with Rome, 242; evil policy of, 244; makes treaty with Antiochus III., 247; defeated at Samos, 248; devastates Attica, 253; military ability of, 254; defeated at Cynoscephalæ, 256; his part in war between Rome and Antiochus III., 277; treatment of, by Rome, *id.*; his domestic troubles and death, 279; his character, *id.*

Philopœmen opposes Cleomenes, 212; general of Achæan League, 241; leaves Greece, 254; returns, 282; his death, 283

Philosophy, rise and spread of, 96, 97; theoretical nature of, at the first, *id.*; obtains public importance, 100; takes a practical tone, 100–103; general effect of, on the age, 107

Plato, theoretical nature of philosophy of, 96, 97; claims pre-eminence for monarchy, 98

Pleiad, the, 152

Plutarch's *Lives*, 59, 67, 85, 163, 173, 215, 305; influence of, on the world, 223

Polybius on Greek trade, 234; life of, 295; history of, *id.*; gives us examples of Græcomania at Rome, 306

Polysperchon appointed Regent, 51; proclaims the liberty of the Greeks, *id.*

Pontus, kingdom of, 90

Popilius Lænas checks Antiochus IV., 298

Perus, death of, 65

Postumius Aulus, Græcomania of, 306

Prusias of Bithynia aids Rhodes against Byzantium, 236

Ptolemies, wars of, with the Seleucids, 113

Ptolemy I. Soter takes government of Egypt, 45; attacked by Perdiccas, 47; wars of, with Antigonus, 58; his descendants, 71; his death, 73

Ptolemy II. Philadelphus marries daughter of Lysimachus. 72; wars of, with Antigonus Gonatas, 117; urges Greeks to claim their liberty *id.*; his policy, 120; his researches, 131; marries his sister Arsinoe, 132; his amours, *id.*

Ptolemy III. Euergetes, marriage of, 119; wars of, with Syria, 157; circumnavigates Arabia, 160; becomes head of Achæan League, 169; death, 215

Ptolemy IV. Philopator attacked by Antiochus III., 228; his character and death, 232, 233

Ptolemy V. Epiphanes, accession of, 248; ceremony at his coronation, 268; his death, 278

Ptolemy VI. Philometor, deposed, 297

Ptolemy VII. Euergetes II. called Physcon, placed on the throne, 297

Punjab conquered by Alexander, 39

Pydna, battle of, 290

Pyrrho, Teacher of Scepticism, 103

Pyrrhus, King of Epirus, 68; checked by Lysimachus, 70; bribed to invade Italy, 73; his youth and marriage, 85; campaigns of, in Italy, Sicily, and Greece, 86, 87; his death and character, 87

R

Raphia, battle of, 229

Representative Government, idea of foreign to Greek mind, 177

Rhakotis, 121

Rhodes, organizes a federation, 57; besieged by Demetrius, 60; neutral policy of, 114; becomes a leader of Hellenism, 159; history of, 190; wars of, with Euergetes, 194; earthquake at, 197; interference of, with Byzantium, 235; defeats Philip, 248; opposition of, to Eumenes, 275; commerce of, destroyed by Rome, 293; intercourse of, with Rome in early times, 300; decadence of, 308

Romance, rise of, 146; new veins of, 152

Rome, attack on, meditated by Alexander, 38; probable effects on, of such a war, 39; friendship of, courted by Ptolemy Philadelphus, 120; applied to by Acarnanians, 184; endeavours to gain a place in Hellenism, 185; war of, with Teuta, 186; successes of, against the Greeks, 200; interference of, in Greece delayed, 218; conquers Illyria, 237; makes treaty with Ætolians, 241; forces Philip to make peace, 242; arbiter of Eastern affairs, 248; becomes guardian of Ptolemy Epiphanes, 252; commences war with Philip V., 254; is victorious, 256; withdraws troops from Greek fortresses, 260; commences war with Antiochus III., 262; operations of, in Asia Minor, 265; becomes powerful over all the Empire of Alexander, 276; Greek states severely treated by, 277; different policies of, 280; inconsistency of dealings of, with Greek states, 286; declares war against Perseus, 289; treatment of Macedonia by, 291; of Epirus, 292; of Eumenes, *id.*; of Rhodes, 293; of Achæan League, 294; interferes with Antiochus IV., 298; intercourse of, with Greece in early times, 300; intercourse of, with Hellenistic world, 301; public immorality of, as compared with Greece, 304; injurious results of Alexander's Empire on, 305; Græcomania at, 306; inability of, to appreciate Greek art, 307; influence of, on manners of the East,

307, 308; transfers to itself Hellenistic arts, 309

Rosetta Stone, discovery of, 268; inscription on, 271

Roxana, wife of Alexander, 33; murdered, 52

S

"Sacred History" of Euemerus, 302
Samos, battle at, 248
Sandracottus, see Chandragupta
Sannazaro, "Arcadia" of, 146
Sardis, taken by Alexander, 19; besieged by Antiochus III., 229
Scepticism, rise of, 103
Science, advance of, at Alexandria, 161; in Hellenistic world, 224
Scipio, Lucius, commander at Magnesia, 264
Scopas of Ætolia, 248; defeated by Antiochus III., 252; his rapacity, 267; his death, *id.*
Sculpture, revival of, 79; at Pergamum, 188
Seleucia captured by Antiochus III., 228
Seleucidæ, wars of, against Ptolemies, 113
Seleucus I. Nicator appointed Chiliarch, 46; made satrap of Babylon, 49; flees to Egypt from Antigonus, 50; restored to Babylon, 58; his Eastern campaigns, 65; takes part in war against Antigonus, 65-67; captures Demetrius, 67; his power, 69; murdered by Keraunos, 73
Seleucus II. Callinicus, wars of, against Ptolemy III., 157; his death, 198
Seleucus III. Soter, death of, 213
Seleucus IV. Philopator, 278; his death, 296
Sellasia, battle of, 215
Septuagint, the, 137, 153
Sicyon joins Achæan League, 168
Society, state of, in Athens, 108, 109
Sogdiana conquered by Alexander, 35; its revolt, 139
Sosibius, minister of Ptolemy Philopator, 229, 232; regent for Ptolemy Epiphanes, 251

Sparta, poverty and insignificance of, 92; takes part in Chremonidean War, 117; institutions of, 171; detached from Achæan League, 238; captured by Philopœmen, 283

Sphærus, Stoic philosopher, 202

Spitamenes, 33

Stoicism, rise of, 101; its teaching, 105; and cosmopolitanism, *id.*; in many respects dissimilar to Epicureanism, 105, 106

Stoics, chiefly foreigners, 106; readiness of, to take part in public affairs, *id.*; influence of, on tone of Athens, 118; opposition of, to Antigonus, *id.*

Stratonice, 135

Swiss Confederation, similarity of, to Ætolian Confederation, 183

Syria, extent of, 90; fall of, 264; finally settled, 299

"Syrian Wars," 113

T

Teuta humbled by Rome, 186

Thebes destroyed by Alexander, 11

Theocritus, pastoral idylls of, 146

Theophiliscus, Rhodian admiral, 248

Theophrastus, peripatetic philosopher, 107

Thermopylæ, battle at, 263

Thermus, capital of Ætolian League, 181; taken by Philip, 238

Thrace, ruled by Lysimachus, 46

Tlepolemus, regent for Epiphanes, 251

Triparadeisus, meeting of Diadochi at, 49

Tylis, kingdom of, established, 235

Tyre taken by Alexander, 23

U

Upper Provinces of the East, revolt in, 138

V

Vergil, indebted to Apollonicus Rhodius, 151; to Aratus, 152

Vulso, Manlius, defeats Celts, 83, 265

X

Xanthippus, satrap of Persia and India, 159

Xenocrates, of the Academy, 100, 107

Xenon, member of Achæan League, 294

Z

Zeleia, scene of battle of Granicus, 15

Zeno, founder of Stoicism, 105

Zenodotus, librarian at Alexandria 144

Zenonians, see Stoics.

UNWIN BROTHERS, PRINTERS
LITTLE BRIDGE STREET, 73A, LUDGATE HILL, E.C.

St. Nicholas Magazine
FOR YOUNG FOLKS.
Edited by Mrs. MARY MAPES DODGE.

Price 1s. Monthly.

With the beginning of the Seventeenth Volume (*November*, 1889) ST. NICHOLAS will be enlarged by the addition of eight or more pages to each number, and the Magazine will be printed in a new and clearer-faced type. During the year there will be four important **Serial Stories** by well-known authors, and also **Notable Papers on Athletics and Outdoor Sports**, as well as a multitude of Occasional Papers, Stories, Illustrated Articles of Character and Adventure, Suggestive of Talks on Natural History, Scientific Subjects, &c. *The price will remain the same.*

The Century
ILLUSTRATED MONTHLY MAGAZINE.
Price 1s. 4d. Monthly.
FOR 1889-90,
Will include among other features:—

The Autobiography of Joseph Jefferson ("Rip Van Winkle"); "**Friend Olivia,**" a Serial Story by Mrs. BARR, Author of "Jan Vedder's Wife," &c.; "**The Merry Chanter,**" in Four Parts, by FRANK R. STOCKTON; **Letters from Japan,** by JOHN LA FARGE; and **The Gold Hunters of California,** being Personal Narratives of most Romantic Interest.

Besides the above Special Features there will be valuable Contributions in Prose and Verse by MARK TWAIN, EDMUND GOSSE, H. H. BOYESEN, HENRY JAMES, EDW. EGGLESTON, &c., &c.

The Century Dictionary.

In 24 Monthly Parts, Price 10s. 6d. each.

PART I. NOW READY.

When completed the work will form Six Volumes, price £2 2s. each.

A LIBRARY IN ONE BOOK,
Purchasers of this Dictionary will obtain a reference library which does away with a great number of other books. They will have—

1. A COMPLETE DEFINING DICTIONARY OF ENGLISH WORDS.
2. A DICTIONARY OF ETYMOLOGIES, UNEQUALLED BY ANY WORK YET PUBLISHED.
3. A STANDARD DICTIONARY OF SPELLING AND PRONUNCIATION.
4. AN ENCYCLOPÆDIA OF GENERAL INFORMATION, PARTICULARLY RICH IN HISTORICAL MATERIAL.
5. A STANDARD DICTIONARY OF MECHANICAL TERMS.
6. A COMPREHENSIVE DICTIONARY OF THE PRACTICAL ARTS AND TRADES, COMMERCE, FINANCE, ETC.
7. A DICTIONARY OF SCIENTIFIC TERMS, GIVING THE RESULT OF THE VERY LATEST THOUGHT IN EVERY DEPARTMENT OF SCIENCE, AS BIOLOGY, BOTANY, ZOOLOGY, MINERALOGY, PHYSICS, ETC.
8. A DICTIONARY OF MEDICINE, SURGERY, PHYSIOLOGY, ANATOMY, ETC.
9. A DICTIONARY OF THEOLOGICAL TERMS.
10. A DICTIONARY OF ART AND ARCHÆOLOGY, MYTHOLOGY, SCULPTURE, MUSIC, ETC., EXQUISITELY ILLUSTRATED.
11. A LAW DICTIONARY.
12. A STANDARD REFERENCE BOOK OF ENGLISH GRAMMAR AND PHILOLOGY.
13. A DICTIONARY OF SYNONYMS.
14. A TREASURY OF QUOTATIONS.

For Terms and Prospectuses apply to

T. FISHER UNWIN, 11, Paternoster Buildings, Paternoster Square, London, E.C.

Catalogue of Select Books in Belles Lettres, History, Biography, Theology, Travel, Miscellaneous, and Books for Children.

Belles Lettres.

The Letters of Horace Walpole. Selected and Edited, with Introduction and Notes, by CHARLES DUKE YONGE, M.A. Portraits and Illustrations. Limited Edition of 750 copies in Two Vols., medium 8vo., cloth, 32s.

The present selection comprises the more valuable portion of the famous letters to Thomas Gray the poet, Sir Horace Mann, and George Montagu, and is designed chiefly for those who, while lacking leisure to attack the bulk of the correspondence, may welcome the opportunity of becoming acquainted with "certainly the best letter-writer in the English language" (*vide* Sir Walter Scott).

The English Novel in the Time of Shakespeare. By J. J. JUSSERAND, Author of "English Wayfaring Life." Illustrated. Demy 8vo., cloth. The work is divided into six chapters:—I. Before Shakespeare; II. Lyly and his Euphues; III. The School of Lyly; IV. Sir Philip Sydney and the Pastoral romance; V. Thomas Nash and the picturesque romance; VI. After Shakespeare.

Light and Shadow: A Novel. By EDWARD GARNETT, Author of "The Paradox Club." Crown 8vo., cloth, 6s.

In Thoughtland and in Dreamland. By ELSA D'ESTERRE-KEELING, Author of "Three Sisters," "Bib and Tucker," &c. Square imperial 16mo., cloth, 6s.; Presentation Edition (uniform with the above), in Box, 7s. 6d

English Wayfaring Life in the Middle Ages (XIVth Century).
By J. J. JUSSERAND. Translated from the French by LUCY A. TOULMIN SMITH. Illustrated. Second Edition. Demy 8vo., cloth, 12s.

"This is an extremely fascinating book, and it is surprising that several years should have elapsed before it was brought out in an English dress. However, we have lost nothing by waiting."—*Times.*

Old Chelsea.
A Summer-Day's Stroll. By Dr. BENJAMIN ELLIS MARTIN. Illustrated by JOSEPH PENNELL. Second Edition. Crown 8vo., cloth, 7s. 6d.

"Dr. Martin has produced an interesting account of old Chelsea, and he has been well seconded by his coadjutor."—*Athenæum.*

The Twilight of the Gods.
By RICHARD GARNETT, LL.D. Crown 8vo., cloth, 6s.

"If imagination and style constitute the true elixir of literary life, Dr. Garnett's 'Twilight of the Gods' should live."—*British Weekly.*

The Coming of the Friars,
And other Mediæval Sketches. By the Rev. AUGUSTUS JESSOPP, D.D., Author of "Arcady: For Better, For Worse," &c. Third Edition. Crown 8vo., cloth, 7s. 6d.

Contents.—I. The Coming of the Friars.—II. Village Life in Norfolk Six Hundred Years ago.—III. Daily Life in a Mediæval Monastery.—IV. and V. The Black Death in East Anglia.—VI. The Building-up of a University.—VII. The Prophet of Walnut-tree Walk.

Arcady:
For Better, For Worse. By AUGUSTUS JESSOPP, D.D., Author of "One Generation of a Norfolk House." Portrait. Popular Edition. Crown 8vo., cloth, 3s. 6d.

"A volume which is, to our minds, one of the most delightful ever published in English."—*Spectator.*

The Romance of a Shop.
By the late AMY LEVY, Author of "Reuben Sachs," "A London Plane Tree, and Other Poems," &c. Crown 8vo., cloth, 6s.

"Miss Levy's story is bright and fresh; there is a dash of originality in the idea and plenty of spirit in its execution."—*Athenæum.*

The Paradox Club. By EDWARD GARNETT. With Portrait of Nina Lindon. Second Edition. Crown 8vo., limp cloth, 3s. 6d.

"Mr. Garnett's dialogue is often quite as good as his description, and in description he is singularly happy. The mystery of London streets by night is powerfully suggested, and the realistic force of his night-pieces is enhanced by the vague and Schumann-like sentiment that pervades them."—*Saturday Review.*

Euphorion : Studies of the Antique and the Mediæval in the Renaissance. By VERNON LEE. Cheap Edition, in one volume. Demy 8vo., cloth, 7s. 6d.

"It is the fruit, as every page testifies, of singularly wide reading and independent thought, and the style combines with much picturesqueness a certain largeness of volume, that reminds us more of our earlier writers than those of our own time."
Contemporary Review.

Studies of the Eighteenth Century in
Italy. By VERNON LEE. Demy 8vo., cloth, 7s. 6d.

"These studies show a wide range of knowledge of the subject, precise investigation, abundant power of illustration, and hearty enthusiasm. . . . The style of writing is cultivated, neatly adjusted, and markedly clever."—*Saturday Review.*

Belcaro : Being Essays on Sundry Æsthetical Questions. By VERNON LEE. Crown 8vo., cloth, 5s.

"This way of conveying ideas is very fascinating, and has an effect of creating activity in the reader's mind which no other mode can equal. From first to last there is a continuous and delightful stimulation of thought."—*Academy.*

Juvenilia : A Second Series of Essays on Sundry Æsthetical Questions. By VERNON LEE. Two vols. Small crown 8vo., cloth, 12s.

"To discuss it properly would require more space than a single number of 'The Academy' could afford. —*Academy.*
"Est agréable à lire et fait penser."—*Revue des deux Mondes.*

Baldwin : Dialogues on Views and Aspirations. By VERNON LEE. Demy 8vo., cloth, 12s.

"The dialogues are written with . . . an intellectual courage which shrinks from no logical conclusion."—*Scotsman.*

Ottilie : An Eighteenth Century Idyl. By VERNON LEE. Square 8vo., cloth extra, 3s. 6d.

"A graceful little sketch. . . . Drawn with full insight into the period described."—*Spectator.*

Introductory Studies in Greek Art.
Delivered in the British Museum by JANE E. HARRISON. With Illustrations. Square imperial 16mo., 7s. 6d.

'The best work of its kind in English."—*Oxford Magazine.*

The Fleet: Its River, Prison, and Marriages. By JOHN ASHTON, Author of "Social Life in the Reing of Queen Anne," &c. With 70 Drawings by the Author from Original Pictures. Second and Cheaper Edition, cloth, 7s. 6d.

Romances of Chivalry: Told and Illustrated in Fac-simile by JOHN ASHTON. Forty-six Illustrations. New and Cheaper Edition. Crown 8vo., cloth, 7s. 6d.

"The result (of the reproduction of the wood blocks) is as creditable to his artistic, as the text is to his literary, ability."—*Guardian.*

The Dawn of the Nineteenth Century in England: A Social Sketch of the Times. By JOHN ASHTON. Cheaper Edition, in one vol. Illustrated. Large crown 8vo., 10s. 6d.

"The book is one continued source of pleasure and interest, and opens up a wide field for speculation and comment, and many of us will look upon it as an important contribution to contemporary history, not easily available to others than close students."—*Antiquary.*

Legends and Popular Tales of the Basque People. By MARIANA MONTEIRO. With Illustrations by HAROLD COPPING. Popular Edition. Crown 8vo., cloth, gilt edges, 6s.

"In every respect this comely volume is a notable addition to the shelf devoted to folk-lore . . . . and the pictures in photogravure nobly interpret the text."—*Critic.*

Heroic Tales. Retold from Firdusi the Persian. By HELEN ZIMMERN. With Etchings by L. ALMA TADEMA. Popular Edition. Crown 8vo., cloth extra, 5s.

"Charming from beginning to end. . . . Miss Zimmern deserves all credit for her courage in attempting the task, and for her marvellous success in carrying it out."—*Saturday Review.*

Pilgrim Sorrow. By CARMEN SYLVA (The Queen of Roumania). Translated by HELEN ZIMMERN. Portrait-etching by LALAUZE. Square crown 8vo., cloth extra, 5s.

"A strain of sadness runs through the delicate thought and fancy of the Queen of Roumania. Her popularity as an author is already great in Germany, and this little work will win her a place in many English hearts."—*Standard.*

Chopin, and Other Musical Essays.

By HENRY T. FINCK, Author of "Romantic Love and Personal Beauty." Crown 8vo., cloth, 6s.

"There are six essays in this compact and well-printed volume. They are all written with great thoroughness, and the interest of each one is admirably sustained throughout."—*Freeman's Journal.*

The Temple: Sacred Poems and Private Ejaculations.

By Mr. GEORGE HERBERT. New and fourth edition, with Introductory Essay by J. HENRY SHORTHOUSE. Small crown, sheep, 5s.

A fac-simile reprint of the Original Edition of 1633.

"This charming reprint has a fresh value added to it by the Introductory Essay of the Author of 'John Inglesant.'"—*Academy.*

Songs, Ballads, and A Garden Play.

By A. MARY F. ROBINSON, Author of "An Italian Garden." With Frontispiece of Dürer's "Melancolia." Small crown 8vo., half bound, vellum, 5s.

"The romantic ballads have grace, movement, passion and strength."—*Spectator.*
"Marked by sweetness of melody and truth of colour."—*Academy.*

Essays towards a Critical Method. Studies in English

Literature. By JOHN M. ROBERTSON. Cr. 8vo., cloth, 7s. 6d.

"His essays are always shrewd and readable. His criticisms on the critics are enjoyable for the irony (conscious or unconscious) that is in them; and the book will not fail to please lovers of literature and literary history, and to prove suggestive to the critical."—*Scotsman.*

The Lazy Minstrel.

By J. ASHBY-STERRY, Author of "Boudoir Ballads." Fourth and Popular Edition. Frontispiece by E. A. ABBEY. Fcap. 8vo., cloth, 2s. 6d.

"One of the lightest and brightest writers of vers de société."
St. James's Gazette.

Caroline Schlegel, and Her Friends.

By Mrs. ALFRED SIDGWICK. With Steel Portrait. Crown 8vo., cloth, 7s. 6d.

"This is a singularly brilliant, delicate and fascinating sketch—one of the most skilful pieces of literary workmanship we have seen for a long time. . . . Mrs. Sidgwick is a writer of very unusual equipment, power and promise."
British Weekly.

Amos Kilbright: His Adscititious Adventures.

With other Stories. By FRANK R. STOCKTON. 8vo., cloth, 3s. 6d.

"Mr. Stockton is the quaintest of living humorists."—*Academy.*

History.

Battles and Leaders of the American Civil War.
An Authoritative History, written by Distinguished Participants on both sides. Edited by ROBERT U. JOHNSON and CLARENCE C. BUEL, of the Editorial Staff of "The Century Magazine." Four Volumes, Royal 8vo., elegantly bound, £5 5s.

LORD WOLSELEY, in writing a series of articles in the *North American Review* on this work, says: "The Century Company has, in my judgment, done a great service to the soldiers of all armies by the publication of these records of the great War."

Diary of the Parnell Commission.
Revised with Additions, from *The Daily News*. By JOHN MACDONALD, M.A. Large crown 8vo.

The End of the Middle Ages:
Essays and Questions in History. By A. MARY F. ROBINSON (Madame Darmesteter). Demy 8vo., cloth, 10s. 6d.

"We travel from convent to palace, find ourselves among all the goodness, the wisdom, the wildness, the wickedness, the worst and the best of that wonderful time. We meet with devoted saints and desperate sinners... We seem to have made many new acquaintances whom before we only knew by name among the names of history... We can heartily recommend this book to every one who cares for the study of history, especially in its most curious and ascinating period, the later middle age."—*Spectator*.

The Federalist:
A Commentary in the Form of Essays on the United States Constitution. By ALEXANDER HAMILTON, and others. Edited by HENRY CABOT LODGE. Demy 8vo., Roxburgh binding, 10s. 6d.

"The importance of the Essays can hardly be exaggerated."—*Glasgow Mail*.

The Story of the Nations.

Crown 8vo., Illustrated, and furnished with Maps and Indexes, each 5s.

"L'interessante serie l'Histoire des Nations formera . . . un cours d'histoire universelle d'une tres grande valeur."—*Journal des Débats.*
"The remarkable series."—*New York Critic.*
"That useful series."—*The Times.*
"An admirable series."—*Spectator.*
"That excellent series."—*Guardian.*
"The series is likely to be found indispensable in every school library."
"This valuable series."—*Nonconformist.*   *Pall Mall Gazette.*
"Admirable series of historical monographs."—*Echo.*

Rome. By ARTHUR GILMAN, M.A., Author of "A History of the American People," &c. Third edition.

The Jews. In Ancient, Mediæval, and Modern Times. By Prof. J. K. HOSMER. Second edition.

Germany. By Rev. S. BARING-GOULD, Author of "Curious Myths of the Middle Ages," &c. Second edition.

Carthage. By Prof. ALFRED J. CHURCH, Author of "Stories from the Classics," &c. Third edition.

Alexander's Empire. By Prof. J. P. MAHAFFY, Author of "Social Life in Greece." Fourth edition.

The Moors in Spain. By STANLEY LANE-POOLE, Author of "Studies in a Mosque." Third edition.

Ancient Egypt. By Canon RAWLINSON, Author of "The Five Great Monarchies of the World." Third edition.

Hungary. By Prof. ARMINIUS VAMBÉRY, Author of "Travels in Central Asia." Second edition.

The Saracens: From the Earliest Times to the Fall of Bagdad. By ARTHUR GILMAN, M.A., Author of "Rome," &c.

Ireland. By the Hon. EMILY LAWLESS, Author of " Hurrish." Third edition.

Chaldea. By Z. A. RAGOZIN, Author of " Assyria," &c. Second edition.

The Goths. By HENRY BRADLEY. Second edition.

Assyria : By ZÉNAÏDE A. RAGOZIN, Author of " Chaldea," &c.

Turkey. By STANLEY LANE-POOLE. Second edition.

Holland. By Professor THOROLD ROGERS. Second edition.

Mediæval France. By GUSTAVE MASSON. Second edition.

Persia. By S. G. W. BENJAMIN. Second edition.

Phœnicia. By CANON RAWLINSON.

Media. By Z. A. RAGOZIN.

The Hansa Towns. By HELEN ZIMMERN.

Early Britain. By Prof. A. J. CHURCH, Author of " Carthage," &c.

Russia. By W. R. MORFILL, M.A., Author of a " A Grammar of the Russian Language."

The Barbary Corsairs. By STANLEY LANE POOLE, Author of " The Moors in Spain," " Turkey," &c.

The Jews under the Roman Empire. By W. DOUGLAS MORRISON, M.A.

Scotland. By JOHN MACINTOSH, LL.D., Author of " The History of Civilisation in Scotland."

(*For further information, see " Nation Series" Catalogue. Sent to any address on application to the Publisher.*)

Biography.

Sir John Hawkwood (l'Acuto). Story of a Condottiere. Translated from the Italian of John Temple-Leader and Guiseppe Marcotti, by LEADER SCOTT. Illustrated. Royal 8vo., bound in buckram, gilt tops. Limited Edition.

Extract from Preface.—" He was for more than thirty years one of the most effective dominators of Italian affairs, and in her history—military, political, and social—he figures as a personage whose character and actions have an importance more than sufficient to justify the simple curiosity of biographical erudition."

The Life & Times of William Lloyd
GARRISON. From 1840—1879. By HIS CHILDREN. Vols. III. and IV., completing the work. Portraits and Illustrations. Demy 8vo., cloth, 30s.

Compiled by Mr. Garrison's two sons, Wendell Phillips Garrison, Literary Editor of the *Nation*, and his brother, F. J. Garrison, the above work is undoubtedly one of the most important contributions yet made to American history and biography. Among those with whom Mr. Garrison was at one time or another during his career associated, may be mentioned Mazzini, John Bright, J. S. Mill, Emerson, James Mott, William E. Channing, Whittier, Maria W. Chapman, Caleb Cushing, Lafayette, Wilberforce, Fowell Buxton, Daniel O'Connell, George Thompson, Zachary Macaulay, Clarkson, Harriett Martineau, Wendell Phillips, Mrs. Opie, Haydon, Lady Byron, Sir John Bowring, the Duchess of Sutherland, and others.

Good Men and True :
Biographies of Workers in the Fields of Beneficence and Benevolence. By ALEXANDER H. JAPP, LL.D. Illustrated. Crown 8vo., cloth, 6s.

CONTENTS:—I. Norman MacLeod, D.D.—II. Edward Denison.—III. Arnold Toynbee.—IV. John Conington.—V. Charles Kingsley.—VI. Bishop Hannington.—VII. The Stanleys: Father and Son.—VIII. Thomas Guthrie, D.D.—IX. Sir Titus Salt.—X. Samuel Plimsoll.

Life & Times of Girolamo Savonarola.
By PASQUALE VILLARI. Translated by LINDA VILLARI. Portraits and Illustrations. Two vols. Second Edition, with New Preface. Demy 8vo., cloth, 32s.

Anne Gilchrist : Her Life and Writings. Edited by Herbert Harlakenden Gilchrist. Prefatory Notice by William Michael Rossetti. Second edition. Twelve Illustrations. Demy 8vo., cloth, 16s.

Charles Dickens as I knew Him : The Story of the Reading Tours in Great Britain and America (1866-1870). By George Dolby. New and cheaper edition. Crown 8vo., 3s. 6d.

"It will be welcome to all lovers of Dickens for Dickens' own sake."—*Athenæum.*

Ole Bull : A Memoir. By Sara C. Bull. With Ole Bull's "Violin Notes" and Dr. A. B. Crosby's "Anatomy of the Violinist." Portraits. Second edition. Crown 8vo., cloth, 7s. 6d.

Johannes Brahms : A Biographical Sketch. By Dr. Herman Deiters. Translated, with additions, by Rosa Newmarch. Edited, with a Preface, by J. A. Fuller Maitland. Portrait. Small crown 8vo., cloth, 6s.

The Lives of Robert and Mary Moffat. By their Son, John Smith Moffat. Sixth edition. Portraits, Illustrations, and Maps. Crown 8vo., cloth, 7s. 6d. ; Popular Edition, crown 8vo., 3s. 6d..

"The biographer has done his work with reverent care, and in a straightforward unaffected style."—*Contemporary Review.*

The German Emperor and Empress : The Late Frederick III. and Victoria. The Story of their Lives. By Dorothea Roberts. Portraits. Crown 8vo., cloth, 2s. 6d.

"A book sure to be popular in domestic circles."—*The Graphic.*

Arminius Vambery : His Life and Adventures. Written by Himself. With Portrait and Fourteen Illustrations. Fifth and Popular Edition. Square Imperial 16mo., cloth extra, 6s.

"The work is written in a most captivating manner."—*Novoe Vremya, Moscow.*

Francis Bacon (Lord Verulam) : A Critical Review of his Life and Character, with Selections from his Writings. By B. G. Lovejoy, A.M., LL.B. Crown 8vo., half-bound cloth, gilt top, 6s.

Theology and Philosophy.

The Treasure Book of Consolation: For all in Sorrow or Suffering. By BENJAMIN ORME, M.A. Popular Edition. Crown 8vo., cloth extra, gilt edges, 3s. 6d.

The Questions of the Bible, Arranged in the Order of the Books of Scripture, with Connective Readings and Tables. By W. CARNELLEY. Demy 8vo., cloth, 7s. 6d.

"The book will be a useful one for theologians and students."—*Fireside News.*

"A book of peculiar value to all who study the Bible."—*Christian.*

The House and Its Builder, with Other Discourses: A Book for the Doubtful. By Dr. SAMUEL COX. Third Edition. Small crown 8vo., paper, 2s. 6d.; cloth, 3s.

"Expositions." By the same Author. In Four Volumes, demy 8vo., cloth, price 7s. 6d. each.

"We have said enough to show our high opinion of Dr. Cox's volume. It is indeed full of suggestion. . . . A valuable volume."—*The Spectator.*

"Here, too, we have the clear exegetical insight, the lucid expository style, the chastened but effective eloquence, the high ethical standpoint, which secured for the earlier series a well-nigh unanimous award of commendation."—*Academy.*

"When we say that the volume possesses all the intellectual, moral, and spiritual characteristics which have won for its author so distinguished a place among the religious teachers of our time . . . what further recommendation can be necessary?"—*Nonconformist.*

The Risen Christ: The King of Men. By the late Rev. J. BALDWIN BROWN, M.A. Second and Cheaper Edition. Crown 8vo., cloth, 3s. 6d.

"We have again felt in reading these nervous, spiritual, and eloquent sermons, how great a preacher has passed away."—*Nonconformist.*

Christian Facts and Forces. By the Rev. NEWMAN SMYTH, Author of "The Reality of Faith." New edition. Crown 8vo., cloth, 4s. 6d.

"An able and suggestive series of discourses."—*Nonconformist.*

"These sermons abound in noble and beautiful teaching clearly and eloquently expressed."—*Christian.*

Inspiration and the Bible: An Inquiry. By ROBERT HORTON, M.A., formerly Fellow of New College, Oxford. Fourth and Cheaper Edition. Crown 8vo., cloth, 3s. 6d.

"The work displays much earnest thought, and a sincere belief in, and love of the Bible."—*Morning Post.*

"It will be found to be a good summary, written in no iconoclastic spirit, but with perfect candour and fairness, of some of the more important results of recent Biblical criticism."—*Scotsman.*

Faint, yet Pursuing. By the Rev. E. J. HARDY, Author of "How to be Happy though Married." Sq. imp. 16mo., cloth, 6s. Cheaper Edition, 3s. 6d.

"One of the most practical and readable volumes of sermons ever published. They must have been eminently bearable."—*British Weekly.*

The Meditations and Maxims of Koheleth. A Practical Exposition of the Book of Ecclesiastes. By Rev. T. CAMPBELL FINLAYSON. Crown 8vo., 6s.

"A thoughtful and practical commentary on a book of Holy Scripture which needs much spiritual wisdom for its exposition. . . . Sound and judicious handling."—*Rock.*

The Pharaohs of the Bondage and the Exodus. Lectures by CHARLES S. ROBINSON, D.D., LL.D. Second edition. Large crown 8vo., cloth, 5s.

"Both lectures are conceived in a very earnest spirit, and are developed with much dignity and force. We have the greatest satisfaction in commending it to the attention of Biblical students and Christian ministers."—*Literary World.*

A Short Introduction to the History of Ancient Israel. By the Rev. A. W. OXFORD, M.A., Vicar of St. Luke's, Berwick Street, Soho, Editor of "The Berwick Hymnal," &c. Crown 8vo., cloth, 3s. 6d.

"We can testify to the great amount of labour it represents."—*Literary World.*

The Reality of Religion. By HENRY J. VAN DYKE, Junr., D.D., of the Brick Church, N.Y. Second edition. Crown 8vo., cloth, 4s. 6d.

"An able and eloquent review of the considerations on which the writer rests his belief in Christianity, and an impassioned statement of the strength of this belief."—*Scotsman.*

The Reality of Faith. By the Rev. NEWMAN SMYTH, D.D., Author of "Old Faiths in New Light." Fourth and cheaper edition. Crown 8vo., cloth, 4s. 6d.

"They are fresh and beautiful expositions of those deep things, those foundation truths, which underlie Christian faith and spiritual life in their varied manifestations."—*Christian Age.*

A Layman's Study of the English Bible Considered in its Literary and Secular Aspects. By FRANCIS BOWEN, LL.D. Crown 8vo., cloth, 4s. 6d.

"Most heartily do we recommend this little volume to the careful study, not only of those whose faith is not yet fixed and settled, but of those whose love for it and reliance on it grows with their growing years."—*Nonconformist.*

The Parousia. A Critical Inquiry into the New Testament Doctrine of Our Lord's Second Coming. By the Rev. J. S. RUSSELL, M.A. New and cheaper edition. Demy 8vo., cloth, 7s. 6d.

"Critical, in the best sense of the word. Unlike many treatises on the subject, this is a sober and reverent investigation, and abounds in a careful and instructive exegesis of every passage bearing upon it."—*Nonconformist.*

The Ethic of Freethought: A Selection of Essays and Lectures. By KARL PEARSON, M.A., formerly Fellow of King's College, Cambridge. Demy 8vo., cloth, 12s.

"Are characterised by much learning, much keen and forcible thinking, and a fearlessness of denunciation and exposition."—*Scotsman.*

Descartes and His School. By Kuno Fischer. Translated from the Third and Revised German Edition by J. P. Gordy, Ph.D. Edited by Noah Porter, D.D., LL.D. Demy 8vo., cloth, 16s.

"A valuable addition to the literature of Philosophy."—*Scotsman.*

"No greater service could be done to English and American students than to give them a trustworthy rendering of Kuno Fischer's brilliant expositions."—*Mind.*

Socrates: A Translation of the Apology, Crito, and Parts of the Phædo of Plato. 12mo., cloth, 3s. 6d.

"The translation is clear and elegant."—*Morning Post.*

A Day in Athens with Socrates: Translations from the Protagoras and the Republic of Plato. 12mo., cloth, 3s. 6d.

"We can commend these volumes to the English reader, as giving him what he wants—the Socratic . . . philosophy at first hand, with a sufficiency of explanatory and illustrative comment."—*Pall Mall Gazette.*

Talks with Socrates about Life: Translations from the Gorgias and the Republic of Plato. 12mo., cloth, 3s. 6d.

"A real service is rendered to the general reader who has no Greek, and to whom the two ancient philosophers are only names, by the publication of these three inviting little volumes. . . . Every young man who is forming a library ought to add them to his collection."—*Christian Leader.*

Natural Causation. An Essay in Four Parts. By C. E. Plumptre, Author of "General Sketch of the History of Pantheism," &c. Demy 8vo., cloth, 7s. 6d.

"While many will find in this volume much from which they will dissent, there is in it a great deal that is deserving of careful consideration, and a great deal that calculated to stimulate thought."—*Scotsman.*

Travel.

Our Journey to the Hebrides. By JOSEPH PENNELL and ELIZABETH ROBBINS PENNELL. 43 Illustrations by JOSEPH PENNELL. Crown 8vo., cloth, 7s. 6d.

"It will be easily understood that we could not plan a route out of our ignorance and prejudice. It remained to choose a guide, and our choice, I hardly know why, fell upon Dr. Johnson."

Studies in the South and West, with Comments on Canada. By CHARLES DUDLEY WARNER, Author of "Their Pilgrimage." Crown 8vo., 10s. 6d.

Studies of Kentucky, The Blue Grass Region, New Orleans, Chicago, etc., etc.

Ranch Life and the Hunting Trail. By THEODORE ROOSEVELT, Author of "Hunting Trips of a Ranchman." Profusely Illustrated. Small 4to., cloth elegant, 21s.

"It contains the highest excellence of letter-press and engraving."—*Saturday Review.*

Rides and Studies in the Canary Isles. By CHARLES EDWARDES. With many Illustrations and Maps. Crown 8vo., cloth, 10s. 6d.

"An honest piece of work done by a capable hand."—*Academy.*

Guatemala: The Land of the Quetzal. By WILLIAM T. BRIGHAM. Twenty-six full-page and Seventy-nine smaller Illustrations. Five Maps. Demy 8vo., cloth, £1 1s.

"A book of laborious research, keen observation, and accurate information concerning a region about which previously scarcely anything was known."
Leeds Mercury.

A Summer's Cruise in the Waters of Greece, Turkey, and Russia. By ALFRED COLBECK. Frontispiece. Crown 8vo., cloth, 10s. 6d.

The Decline of British Prestige in the East. By SELIM FARIS, Editor of the Arabic "El-Jawaïb" of Constantinople. Crown 8vo., cloth, 5s.

"A perusal of his book must do the English reader good."—*Asiatic Quarterly Review.*

Daily Life in India. By the Rev. W. J. WILKINS. Illustrated. Crown 8vo., cloth, 5s.

"A very able book."—*Guardian.*

Modern Hinduism: An Account of the Religion and Life of the Hindus in Northern India. By Rev. W. J. WILKINS. Demy 8vo., cloth, 16s.

"A valuable contribution to the study of a very difficult subject."—*Madras Mail.*

Central Asian Questions: Essays on Afghanistan, China, and Central Asia. By DEMETRIUS C. BOULGER. With Portrait and Three Maps. Demy 8vo., cloth, 18s.

"A mine of valuable information."—*Times.*

The Balkan Peninsula. By EMILE DE LAVELEYE. Translated by Mrs. THORPE. Edited and Revised for the English Public by the Author. Map. Demy 8vo., cloth, 16s.

"Likely to be very useful at the present time, as it is one of the best books on the subject."—*Saturday Review.*

Tuscan Studies and Sketches. By LEADER SCOTT, Author of "A Nook in the Apennines," "Messer Agnolo's Household," &c. Many Full-page and smaller Illustrations. Sq. imp. 16mo., cloth, 10s. 6d.

"The sketches are of that happy kind which appeal to the learned through their style, and to the simple through their subjects."—*Truth.*

Letters from Italy. By EMILE DE LAVELEYE. Translated by Mrs. THORPE. Revised by the Author. Portrait of the Author. Crown 8vo., 6s.

"A most delightful volume."—*Nonconformist.*
"Every page is pleasantly and brightly written."—*Times.*

Miscellaneous.

The Letters of the Duke of Wellington to Miss J., 1834-1851. Edited with extracts from the Diary of the latter by CHRISTINE TERHUNE HERRICK. Crown 8vo., paper boards, 6s.

How Men Propose. The Fateful Question and Its Answer. Love scenes from popular works of Fiction, collected by AGNES STEVENS. Square Imp. 16mo., cloth, 6s.; Presentation Edition, cloth elegant, bevelled boards, gilt edges, in box, 7s. 6d. (Uniform with "How to be Happy Though Married.")

This work presents a collection of extracts from the works of prominent novelists, showing the many and various ways in which they treat the marriage proposal. No effort has been spared to include the widest range of authors and varieties of treatment.

Sylvan Folk. Sketches of Bird and Animal Life in Britain. By JOHN WATSON, Author of "A Year in the Fields," &c. Crown 8vo., cloth, 3s. 6d.

"His descriptions are so fresh that they will give genuine pleasure to everyone who reads them. The book will be especially interesting to young readers."
Nature.

Industrial Rivers of the United Kingdom.
By various well-known Experts. With numerous Illustrations. Crown 8vo., cloth, 7s. 6d.

These Chapters are not confined to the commerce and industries which characterise the great rivers: the history of each stream is traced from the earliest times. The foundation of the trade and manufactures which distinguish the several ports and districts are noticed; and the improvement of the rivers and harbours, and the development of the trade and commerce, up to the latest possible period, are dealt with at length.

Crime: Its Causes and Remedy. By L. GORDON RYLANDS, B.A. (Lond.) Crown 8vo., cloth, 6s.

A treatise on crime and its causes, presenting many interesting statistics and tables on its fluctuations, and suggesting remedies and a new method of meeting it.

The Five Talents of Woman. A Book for Girls and Young Women. By the Rev. E. J. HARDY, Author of "How to be Happy though Married," &c. Sq. Imperial 16mo., cloth, 6s.; Presentation Edition, bevelled boards, gilt edges, in box, 7s. 6d.

How to be Happy though Married. Small crown 8vo., cloth, 3s. 6d. Bridal Gift Edition, white vellum cloth, extra gilt, bev. boards, gilt edges, in box, 7s. 6d.

"We strongly recommend this book as one of the best of wedding presents."
Pall Mall Gazette.

"Manners Makyth Man." By the Author of "How to be Happy though Married." Popular Edition, small crown 8vo cloth, 3s. 6d.; imp. 16mo., cloth, 6s.

Representative British Orations. With Introductions, &c., by CHAS. K. ADAMS. 16mo., Roxburgh, gilt tops, 3 vols., in cloth box, 15s. The volumes may also be had without box, 13s. 6d.

Jottings from Jail. Notes and Papers on Prison Matters. By the Rev. J. W. HORSLEY, M.A., Oxon., late (and last) Chaplain of H.M. Prison, Clerkenwell. Second edition. Crown 8vo., cloth, 3s. 6d.

Literary Landmarks of London. By LAURENCE HUTTON. Fourth, revised, and cheaper edition. Crown 8vo., Illustrated cover, 2s. 6d.; cloth, 3s. 6d.

English as She is Taught. Genuine Answers to Examination Questions in our Public Schools. With a Commentary by MARK TWAIN. Demy 16mo., cloth, 2s.; parchment, 1s.

MARK TWAIN says: "A darling literary curiosity. . . . This little book ought to set forty millions of people to thinking."

Proverbs, Maxims and Phrases of all Ages. Classified subjectively, and arranged alphabetically. By ROBERT CHRISTY. 2 vols., half cloth, gilt tops, 21s.

Books for Children.

Daddy Jake, the Runaway; And Short Stories told after Dark. By "UNCLE REMUS" (Joel Chandler Harris). Many Illustrations. Medium 4to., cloth, gilt edges, 6s. (Uniform with "The Brownies.")

When Mother was Little. By S. P. YORKE. Thirteen Full-page Illustrations by HENRY J. FORD. Small square 8vo., cloth, 3s. 6d.

The Butterfly : Its Nature, Development, and Attributes. By JOHN STUTTARD. Dedicated to Sir John Lubbock, Bart. Illustrated. Fscap. 8vo., limp cloth, 1s.

Æsop's Fables for Little Readers : Told by Mrs. ARTHUR BROOKFIELD. Twenty-five Illustrations by HENRY J. FORD. Small 4to., cloth, 3s. 6d.

"In their present shape, the fables should be very popular among the inmates of the nursery, more particularly as they are illustrated with nearly thirty clever drawings by Henry Ford, which are beautifully printed in monochrome."
Scottish Leader.

Six Girls. A Home Story. By FANNIE BELL IRVING. Illustrated by F. T. MERRILL. Crown 8vo., cloth, 5s.

"The six main characters are drawn carefully, and well differentiated. The book has many a touch of simple pathos, and many a passage of light-hearted high spirits."—*Scotsman.*

The Brownies : Their Book. By PALMER COX. Reprinted from *St. Nicholas*, with many new Poems and Pictures. Third and Cheaper Edition. Medium 4to., cloth, gilt edges, 6s.

New Fairy Tales from Brentano. Told in English by KATE FREILIGRATH KROEKER, and Pictured by F. CARRUTHERS GOULD. Eight Full-page Coloured Illustrations. Square 8vo., illustrated, paper boards, cloth back, 5s.; cloth, gilt edges, 6s.

"A really charming collection of stories."—*Pall Mall Gazette.*

Fairy Tales from Brentano. Told in English by KATE FREILIGRATH KROEKER. Illustrated by F. CARRUTHERS GOULD. Popular Edition. Sq. imp. 16mo., 3s. 6d.

"An admirable translator in Madame Kroeker, and an inimitable illustrator in Mr. Carruthers Gould."—*Truth.*

In the Time of Roses: A Tale of Two Summers. Told and Illustrated by FLORENCE and EDITH SCANNELL, Author and Artist of "Sylvia's Daughters." Thirty-two Full-page and other Illustrations. Sq. imp. 16mo., cloth, 5s.

"A very charming story."—*Scotsman.*
"A delightful story."—*Punch.*

Prince Peerless: A Fairy-Folk Story-Book. By the Hon. MARGARET COLLIER (Madame Galletti di Cadilhac), Author of "Our Home by the Adriatic." Illustrated by the Hon. JOHN COLLIER. Sq. imp. 16mo., cloth, 5s.

"Delightful in style and fancy."—*Scotsman.*
"A volume of charming stories."—*Saturday Review.*

When I was a Child; or, Left Behind. By LINDA VILLARI, Author of "On Tuscan Hills," &c. Illustrated. Square 8vo., cloth, gilt edges, 3s. 6d.

"A finer girl's book could not be had."—*Scotsman.*

The Prince of the Hundred Soups: A Puppet Show in Narrative. Edited, with a Preface, by VERNON LEE. Illustrated. Cheaper edition. Square 8vo., cloth, 3s. 6d.

"There is more humour in the volume than in half-a-dozen ordinary pantomimes."—*Spectator.*

The Bird's Nest, and other Sermons for Children of all Ages. By the Rev. SAMUEL COX, D.D., Author of "Expositions," &c. Cheap and Popular Edition. Imp. 16mo., cloth, 3s. 6d.

"These beautiful discourses were addressed to children of all ages, and must have found an echo in the hearts of many youthful listeners."—*St. James's Gazette.*

Spring Blossoms and Summer Fruit; or, Sunday Talks for the Children. By the Rev. JOHN BYLES, of Ealing. Crown 8vo., cloth, 2s. 6d.

"They are of simple and instructive character."—*Dundee Advertiser.*

Arminius Vambéry: His Life and Adventures. Written by Himself. With Introductory Chapter dedicated to the Boys of England. Portrait and Seventeen Illustrations. Crown 8vo., 5s.

"We welcome it as one of the best books of travel that our boys could have possibly placed in their hands."—*Schoolmaster.*

Boys' Own Stories. By ASCOTT R. HOPE, Author of "Stories of Young Adventurers," "Stories out of School Time," &c. Eight Illustrations. Crown 8vo., cloth, 5s.

"This is a really admirable selection of genuine narrative and history, treated with discretion and skill by the author. Mr. Hope has not gathered his stores from the highway, but has explored far afield in less-beaten tracts, as may be seen in his 'Adventures of a Ship-boy' and 'A Smith among Savages.'"—*Saturday Review.*

The Adventures of Robinson Crusoe. Newly Edited after the Original Editions. Nineteen Illustrations. Large crown 8vo., cloth extra, 5s.

Two Little Confederates. By THOMAS NELSON PAGE. With eight full-page illustrations by E. W. KEMBLE and A. C. REDWOOD. Square 8vo., cloth, 6s.

"A charming story."—*American Traveller.*

THE CAMEO SERIES.

Half-bound, paper boards, price 3s. 6d. each. Fine Edition, bound in parchment, printed on Japan paper, numbered and signed, 30 copies only printed, 25 being for sale; terms on application from Booksellers or the Publisher.

The Lady from the Sea. By HENRIK IBSEN. Translated, with the Author's permission, from the Norwegian by ELEANOR MARX AVELING. With a Critical Introduction by EDMUND GOSSE. Portrait of the Author and Autograph.

A London Plane-Tree, and Other Poems. By the late AMY LEVY, Author of "The Romance of a Shop," "Reuben Sachs," &c. Illustrated by J. BERNARD PARTRIDGE.

Wordsworth's Grave and Other Poems. By WILLIAM WATSON, Author of "The Prince's Quest," & Frontispiece.

Sakuntala; or, The Fatal Ring. An Indian Drama by KALIDASA. Translated by Sir WILLIAM JONES, and Edited, with an Introduction, by T.W. RHYS DAVIDS, Ph.D., LL.D.

"UNWIN'S NOVEL SERIES."

The Volumes average about 300 pp., small cr. 8vo., limp cloth, price 2s. each.

Gladys Fane. By T. WEMYSS REID. Fifth Edition.

Mrs. Keith's Crime. By Mrs. W. K. CLIFFORD.

Concerning Oliver Knox. By G. COLMORE.

Miss Bayle's Romance; Or, An American Heiress in Europe. By W. FRASER RAE.

Isaac Eller's Money. By Mrs. ANDREW DEAN.

Chronicles of a Health Resort. By A. HERDER.

LONDON: T. FISHER UNWIN, PATERNOSTER SQUARE, E.C.

www.ingramcontent.com/pod-product-compliance
Lightning Source LLC
Chambersburg PA
CBHW020300240426
43673CB00039B/656